Bull Connor

BULL
CONNOR

William A. Nunnelley

THE UNIVERSITY OF ALABAMA PRESS
TUSCALOOSA AND LONDON

The paper on which this book is printed meets the minimum requirements of
American National Standard for Information Science-Permanence of Paper for
Printed Library Materials, ANSI Z39.48–1984.

Library of Congress Cataloging-in-Publication Data

Nunnelley, William A., 1940–
Bull Connor / William A. Nunnelley
p.   cm.
ISBN 0–8173–0495–9 (alk. paper)
1. Connor, Theophilus Eugene, 1897–1973. 2. Birmingham (Ala.)—
Officials and employees—Biography. 3. Birmingham (Ala.)—Race
relations. 4. Civil rights demonstrations—Alabama—Birmingham—
History—20th century. 5. Civil rights movements—Alabama—
Birmingham—History—20th century.   I. Title.
F334.B653C666   1991
976.1′781063′092—dc20   89–78196
[B]   CIP

British Library Cataloguing-in-Publication Data available

*To Carol and Meg,
and the memory of Richard A. Nunnelley*

Contents

Acknowledgments

I owe a debt of gratitude to a number of people who assisted me while I worked on this project. At the risk of omitting the names of others who were helpful along the way, I would particularly like to thank the following. Dr. Leah R. Atkins and Dr. Marlene Rikard of the Samford University Department of History and Political Science provided numerous valuable suggestions regarding research and writing; Dr. Atkins is now Executive Director of the Auburn University Center for the Arts and Humanities. All my interview subjects were patient and generous with their sharing of material. Attorneys Henry Simpson and Thomas King not only took time to be interviewed but made files available which enabled me to deal with my subject more completely. Chriss Doss, Director, and Linda Dukes, Staff Attorney, of the Samford University Center for the Study of Law and the Church rendered valuable assistance researching court cases. I have found librarians to be a helpful breed, and this was particularly true of the staffs of the Birmingham Public Library Archives and Southern History departments and the Samford University Special Collections Department. I should also thank the family of Eugene "Bull" Connor for making scrapbooks available to me at the time this project began as a Master's thesis. James Jacobson, Editor, and Laurie Dean, Reference Librarian, of *The Birmingham News* helped me greatly as I searched for photographs with which to illustrate this volume. Finally, my wife Carol—a skilled editor—offered excellent suggestions that made the book more readable. For all of your help, I sincerely thank you all.

WILLIAM A. NUNNELLEY

Bull Connor

1

City of Fear

When Martin Luther King, Jr., brought his civil rights demonstrations to Birmingham, Alabama, during the spring of 1963, he sought a confrontation that would dramatize his efforts to break down the walls of segregation in America. King came to Birmingham in frustration, mindful that his most recent antisegregation campaign—in Albany, Georgia—had produced only modest results. Some called the Albany campaign a failure; King himself admitted that mistakes had been made and that the effort could be best described as a learning experience.[1]

King had vaulted into the public eye by leading a successful 1955 bus boycott in Montgomery, Alabama, chipping away at segregation's ramparts in the Cradle of the Confederacy. By the start of the Albany campaign in 1961, he had become the nationally acknowledged leader of the civil rights movement. The movement leaders chose to attack all vestiges of segregation in Albany, rather than concentrating on one or two such as bus segregation or the all-white police force. The result was an incohesive, uncoordinated effort that prompted one observer, movement veteran Ruby Hurley, to remark, "Albany was successful only if the goal was to go to jail."[2] King's biographer David L. Lewis asserts that blacks demanded the wrong things at the wrong time in Albany "because there was too little coordination, trust, and harmony within the Movement."[3]

Albany taught King and his Southern Christian Leadership Conference (SCLC) that strong leadership and organization were essential to the success of a campaign dependent upon what Lewis
termed an "anarchic and querulous mosaic of inexperienced
groups."[4] In the wake of Albany, King sought to rekindle the antisegregation struggle against a new target. He cast his eyes in the
direction of Birmingham and its segregationist police commissioner Eugene "Bull" Connor. Project C, for "confrontation," thus
was born.

Birmingham—a city established in 1871 by speculators and industrialists—was a creation of the New South. Unlike its sister
cities of Mobile and Montgomery, it had no antebellum tradition
and developed along the lines of an overgrown mining town. During its first half century, Birmingham sprang from a cornfield to
become the South's third most populous municipality,[5] a great
workshop town hailed by boosters as "The Magic City." For all
its magic growth, however, Birmingham owed its existence to one
industry—steel—or more accurately, to the production of raw materials for the steel industry. The majority of its people were
"working class, sparsely educated, economically insecure, and racially divided."[6] The depression hit the South hard and Birmingham even harder, and steelworkers typified the feeling of the community as they muttered, "Hard times come here first and last
longest."[7] The city rebounded with a burst of prosperity during
World War II; the mills, plants and furnaces operated at capacity.
But stagnation set in after the war. As one mid-1940s report stated,
"Birmingham, the industrial center of the South, has civic anemia."[8] The steel city had almost overtaken Atlanta in the 1940
census, but by 1950 Birmingham lagged far behind, despite a late
1940s effort to diversify industry. By 1960 Birmingham's dream
of challenging Atlanta for preeminence in Dixie had become a forlorn hope.

Absentee ownership in Birmingham's primary industries played
a role in the city's failure to realize its early potential. The efforts
of U.S. Steel Corporation to control its Birmingham subsidiary,
Tennessee Coal and Iron Company, hampered the major industry
of the Alabama city.[9] In addition to practicing "Pittsburgh-plus"
pricing (charging Southern customers more than Northern cus-

tomers paid in Pittsburgh), U.S. Steel moved managers in and out of its Birmingham office at will. "So much depended on the Tennessee company," recalled Lee C. Bradley, Jr., a 1921 Harvard Law School graduate who returned home to head one of Birmingham's leading law firms. "Their big interests were in the North, so they would send men down here that were on their way up. This was a training ground." Other corporations followed similar management patterns. "The important businessmen, most of them, were from the North," said Bradley.[10] While serving their stints in Birmingham, corporate managers tended to reside outside the city in affluent suburbs such as Mountain Brook, and they failed to develop a true community spirit. The head of one large corporation "is so uninterested in the welfare of the community that he does not have a Birmingham bank account and pays his bills with checks on an Atlanta bank," business reporter Irving Beiman wrote during the 1940s.[11] The economic leaders took a "hands off" approach to local politics, caring little about who held office as long as business remained unthreatened by local governmental policies. This laissez-faire attitude contributed to a leadership void resulting in a succession of undistinguished political leaders.

Birmingham was a blue-collar city with a history of violence. The reborn Ku Klux Klan boasted between 15,000 and 20,000 members during the mid-1920s,[12] and its influence continued to be felt into the 1960s. Birmingham answered the growing call for equal rights that followed World War II with a series of violent episodes, which earned the city such nicknames as "Bombingham" and "the most segregated city in America." Birmingham's zoning ordinances enacted in 1926 required blacks and whites to live in separate neighborhoods. When the ordinance was struck down during the late 1940s, blacks began to inch closer to white neighborhoods. During the summer of 1947, the first in a series of home and church bombings in black neighborhoods occurred. One night in 1949, three black homes were bombed within minutes of each other. Generally, the bombings occurred at unoccupied dwellings, but the message was clear. As Bull Connor told a black man who bought property near a white neighborhood during the late 1940s, his presence "might lead to violence and if he were in his place he would move immediately."[13]

The bombings ceased during the early 1950s, but resumed following the 1954 ruling in the *Brown* v. *Board of Education* case. The church and home of the Reverend Fred L. Shuttlesworth, Jr., a black pastor active in the civil rights movement, was dynamited on Christmas night in 1956; three other black homes were bombed within the next eleven months. The violence took other forms as well during the late 1950s; crosses were burned in various parts of the city, singer Nat King Cole was attacked by white toughs while performing a concert at Birmingham Municipal Auditorium, Shuttlesworth was beaten as he attempted to enroll black children in an all-white school, and a black named Judge Aaron was castrated by a band of night riders. In a 1958 article entitled "Integration's Hottest Crucible," *Time* magazine described Birmingham as a city "where a smelter economy, stamped onto Alabama's rural culture, makes a melting pot of raw men as well as raw materials."[14]

Bull Connor was first elected police commissioner in 1937 and served four terms before declining to run for reelection in 1953. After one term away, he jumped back into the political arena, riding the segregation issue to a narrow victory over a political moderate in 1957. Back in city hall, he promised to uphold Birmingham's segregation ordinances "to the utmost of my ability and by all lawful means."[15] Connor was the quintessential segregationist; his instrument of enforcement was the last all-white police force in a U.S. city of more than 50,000,[16] a department in which racism predominated and "blacks had no rights whatsoever," according to Jack A. Warren, who rose to the rank of acting chief during a forty-two-year career on the force.[17]

As commissioner of public safety, Connor was responsible under the city commission form of government not only for Birmingham's police department, but for the fire department, the board of education, the public library system, and other areas as well. But he enjoyed the power and attention afforded the police commissioner role and placed his emphasis there, running the police department with an iron hand. "He would brook no interference with his management of the police department," recalled James C. Parsons, a twenty-five-year veteran of the department who became police chief during the 1970s, a decade after Connor left office. "It was one of those dictatorial regimes where you liked it or you lumped it and got out. The chief, under Commissioner Connor, had no power. There was absolutely nobody that would stand up to him."[18] Connor earned a reputation as an honest and dedicated crimefighter during his early years in office, when he conducted continuing campaigns to rid Birmingham of gambling and vice. Connor "has run gamblers out of Birmingham so often and so completely that dice-shakers from Seattle to Miami cuss him as a poor sport," gushed *Alabama* news magazine in 1948.[19] But from the late 1940s on, he was better known for his bitter opposition to integration and the civil rights movement.

By 1960 Birmingham had become economically depressed and racially polarized. The steel industry—still the heart of Birmingham's economy—was slow to recover from a series of 1950s recessions. Blacks represented one-third of Birmingham's population but enjoyed few rights. Black reporter and local historian Geraldine H. Moore wrote that Birmingham "before the sixties was a city in which two separate and distinct communities existed, and to a large extent, were hostile to each other."[20] Birmingham whites placed a low priority on race relations and were incensed by a 1960 *New York Times* profile headlined "Fear and Hatred Grip Birmingham." *Times* reporter Harrison Salisbury, after visiting the city and conducting a series of interviews, wrote that "every channel of communication, every medium of mutual interest, every reasoned approach, every inch of middle ground has been fragmented by the emotional dynamite of racism, enforced by the whip, the razor, the gun, the bomb, the torch, the club, the knife, the mob, the police and many branches of the state's apparatus."[21]

Birmingham newspapers reacted angrily to the article, taking the position that the city had been slandered and that the *Times* article had been overly dramatic. The *Birmingham News* called the Salisbury article "another journalistic and literary libel against the South" and described it as "an amazing recital of untruths and semi-truths" providing a picture of Birmingham that was "maliciously bigoted, noxiously false, viciously distorted."[22] Connor said "the mighty *Times* is stooping again to gain circulation among those who seek sensationalism at our expense" and called the article "a cheap attempt to smear our city and state."[23] These comments reflected the siege mentality that enveloped Birmingham as, increasingly, the city was portrayed by outside media as the symbol of hard-line Southern racism. But a year later, when white toughs attacked a group of black and white Freedom Riders at a Birmingham bus station without interference from police, the *Birmingham News* wrote, "Fear and hatred did stalk Birmingham streets yesterday." In a front-page editorial, the *News* said that the people and the police permitted the attack and asked, "When will the people demand that fear and hatred be driven from the streets?"[24] The same week, CBS News aired an hour-long special entitled "Who Speaks for Birmingham?" replaying for a national television audience the now-familiar themes of racial division and brutality within the steel city. CBS reporter Howard K. Smith was in Birmingham gathering material for the program the day of the Freedom Riders attack; his film footage included the aftermath of the bus station assault.

Bull Connor was riding high at the time of the Freedom Riders attack. Less than two weeks earlier, he had been reelected to a sixth term by the largest margin of his political career, strengthening his determination to resist integration by all available means. But the Freedom Riders episode convinced the same business and civic leaders who had disagreed with Salisbury's assessment that, for Birmingham to go forward, a change in city hall leadership was necessary. "We're suffering from a severe case of Bull Connorism," one Birmingham resident told *Atlanta Constitution* columnist Ed Hughes, a Birmingham native. Connor typified "the ultimate in conservatism and racial bitterness," wrote Hughes.[25] This was underscored in January 1962, when Connor and fellow commissioners Art Hanes and James T. "Jabo" Waggoner closed Birmingham's city parks rather than submit to court-ordered integration. The progressive Young Men's Business Club led a campaign to change Birmingham's form of government during the fall of 1962, and voters approved the change in November. Thus, as the spring of 1963 approached, Birmingham stood poised to choose new leadership, and Martin Luther King, Jr., hurriedly laid the groundwork for massive demonstrations in the city before Bull Connor could retire.

Connor was the perfect adversary for a civil rights movement desperately in need of additional thrust. "We knew when we came that Connor would do something to help our movement along," recalled King's aide Wyatt Tee Walker, who planned SCLC activities.[26] "We didn't want to march after Bull was gone." Albany had provided "no real dramatization to the nation of what segregation was like," said Walker, but Birmingham "would provide that kind of platform." SCLC felt that "as Birmingham went, so would go the South," and, Walker added, "if we could crack that city, then we could crack any city."[27]

On 3 April, the day after Connor lost a mayoral runoff election to moderate segregationist Albert Boutwell, Birmingham blacks began a series of marches protesting the city's segregation ordinances and the discriminatory practices of employers, who traditionally relegated blacks to the lowest paid and most menial jobs. Birmingham police were restrained in their handling of the early marches but became less so as the number of participants grew in late April. The demonstrations reached full crescendo in the first week of May, and Connor's policemen and firemen responded with force.

"Hell, there must have been three thousand, four thousand [demonstrators] out there," recalled retired policeman Jack Warren, head of the Patrol Division in 1963. "I mean, it was just solid, the park [Kelly Ingram], every street around there west of 17th Street. So they were coming up Fifth Avenue. And when they got up there, their numbers, their attitudes, their mannerisms, what they were doing, they were going to City Hall. And the orders were, they can't come. So, at that time, when it was obvious they were going to keep coming, that's when the fire hoses and the dogs were turned loose.

"If you're a policeman," said Warren, "and 10 or 15 [policemen] are out at the intersection, and you're aware of the fact that you're going to get walked over, you've either got to do something or run. It's a hard damn decision. But the orders were, they can't come."[28]

When Connor attempted to quell the demonstrations with fire hoses and police dogs, a shower of national media coverage focused attention on the plight of blacks in segregated areas. Following the Birmingham campaign, Pres. John F. Kennedy—mindful of his campaign commitment to civil rights—proposed an omnibus bill designed to bring minorities to positions of equality in American life, and Congress took the first steps toward his legislation. Project C was thus a success.

Walker said in later years that SCLC "did with design precipitate crises, crucial crises in order to expose what the black community was up against,"[29] adding that he and King were delighted with Connor's reaction. "Bull Connor had something in his mind about not letting these niggers get to City Hall," Walker recalled. "I prayed that he'd keep trying to stop us. . . . Birmingham would have been lost if Bull had let us go down to the City Hall and pray; if he had let us do that and stepped aside, what else would be new? There would be no movement, no publicity. But all he could see was stopping us before we got there."[30]

Connor's use of police dogs and fire hoses to curb SCLC demonstrations dominated the fifteen-minute national television news shows, prompting the Kennedy administration to redouble its efforts in the area of civil rights reform. King had called his Birmingham campaign Project C for "confrontation." Renaming it for Connor would have been appropriate.

2

"Me and Plato"

Theophilus Eugene Connor was a son of the Black Belt, that rural region of west-central Alabama noted for its rich soil and Old South mentality. Connor was born on 11 July 1897 in Selma, where his father worked as a railroad dispatcher. Eugene, as he was called, was the second—and eldest surviving—of five sons born to King Edward Connor and his wife, the former Molly Godwin of nearby Plantersville. A son born prior to Eugene had died at four months of age. Railroad employees were subject to frequent relocations during this era, and Eugene became a traveler at an early age. By 1905, when he was eight, the family had taken up residence in Atlanta, Georgia. Here tragedy struck when Mrs. Connor caught pneumonia and died four months after the birth of her fifth son, Ed.

As a boy Connor lived for a time in North Birmingham with his aunt and uncle, Mr. and Mrs. John Godwin, and attended school there. During this period a playtime accident blinded Eugene in one eye; he peeped through a hole in a fence just as a young friend shot an air rifle through the opposite side of the fence hole. Connor traveled extensively with his father during his boyhood years and once claimed to have resided in thirty-six of the American states. From his father, he learned the art of telegraphy.

During the summer of 1916 Connor made one of his periodic visits to Plantersville to spend time with another aunt, Lula Fulford. On this visit he met Beara Levens, the daughter (and one of eleven children) of a timber company vice president. Eugene became a frequent visitor and occasional resident of Plantersville during the next several years, and he and Beara continued to see each other regularly. A romance blossomed, and on 29 September 1920, the couple was married at the home of the Methodist minister in Selma. By this time, Connor—who dropped out of school and never completed his high school degree—had begun work as a railroad telegrapher. A job opened in New Orleans, Louisiana, and Eugene accepted it. After the wedding, the young couple boarded a train and headed for the Crescent City, where they honeymooned briefly before Connor began his employment.

New Orleans was merely the first stop on an extensive tour of jobs and cities during the early months of their marriage. A telegrapher enjoyed instant communication with a network of colleagues at distant sites. Each time Eugene received word of a more desirable opportunity elsewhere, he and Beara packed their suitcases and caught a train. Residing in hotels and boarding homes made moving a simple matter. "My wife and I lived in seven different states the first year we were married," Connor once recalled.[1]

By the summer of 1921 Connor had left a job in Memphis, Tennessee, and moved to Dallas, Texas. Always a sports enthusiast, with a keen interest in baseball, he enjoyed following the progress of the local team. One day in Dallas, he attended what was known as a baseball "matinee," a re-creation of a game by an announcer using telegraph reports. Fans unable to attend an actual game could follow the progress of their team at a matinee in a downtown storefront studio. On this particular day the regular announcer became ill and sought a replacement from the audience.

"The man came out in the audience and asked if there was an operator in the audience," Connor recalled during a 1931 interview. "I hung back—you know, modest like, that's Bull all the time—but didn't noboby else go up, then I did and told him I was an operator. He said he was sick and couldn't stand up and would I call the game. I told him I couldn't do that, but he insisted and said he'd give me $5. Well, $5 was a lot of money in them days, so I said I'd do it—least I'd try."[2]

Connor thus took the first step toward a new career as a sportscaster. Most matinee broadcasters required a telegrapher to feed them information. Connor had the advantage of taking the action directly from the wire, which enabled him "to get the play on the air," he estimated, "within five seconds after it is over."[3] This delighted the matinee patrons, as did Connor's down-home delivery.

"I'm still modest, but I'm tellin' you I made a big hit," he remembered. "The next day when the other man came out to call the game, the fans yelled for me. They kept on yelling until the other man asked me to come on up and work again. That day he gave me $10. And after that he hired me regular."[4]

Connor returned to Birmingham on 10 February 1922—Beara's twenty-third birthday. He opened his own baseball matinee, charging customers thirty-five cents admission to hear him call Birmingham Barons games. Later he took a job with the *Birmingham News* operating the "telepic" machine that sent photographs over telegraph wires. At the same time, he worked extra at Birmingham radio stations taking sports results from the wire for the regular announcers.

"One Sunday afternoon I went to work at the studio at WKBC," Connor recalled. "I got my little table and my typewriter all ready . . . lighted up my cigaret . . . when in came Dud Connally, and Dud asked me how I was. Right away I got suspicious, because ordinarily an operator don't get asked how he is. But I told him I was all right, then I waited. Then he told me. 'Bull,' he said, 'you're gonna call this game this afternoon.'

"'Oh, no, I ain't,' I said, and lighted another cigaret. 'I got a wife and baby, and I don't want to get killed.'"

Connally convinced Connor to call the game, and Bull agreed to try, "provided he didn't use my name." Once more, the voluble Connor was a hit despite his fear that he would "get up there and talk like a countryman and have people laugh at me."[5] His sudden popularity won Connor a regular job as the voice of the Barons; and his personal economic situation took a turn for the better when he became a salesman for Hood-McPherson Furniture Company, which sponsored Baron broadcasts.

During this time, he earned a nickname that would stay with him throughout his life. Connor was short—five feet eight inches—but possessed a booming voice and an affinity for chatter.

While broadcasting baseball road games from a local studio, he received only minimal information from the ticker tape but filled dead air time between pitches by "shooting the bull," or relaying contrived word descriptions about imagined action on the field. As it happened, the *Birmingham Post* ran a popular front-page feature during this period about a caricature character named "Dr. B.U.L. Conner." This combination of factors prompted Eugene's friends to call him "Bull."[6] He enjoyed the nickname and always signed his correspondence Eugene "Bull" Connor.

Minor league baseball enjoyed a golden age in Birmingham in the 1920s, providing diversion from the drudgeries of the mines, mills, and plants. Baron fans followed the fortunes of their favorites over the radio with Bull Connor doing the play-by-play. Such phrases as "There he goes!" and "Did you hear that?" were Connor bywords, but the term that listeners most associated with Bull was a dramatically drawn-out version of "He's o-u-u-t-t-t!" He also broadcast college football games and professional boxing matches and often read election results off the wire, broadcasting them to audiences at downtown theaters. Baseball was his favorite, however, and the activity that earned him his large following. A typical message from a fan read: "Please find enclosed a four leaf clover & horseshoe embroidered on a piece of material, hope this will bring you good luck. & also the Barons. from a Radio fan, a lady 74 years young. Mrs. Hovel."[7] A national baseball publication, *The Sporting News*, called Connor "one of Dixie's most popular announcers" and noted that he "tells all about the game in a homely style all his own that has earned him a following second to none throughout the Southern Association."[8]

Connor decided to run for the Alabama House of Representatives in 1934 "partly for the fun of it and partly to see how many friends I had."[9] His platform opposed higher taxes in any form—especially a state sales tax—and supported reductions in the cost of auto tags, gas and oil taxes, and the expense of government. He also favored legalizing beer sales and state regulation of other liquors with local options by counties, as well as "strict civil service laws for all state, county and city employees."[10] Whatever his motivation for running, and despite having "no more idea of being elected than I had of beating Lou Gehrig out of first base with the Yankees,"[11] Connor won election on 6 November as one of Jefferson County's seven representatives.[12] *The Birmingham News* noted that Connor won his race "without the support of a political organization," saying, "He made a few speeches, kissed a few babies, and made no rosy promises to voters, except beer 'with a tax on it' and hard liquor if they wanted it."[13]

In the legislature Connor became known for his pointed questioning of speakers, his "trick" bills, and his unbounded enthusiasm when taking part in a floor fight. Connor believed ridicule could be far more effective at times than cold logic could be. To further his opposition to a proposed state sales tax, he introduced a bill that would appropriate one million dollars to enlarge jails to hold all the people who would refuse to pay the tax, should it be levied.[14]

Among those elected to the legislature with Connor in 1934 was attorney James A. Simpson, who became Jefferson County's lone senator and, as such, the acknowledged leader of the county delegation. A proponent of efficient government, Simpson opposed the spoils system that permeated state and local politics. Traditionally, winning candidates fired city and county workers after each election in order to fill the jobs with their own friends, relatives, and supporters; in depression-era Birmingham, the ability to provide jobs was especially important. As a result, infighting had developed at city hall, where first-term associate commissioners W. O. Downs and Lewey Robinson had gone so far as to fire appointees made by Mayor James M. "Jimmie" Jones, who had served since 1925. Jones appealed to the county legislative delegation for help, and Simpson took up the cause.[15]

In a meeting in Simpson's office on 3 March 1935, Connor and the rest of the delegation "pledged unanimously" to support a civil service law that would end the fractious situation at city hall.[16] During the regular legislative session of 1935, the delegation proposed House Bill 737 "to create and establish in each county with a population of 200,000 or more people, according to the latest Federal census, . . . a County wide Civil Service System." Connor, as chairman of the Standing Committee on Local Legislation Number Two, reported that his committee had ordered the bill returned "with a favorable report."[17] The bill passed the House by a 72–13 margin and was sent to the Senate on 30 July. Connor and a majority of the House opposed a last-minute attempt to make passage of the bill subject to voter approval, and that amendment was tabled, 51–40. The Senate passed the civil service bill on 20 August and the measure was delivered to the governor, Bibb Graves, on 26 August.[18] The fear that Graves might veto the measure to satisfy Jefferson County supporters proved unfounded, and the bill went on to survive a challenge before the Alabama Supreme Court in 1939.[19]

While fighting successfully for passage of the civil service law, Connor and Simpson began a lifelong friendship and political association. Simpson viewed Connor and Bessemer lawyer William S. Welch as his best allies in the fight, and he was impressed with Connor "as a loyal and honest representative."[20] Connor "had enough political instinct to know that he needed somebody to guide him right," recalled James T. "Jabo" Waggoner, who served with Connor on the Birmingham City Commission during the 1950s and '60s. Simpson, a corporate lawyer who had served an earlier term in the legislature, "took Bull under his wing and advised him."[21]

Like Simpson, Connor supported legislative reapportionment and fiscal responsibility in government. Connor introduced a reapportionment bill that would have increased Jefferson County's representation in the legislature; he supported a measure requiring city commissioners to itemize expense accounts, but opposed a legislative pay raise (from four dollars to six dollars a day) and a two-week paid Christmas holiday for legislators. He backed bills to create the Alabama Department of Labor and to liberalize the state Workmen's Compensation Act, but fought a measure legalizing horse-racing and an antisedition law. The *Birmingham News* gave Connor good marks for his legislative performance, noting that he had "made a record which commended him to the voters of Birmingham" and that he had "shown he had the capacity for learning and developing while serving in Montgomery."[22]

As the 1937 Democratic primary for the Birmingham City Commission neared, Connor decided to run for the job of associate commissioner. He was encouraged by Simpson and Birmingham businessmen such as Chevrolet automobile dealer Al DeMent.

Factionalism continued at city hall. The turmoil began at the top, where Associate Commissioners Downs and Robinson paired their votes to strip the influence of Mayor Jones, and spread through the ranks of city government. Connor joined seven candidates, including incumbents Downs and Robinson, in the associate commissioner's race; Jones faced four mayoral aspirants.

Campaigning started slowly, and not until election eve did anything resembling fireworks begin. Breaking the lethargy on the Saturday prior to voting on Tuesday 4 May, Connor lashed out at the administration of Governor Graves for sending men to Birmingham to work against his candidacy. Using radio, a medium with which he was highly familiar, Connor said four men on the state payroll had been in Birmingham a week "moving Heaven and earth" in an effort to defeat him because he had opposed the Graves sales tax proposal in the legislature. In a Sunday speech, Connor upped the number of those working against him to seven.[23]

Whether this sudden shattering of the campaign calm helped was difficult to measure, but two days later Connor led the field of associate commissioner candidates with 11,543 votes, coming within 756 votes of winning without a runoff. John H. Taylor, who earlier had served three terms as police commissioner, ran second with 9,837 votes; James W. Morgan third with 8,359; and incumbent Commissioner of Public Improvements Lewey Robinson fourth with 6,020. Commissioner of Public Safety W. O. Downs failed to make the runoff, polling 5,306 votes for the fifth spot. Meanwhile, the electorate gave Mayor Jones a resounding vote of confidence, sending him back to his fourth term with 56 percent of the 24,596 votes cast.[24]

Lewey Robinson opened campaigning for the 18 May runoff with an immediate explosion, attacking Morgan and Taylor on the first day after the primary and urging voters to support him and Connor. Momentarily taken aback, Connor assured the electorate that he was opposed to alliances and was "still running my own race and nobody else's." Recovering from his surprise, he added quickly, "I naturally want all the votes I can get and would like to see the other two candidates endorse me."[25]

As the runoff drew near, the other three candidates quickened their sniping at each other while Connor ran a relatively positive

campaign. He said he believed his opponents to be "very good fel-
lows" and attacked only those outsiders from Montgomery who,
he alleged, were trying to engineer his defeat. When others raised
the question of whether the next police chief (appointed by the
public safety commissioner) would be chosen from within or outside department ranks, Connor said such appointments "should
be kept out of politics and out of political campaigns."[26]

Connor's theme was "I am the people's candidate, just as I was
when I ran for the legislature, and I'm running on my legislative
record." He told a rally at Barrett School in East Lake, "My legislative record is in the House journal in black and white, and I sol-
emnly pledge the people that if I am elected I will not vote to
raise your taxes or increase your licenses. They have money
enough at Montgomery and at City Hall here to run the state and
city governments, and they can do it if the politicians do as private individuals have to do—live on their incomes." He repeated
his belief in civil service and promised to stand on the principles
of civil service "regarding all city employees."[27]

By 13 May the *Birmingham News* was ready to declare Connor
a winner. Political reporter Fred Taylor described him as the man
"who led the first primary and whose election next Tuesday is
apparently assured." Three days later, in the second paragraph of
a front-page article, the *News* said, "Eugene (Bull) Connor, whose
election is conceded, made no speech, nor was his name mentioned other than in the light of a certain winner."[28]

Election day proved Fred Taylor right. Connor piled up 18,600
votes, carrying every city box except one, Ensley. Morgan polled
10,745 votes, finishing ahead of John H. Taylor's 10,356 and Robinson's 6,091. The practice was for the three-man commission to
vote on which post each of the two associates would fill after the
candidates expressed their preferences; law prohibited running for
either post specifically. Because Connor had expressed an interest
in becoming public safety commissioner and Morgan in serving
as the public improvements commissioner, the matter was settled
amicably.

Connor was elated by the victory, which he interpreted as an
endorsement of his "legislative activities against the tax-raising,
license-raising policy of Governor Graves." He told the voters,

"My heart is too full right now to tell you how I feel. I can only say thank you." Then he added, "I can promise you this: I shall give you at the city hall everything that's in me. I shall do my very best to merit your confidence. And when I make [mistakes]—as I certainly shall—I only ask that you come to me and discuss them with me and give me an opportunity to rectify them. My office shall be open to every citizen. I invite you to see me. I need and want your advice. And I pledge myself again to carry with me into the city hall the same ideals which guided me when I was your representative in the Legislature."[29]

While Connor saw his election as a reaction against higher taxes, the *News* interpreted it as a repudiation of the dissension-ridden administration of 1933–37. Commenting editorially after the election, the paper said the defeat of incumbents Downs and Robinson "can only be regarded as a sign of public disapproval of the general policies which they have followed, especially in light of the huge vote given Jimmie Jones." Not only was the election a vote of confidence for Jones, but "a strong indication of the public's desire for more harmony at City Hall." The same editorial praised Connor and Morgan as "highly esteemed" men who "give promise of being able to develop on the job" and "both are known as clean and honest men."[30]

In another sense, the 1937 election—the first since enactment of the Connor-backed Civil Service Bill—was unlike any held previously in Jefferson County. By extending civil service protection to city employees, the law prevented candidates "from offering jobs by the wholesale in exchange for votes" during the primary.[31] Eliminating this source of winning votes helped a political newcomer such as Connor to neutralize an incumbent's advantage.

More than five months later, with the formality of an October general election behind him, Connor sat in a Birmingham restaurant the day before his inauguration and discussed his political philosophy with *News* columnist James Saxon Childers. Four of every five men who went past their table spoke to the commissioner-elect, and Connor wondered aloud why the reporter wanted to interview him because "they all know me anyhow."

"See what I'm telling you," said Connor. "They all know old Bull. And something else I want you to notice. You don't hear any of them calling me Mr. Commissioner, do you? No. And what's more I don't want anybody to start it. I've been Bull Connor. I'm still Bull Connor. If I ever got to be president of the United States and began making fireside chats, I expect I'd occasionally lapse into a little rooting for Uncle Bud Clancy to slam one into the right field stands. I'd know I'd still be Bull. I've always been Bull to my friends, and I always want to be. If they were to start treating me any other way, I'd get worried and figure they didn't like me any more."

Connor told Childers he had no more business going into politics than he would "going into a beauty contest" because he had no training or background in politics. The voters elected him to the legislature because "they had heard me call baseball games and because they had learned to like me.

"That's one of the faults in the way we put men into office," he added. "We elect men who are popular, not necessarily those who are gifted for the job." He said a plan should be worked out "by which men are elected to public office who have been trained to hold public office."

"Bull, Plato had that same idea a good many years ago," said Childers.

"Me and Plato," Connor responded. "Can I help it if he agrees with me?"[32]

Mayor Jones and Commissioners Connor and Morgan were sworn into office on 1 November 1937, and Connor was appointed President Pro Tempore of the commission to preside in the absence of the mayor.[33] In his remarks, Connor said he knew "many difficulties are facing me" and pledged once more to do his best.

"I am not a reformer," he said. "I am not planning to revolutionize my department. But I am going to try to work out its problems gradually and make that department worthy of your respect and confidence. If I make changes at City Hall, they will come after I have carefully studied conditions. And these changes—if any— will be made because I think the best interests of Birmingham demand them. None will be made for political reasons."[34]

Connor said he would work hard to remove the Police Department from politics and added, "This cannot be done unless our laws are enforced impartially." He told the people not to expect or even request personal favors. Then he stressed again his political independence, saying, "Let me tell you again what I told you during the campaign: I owe no political debt. I have made no private promise. I have no political tieup. I am free to devote my efforts and energy to the interests of Birmingham, without any entangling alliance of any kind, shape or character."[35]

The *Birmingham Age-Herald* commented editorially that the public "has every good reason to expect a business-like administration, divorced from petty personal politics."[36] Connor then set about making changes he said would advance his goals of enforcing the law impartially and eliminating dissension from Police Department ranks.

Although he disclaimed the role of reformer, Connor indicated almost immediately a clear determination to set the public safety house in order. His changes during the first forty-five days ranged from such major moves as the naming of new police and fire chiefs to the repainting of city police cars from red to black. His goal: to make the public safety department "more responsive and more professional."

"Wear a smile," Connor told Birmingham's 233 policemen. He also told them to enforce all laws strictly and impartially without regard to a person's creed, church, how much money he or she had in the bank, or color, because "favoritism is out the window."[37] The commissioner assigned one man to break up double parking downtown and voided more than 800 special parking tags which permitted the holders to park anywhere anytime without fear of being ticketed.[38] Both situations had produced outcries of public resentment.

"From now on, dice games anywhere in the Birmingham district are going to be very scarce," Connor warned the area "social clubs." When a fire hose salesman told him that kickbacks were not unusual in his business, the commissioner replied, "It may be customary, but not in Birmingham." Then he gave the story to the newspapers. To lessen the backlog of Recorder's Court cases, he began requiring Judges Henry J. Martin and Frederick V. Wells to work full days rather than the half-day schedule to which they had been accustomed.[39]

On 23 November Connor appointed a parole board to handle

Home life for Eugene "Bull" Connor and his wife Beara during the mid-1930s included an occasional piano concert by their daughter Dora Jean. (Courtesy the Birmingham News)

all clemency in Recorder's Court cases and named as chairman community leader Dr. Henry M. Edmonds, the liberal, social activist pastor of Independent Presbyterian Church. His reason: "To remove this function entirely from the influence or even suggestion of politics." The *Age-Herald* noted that, "The public and officials are beginning to show a more healthy interest in the problem of paroling prisoners" and commended Connor for choosing Dr. Edmonds as chairman.[40]

One of Connor's first acts as commissioner was to tell the Police Department that dissension must stop. "If you can't say anything good about a fellow officer, keep your mouth shut," he ordered. "There isn't any room in this department for cliques."[41] Connor underscored his commitment to having a more harmonious police force by appointing T. A. Riley, a veteran detective who towered six feet six inches in height, as chief in place of E. L. Hollums, who was made chief of detectives. Connor said there was "nothing personal or political in the change," but that it was "in the best interests of the Police Department."[42] One week later, Alf Brown, who had been first assistant fire chief for fifteen years, was appointed fire chief, succeeding B. O. Hargrove.[43] Each change was accomplished by unanimous commission vote at the suggestion of Connor. His message to the two departments was clear: friction must be eliminated and harmony and professionalism increased.

By mid-December, when Connor announced, "I'm through [making changes] now," the *Birmingham Post* was ready to declare that the new Commissioner of Public Safety had accomplished one of his major goals. No more changes were contemplated, the *Post* said, because "the two factions into which the [Fire] department was split during the last administration at City Hall have buried the hatchet," and the same was true of the Police Department "since Mr. Connor delivered the ultimatum that he would not tolerate any dissension or factionalism on the force."[44]

Connor's radio experience had taught him the value of clear, positive reports to the public. He had made effective use of the media during his legislative days and his campaign for the commission, and he continued to do so as police commissioner. He was always ready with a quotable statement and encouraged members of the press to cover him. As soon as he had been sworn in, he called carpenters to remove all office partitions and doors to his office, saying he did not believe in secret meetings. The *Post* covered this pictorially on 1 December 1937, with a caption reading "Connor's Door Is Always Open."[45] His reputation as a man of the people grew with such episodes as his stand against courthouse "fixers" who preyed on people by pretending to be able to help them receive lighter sentences—for a fee. On 26 November Connor issued a statement saying such fixers would be "vigorously prosecuted." On 7 January 1938, the commissioner himself caught professional bondsman Alan Seigal outside a courtroom telling a youth he could fix the boy's traffic offense for five dollars. "I caught him redhanded," Connor told the press, adding, "I have been

watching Seigal and several other so-called 'fixers' and I intend
to run them away from City Hall." The headline read, "Connor,
in new role as detective, nabs bondsman," and received ample display on the front page.[46]

Connor's name as a crime-fighter spread, especially after the
Associated Press carried a story on his "war to the finish" with
gangsters engaged in "the policy racket." Popular during the late
1930s, policies, or "numbers," were illegal games of chance in
which a person bought one of a group of numbers and the winner
was selected by a drawing. On 22 January 1938, Connor announced
that Birmingham police would begin using high-speed cars
equipped with hydraulic steering stabilizers to prevent their over-
turning in chases with policy racketeers, who used supercharged
autos to elude police officers. The "numbers racket" in Birmingham "is an open challenge to every law enforcement officer," Connor said, noting that, "In other cities, its widespread ramifications
have led to political corruption, organized crime and vice and fel-
ony. That must not happen here."[47]

Connor's first few months in office set the tone for his initial
term. He continued to play an active, vocal role in law enforcement and was accorded favorable coverage by the Birmingham
press. He remained on good terms with reporters, frequently
feeding them stories. "I can still see him in the City Hall press
room, with his feet propped up on the table talking to reporters,"
veteran *Birmingham News* reporter Tommy Hill recalled in 1978.[48]
That the voters approved of his first-term performance was demonstrated convincingly during the spring of 1941, when he was reelected without a runoff.[49]

The early Connor generally was a progressive. He opposed the
sales tax, supported reapportionment, fought antisedition measures, favored workmen's compensation, and removed the local
parole board from politics. In supporting a civil service law that
severely curtailed patronage in local politics, Connor actually was
opposing the remnants of the Ku Klux Klan, which tended to bene-
fit from the spoils system. To some extent, Simpson's influence
is evident. The Simpson of the 1920s and '30s held high the progressive movement ideals of honest government, merit systems,
elimination of influence and corruption, and fiscal responsibility.[50]

Connor played these same themes throughout his days in the legislature, his first commission race and beyond. "'Me and Jim' was one of Connor's favorite expressions when discussing pending legislation," wrote Irving Beiman in the 1940s. "Whatever Simpson favored in the State Senate, 'Bull' fought for in the lower house."[51]

Yet Connor more than Simpson represented the kind of person Birmingham voters selected to lead their city commission during most elections after about 1913. Voters, nearly all of them white, elected men "classified with middle-ranking economic groups" who "had made modest beginnings and achieved moderate business or professional success in Birmingham."[52] Connor's modest beginnings, his professional success as a sportscaster, and his amiable nature made him all the more appealing to Birmingham's largely blue-collar electorate. Bull Connor learned the art of politics well during his early years in the legislature and at city hall, both from his mentor Jim Simpson and from the electorate. The lessons paid dividends for years to come.

3

The Issue Changes

hroughout the 1940s, Birmingham's predominantly white and solidly Democratic electorate reaffirmed its confidence in the leadership of Mayor W. Cooper Green (elected by a seven-to-one margin following the death of Mayor Jimmie Jones in 1940[1]) and Associate Commissioners James W. Morgan and Eugene "Bull" Connor. Voters reelected this triumvirate three times—in 1941, 1945, and 1949—and on each occasion thrust the commissioners back into office without so much as a runoff election. Mayor Green ran without opposition in 1941 and 1945. Morgan, who had been elected to the commission with Connor in 1937, led the balloting for associate commissioner in each of the 1940s elections. And Connor, while he encountered the most serious opposition of the three incumbents, polled no less than 53 percent of the vote in any of the three elections. Voter satisfaction was reflected in a series of unemotional campaigns, each being described by the *Birmingham News* as the quietest in the history of city commission elections.[2]

After winning as a reform candidate in 1937, Connor based his 1941 campaign on his record in office. He had inherited a police department that employed both patrolmen and detectives who "couldn't write their own name(s)." Implementation of the civil service law for which Connor worked resulted in better-educated candidates for the police and fire departments. "At least, they would have had to have had some education, to be able to read and write," said George A. Palmer, who successfully completed Birmingham's first civil service examination during August 1936 and became a city policeman. The civil service law, coupled with Connor's practice of giving the older detectives "some reason to retire," improved the calibre of the police force. "It was easy to see that some progress had been made," said Palmer.[3] Connor also encouraged Police Chief T. A. Riley to form a Birmingham Police Department Crime Laboratory during his early tenure as commissioner, and the two sought the help of the Federal Bureau of Investigation in doing so.[4]

As the 1941 primary approached, Connor pointed to improvements in the police and fire departments, and to such first-term achievements as the establishment of a modern city parole system, a reduction in fire hydrant and fire insurance rates, and the purchase of fire equipment at "greatly reduced prices." He vowed to continue his fight against "gambling and slot machine racketeers" and "other vice conditions." As in 1937, when his candidacy was approved by several Birmingham area labor leaders, Connor won a radio endorsement from union official Stanley Gibson. According to Gibson, Connor had "come through the school of hard knocks, had been a working man, was still a member of the telegraph operators' union and was fair and sympathetic to organized labor."[5] Morgan polled 14,396 votes and Connor 10,895 of the 18,152 cast to win reelection to second terms. Connor viewed the victory as "an endorsement, not of me, but of the things that I have stood for during my stay at City Hall" and vowed to "do a better job during my next term."[6]

While some gave Connor credit for improving the police department, others questioned his motives for change. George Palmer, who advanced from patrolman to city detective on 1 May 1942, believes Connor began pushing the older detectives to retire "so that he could put his people up there." The commissioner learned during his first term "that he needed to have them up there" to maintain control of the department. Connor made much over his promise that "favoritism was out the window" during his early days on the commission, even making certain that his own brother paid a traffic ticket. But over the next few years, the commissioner began identifying his favorites and treating them accordingly, said

Palmer. Connor called his favorites "my nigguhs," Palmer recalled, adding, "Anybody that would do what Bull wanted was his 'nigguh.'"[7]

Although the civil service law had a positive effect, the measure was diluted by the practice of reducing recently promoted officers to their former rank before their probationary period ended, according to Palmer. "You were on probation for a year, and they could set you back [during this period] and not have to give you any reason for it," he said.[8] Later, Connor moved officers in and out of the position of police chief regularly to exert control over the department, according to Jamie Moore, a thirty-six-year veteran of the force and its chief from 1956 until 1972.[9] The chief had "absolutely no power" under Connor, said James C. Parsons, another force veteran who became chief after the Connor era. The chief "just sat there in that seat."[10]

As the Democratic primary of 1945 approached, the overriding topic of coverage in the newspapers was World War II. The tide of war had swung heavily in favor of the Allies, and the bombs and mortar shells fell far from Birmingham. But the pages of the papers daily carried sad reminders of the closeness of war—the obituaries of young Alabamians killed in combat. Connor made a practice of reading these accounts and writing families of deceased servicemen offering his condolences. Mr. and Mrs. Frank A. Beavers, Sr., of Birmingham received such a letter in June 1944 in which the public safety commissioner said:

> I was so grieved to read in the paper the sad word that your son had been reported a casualty over the South Pacific area. Although I was not acquainted personally with your splendid boy, I know your heart is sorely grieved and I hasten to send you this little word of assurance of my sympathy. My prayer is that you may find great consolation in the thought that some day, in God's own good time you shall see your boy again.[11]

Within the context of war on an international scale, local politics paled to insignificance. Only two city commission candidates even bothered to open campaign headquarters for the 1945 primary. With no opposition, Mayor Green did little more than announce his candidacy. No mass meetings were held, and the few issues that surfaced were fought almost entirely over radio broadcasts. The race livened up during the final week of the campaign in late April, however, with Connor as the target.[12]

The police commissioner once again based his campaign on his record as a crime fighter and guardian of public safety. In addition to his efforts to rid Birmingham of "numbers racketeers" and vice, Connor was given to such ploys as having Birmingham detectives check all liquor store patrons "to determine whether or not they were complying with the Selective Training and Service Act and if they were not they would be reported to the FBI."[13] A Connor advertisement credited the commissioner with making Birmingham "a clean and law-abiding city" through effective law enforcement programs.

Former police captain Chester Mullins, who was running for a commission seat, disputed the claim. Calling Connor "the madman of city hall," Mullins charged the police commissioner with having driven numerous veteran officers to retirement as soon as they were eligible for their pensions through his overbearing manner and meddlesome administration. A Mullins advertisement quoted former chief E. L. Hollums—replaced by Connor in 1937—as saying the Police Department had improved "NOT because of Mr. Connor but IN SPITE OF Mr. Connor." Hollums cited Connor's "loud, boisterous language in the presence of my secretary as well as other ladies of the police department . . . together with his over-bearing and interference with the efficient operation of my department" as the leading cause of his retirement.[14] Another candidate, Circuit Court Clerk Osa L. Andrews, accused Connor of not enforcing liquor laws stringently.[15]

Connor ignored the criticism until four days before the election, then went on radio to condemn such "mudslinging," vowing not to practice the technique himself. Connor said his defeat was sought by criminal elements wanting to regain a foothold in Birmingham "and a small group of disgruntled Mr. X's—mostly ex-police officers who were in the saddle before Connor cleaned up Birmingham."[16] Despite the last-minute outbursts, Connor retained his post, polling 9,443 of the 17,883 votes cast (53 percent).

Andrews received 7,518, Mullins 2,265, John Rogers 1,467, and Marion Hogan 1,057. Morgan led the associate commissioner race with 14,016 ballots.[17]

Connor's success with the electorate was based primarily on his personal appeal and not on membership in any political clique. By the time his third city commission race rolled around, he had become adroit at monitoring the electorate, using policemen and other acquaintances to keep his hand on the pulse of the voters. "People that wanted something out of Bull" supplied Connor with information regularly, according to Palmer, and the practice was widespread among "his nigguhs" on the police force.[18]

Connor men were rewarded with more attractive assignments, according to Palmer and Parsons, whereas those not sympathetic to the commissioner might find themselves working the "morning shift," from 11 P.M. until 7 A.M., or walking a beat in an out-of-the-way neighborhood such as Wylam or Pratt City.[19] This encouraged policemen to cooperate totally with the commissioner. Connor men were expected to work in behalf of and to vote for their leader. At various times, Parsons recalled, police officers would solicit political contributions for Connor campaigns, approaching such individuals as restaurant owners who owed their business licenses to the city commission.

"A lot of them [restaurant owners] felt the whip when they didn't chip in political contributions," said Parsons. "You'd find some guy that looked like he was 30 that was 20 that would come in that place to buy a drink. And all at once the vice squad [which was handpicked by Connor] would swoop in and then the City Commission would take his license for a period of time until he came in line. That's happened a number of places."[20]

Policemen who gained the reputation of not supporting Connor paid the consequences. As early as 1941 Connor had Capt. A. M. ("Blinks") Ellis, a twenty-six-year veteran who headed the Traffic Division, fired because, according to Ellis, he "didn't work" for Connor during the campaign.[21] Palmer, a stubborn individual, recalled a superior officer, "Red" Cardwell, asking him, "Can't you be for him [Connor]?"

"Naw, I can't be for him, no way or other," Palmer replied.

"We're going to put you on the morning shift," said Cardwell.

"Well, I don't give a damn if you do it," said Palmer, who then spent fourteen months working at night.[22]

Palmer found himself "in the doghouse" periodically during a sixteen-year stint on the police force. Most of his problems occurred after the 1945 city commission race, during which Connor learned that Palmer's father-in-law, East Thomas grocer W. O. Holcombe, opposed the police commissioner's candidacy.

Conversely, Connor favorites "could do anything they wanted to, and get by with it." Palmer cited examples of one officer who "ran a carnival in the city of Birmingham from lot to lot to lot" and another who "never owned an automobile himself" but used a city car to attend classes at Howard College.[23] "If you were his friend, he was all for you," recalled Jamie Moore, "but if you were his enemy, he was all against you. It was all or nothing."[24]

Jack A. Warren joined the police department in late 1945 after service in World War II, beginning a forty-two-year tenure that ultimately led to the rank of acting chief. He recalls "continuous improvement" in the police department during his early years on the force—better people, improved training, new uniforms, and more modern equipment. "We got radios in the cars not long after I started, and this made one hell of a difference," he said. Warren excused Connor's favoritism as "a human failing done all over the country." Connor knew many policemen personally, he recalled, and received widespread support from the department rank-and-file. "They all liked him with few exceptions," said Warren.[25]

Connor enjoyed his image as a man of the people, essentially free from the influence of behind-the-scenes advisers. But his lengthy association with Jim Simpson—a spokesman for Birmingham's big industrial interests—made Connor susceptible to influence from the "big mules." Simpson, Connor's legal adviser and political confidant from their early days in the legislature, was "one of the few people Bull would listen to," recalled Jamie Moore.[26] Connor "called Jim Simpson every day of his life," said Jabo Waggoner.[27] "Bull was close to the corporate interests, and would carry out what they wanted," remembered *Birmingham News* business editor Irving Beiman, "but he stayed on the good side of the union people as well. He was shrewd. He received support from both groups."[28]

Simpson was the antithesis of Connor. Whereas Connor had only a rudimentary formal education and enjoyed playing dominoes with "his boys" at police and fire stations, Simpson was a Vanderbilt University-educated corporate lawyer who moved in the circles of Alabama's business and industrial elite. A veteran state legislator, Simpson was a political conservative who ran strong races for the U.S. Senate against Lister Hill in 1944 and John Sparkman and Frank Boykin in 1946. As an anti–New Deal candidate in 1944, he based his campaign on the race issue and "foreshadowed its importance in future" elections by winning more than 100,000 of 228,000 votes cast.[29] During the course of this campaign, Simpson relied on Connor to supply information on the local political climate.[30] In 1946 both Simpson and Boykin used the race issue as the basis of their campaigns, thus splitting their appeal and enabling the more liberal Sparkman to win 50.1 percent of the vote.[31] Despite losing the two statewide elections, Simpson recognized the potential for exploiting the race issue in state and local campaigns aimed at heavily white electorates. It was an experience from which his old political friend, Bull Connor, would profit more than Simpson did.

Through his first two terms on the commission and into his third, Connor built his reputation on the law enforcement issue. He was quick to enforce the city's myriad segregation statutes, as he did in 1938 to halt integrated meetings of the Southern Conference for Human Welfare (SCHW), a Southwide meeting on the civil rights of workers and blacks. Such notables as First Lady Eleanor Roosevelt, Sen. Lister Hill, Supreme Court Justice Hugo Black, and Gov. Bibb Graves were among several hundred attending the conference; the organization was a New Deal-inspired regional coalition of liberals and radicals perceived broadly as a racial equality group.[32]

"Negroes and whites would not segregate together" in Birmingham as long as he was commissioner, Connor announced during the gathering.[33] Delegates complied with the commissioner's dictate, but resolved against holding segregated meetings in the future.[34] Later Connor denied misusing the word "segregate." But his assistant, Claude Kitchin, told reporter Irving Beiman, "He said it. I heard him."[35]

Despite Connor's headline-grabbing action replete with racial overtones during the SCHW meeting, his appeal to voters during the 1930s and early 1940s stemmed from his image as an energetic and dedicated crime fighter. The most frequent target of his political rhetoric was the criminal element. For Connor, as well as for the vast majority of Southern officeholders, segregation was the foregone conclusion in the South; highblown oratorical support of the dual society was unnecessary. As attitudes toward racial accommodation began to change during the mid-1940s, however, so too did Connor's emphasis on issues. The lessons that Jim Simpson learned in 1944 and 1946 were to serve Connor well during his 1948 campaign for delegate-at-large to the Democratic National Convention as well as in later races for the city commission.

A progression of civil rights developments in the mid-1940s aroused the ire of segregationists across the South. In 1944 the U.S. Supreme Court declared unconstitutional the white primary, which restricted voting in Democratic primaries to whites.[36] In the one-party South of that era, the Democratic primary generally was tantamount to election. During the fall of 1947, Pres. Harry S. Truman's Committee on Civil Rights presented recommendations for the protection of minority civil rights,[37] and on 2 February 1948 President Truman sent a message to Congress that contained proposals for an antilynching law, a Fair Employment Practices Commission, an end to Jim Crow laws in interstate commerce, and protection of voting rights for minorities. A few days later, the Southern Governors Conference responded with notice that the Democratic administration should halt its attacks on white supremacy or face full-fledged revolt in the South.[38] The governor of Mississippi, Fielding L. Wright, called on Southern governors to make a stronger statement that would include calling a 1 March meeting in Jackson, Mississippi, to consider a possible bolt from the party.[39] Although Wright's proposal died for lack of a second, the stage was set for drastic action on the part of the Democratic party's Southern wing.

The realization that President Truman was committed firmly to civil rights programs that would end segregation had a great mobilizing effect on old-line political leaders in the South. Across Dixie, the white supremacists who controlled local and state government began devising ways to thwart the Truman proposals, or else—the latter meaning party revolt. The most intense support for this drastic measure came from the states having the largest black populations—Mississippi and South Carolina[40]—but Alabama was firm in its opposition as well.

Although Bull Connor had announced his support of Truman at the outset of his delegate-at-large campaign on 29 January, he renounced his endorsement after the president's 2 February message to Congress. During his campaign, Connor stressed that the race question should be left to the states to handle and that, in Alabama, "segregation is absolutely necessary and must be maintained to avoid serious difficulties." He also tied the questions of race and communism together, saying, "It is part of the Communist program to stir up strife between white and Negro people and keep it stirred up,"[41] a familiar Connor refrain through the cold war era and beyond.

"It is my hope," Connor announced in a campaign flyer, "that, as one of your delegates, I can help roll back the attempt of meddlers, agitators and Communist stooges, to force down our throats, through our own Democratic Party, the bitter dose they are now offering us under the false name of Civil Liberties."[42]

The Alabama Democratic Executive Committee went on record as supporting electors pledged to vote against any candidate favoring a civil rights program at the 1948 convention; it also urged delegates to walk out of the convention should civil rights be included in the party platform. A fight brewed between loyalists who would remain committed to the Democratic standard-bearer and states' righters who would bolt rather than support a civil rights candidate.[43] Connor committed to the states' rights faction and won election as a delegate-at-large.

Almost on the eve of the delegate election, Connor became involved in an episode that allowed him to underscore his opposition to integration and communism, and to reap national media coverage as well. The Southern Negro Youth Conference (SNYC), an organization listed on the Department of Justice roster of communist-inspired groups, scheduled a meeting in Birmingham for Saturday, 1 May. When Connor discovered the proposed meeting, he pressured several local black ministers into refusing to host the conference at their churches. "There's not enough room in town for Bull and the Commies," the police commissioner announced.[44]

Finally, a small black church, the Alliance Gospel Tabernacle, agreed to serve as the meeting site for the conference, which was to be attended by about one hundred blacks—mostly college students—and fifty whites. One of the speakers was Sen. Glen H. Taylor of Idaho, a flamboyant one-time cowboy band leader who was Progressive party candidate Henry Wallace's vice presidential running mate. By the time Senator Taylor arrived on Saturday night, Birmingham police had already arrested three white people for ignoring the city ordinance against integrated meetings. After the arrests, the church erected temporary partitions between pews and labeled the front entrance "Colored" and the rear entrance "White." A number of policemen and several reporters surrounded the building as Taylor approached. He asked a reporter about the presence of the policemen and was told of the separate entrances. "I'm going in the front way," he asserted.[45]

As Taylor attempted to enter the "Colored" entrance, a policeman and four detectives hustled him to a police car and arrested him. He was taken to the city jail, charged with "disorderly conduct," fingerprinted, and released under $100 bond. Afterward, the senator complained of the manner in which he had been handled. "They treated me very rough," he said, "anything but gentlemanly. God help the ordinary man."[46]

Later, he added, "I was unceremoniously hustled into the police station and searched. I was also shown in jail how Negroes are treated. An officer told a tall, slim Negro to 'turn around, Nigger, before I knock your head off.'"[47] Taylor noted that he had sung the song "Birmingham Jail" many times, but that the incident had given it "new meaning for me."[48]

Connor defended the arrest, which received national coverage, saying Taylor would "follow the law just like any other person." He added, "This was just what he wanted because he was looking for notoriety and a big splurge in the Eastern newspapers."[49] Taylor was convicted in Recorder's Court a few days later, fined fifty dollars and costs, and sentenced to 180 days in jail. The sentence was suspended and the senator placed on probation for six months.

He never served a day, and in later years, Connor was fond of reminding' people that Taylor "still owes the city 180 days."

In a postscript to the incident, the SNYC expressed its "appreciation" to Connor for providing "a spark of spirit and purpose" to the meeting. Connor's actions, said delegate Thomas Boyd of Haskins, North Carolina, "have made us more determined than ever to fight for our rights as American citizens. . . . Had he not done what he did," said Boyd, a minister, "then this meeting would have been a dull, routine conference without much spirit. Mr. Connor supplied us with that needed spirit and purpose."[50] This ironic result forecast the impact Connor would have on Martin Luther King's civil rights campaign in Birmingham fifteen years later.

The Alabama delegation to the 1948 Democratic National Convention in Philadelphia was comprised of fourteen states' righters and twelve loyalists. As the convention opened on 12 July, Southerners began proposing alternate civil rights packages to the one supported by Truman. After rejecting three such measures, the convention also rejected Truman's proposal and passed an even stronger civil rights statement.[51] At the opening of the next session that night, the roll call of states for presidential nominations began, with Alabama first. Handy Ellis, chairman of the delegation, rose and told the convention that the majority of the Alabama group had been elected on a pledge to walk out of the gathering should a strong civil rights platform be adopted. He then said, "At this time, without fear but with disillusionment, we are carrying out our pledge to the people of Alabama. We bid you good by."[52] Leaving the loyalists behind, including a young man from Barbour County named George C. Wallace, Alabama states' righters strode out of the convention hall, with Bull Connor bearing the Alabama standard. Mississippi delegates joined the walkout.

A few days later, states' righters and segregationists from across the South convened in Birmingham to form the States' Rights Democrat, or "Dixiecrat" party, with plans to oppose the major parties in the 1948 election. Connor welcomed a crowd estimated at six thousand people to the opening session in Municipal Auditorium, saying the facilities in Birmingham would be better than those in Philadelphia "and the people a lot more friendly."[53] The Dixiecrats nominated South Carolina governor J. Strom Thurmond

Connor, third from left, visits with fellow Alabama delegates prior to the 1948 Democratic National Convention in Philadelphia. With him are, from left, Tom King, Anniston; Handy Ellis, Columbiana; Albert Stapp, Birmingham; Hardy Riddle, Talladega; Graham Wright, Talladega; and Jess Edwards, Brighton. Fourteen Alabama delegates including Connor walked out of the Convention in protest of a proposed civil rights plank in the national platform. The protest led to formation of the States' Rights Democrat, or "Dixiecrat" Party, which opposed the national parties in the 1948 election. (Courtesy the Birmingham News*)*

as their presidential candidate and Mississippi governor Wright as vice president, and adopted a platform calling for "loyal Americans" to join the Dixiecrats in "ignominiously defeating Harry S. Truman and [Republican] Thomas E. Dewey" in the 1948 election.[54] The Dixiecrats fell far short of that goal, however, carrying only the states of Alabama, Louisiana, Mississippi, and South Carolina to earn thirty-nine electoral votes as Truman won reelection.

While national developments such as the Supreme Court decision against the white primary invoked the wrath of Southern politicians, a decision by a local federal district judge produced a much more violent reaction in Birmingham during the summer of 1947. On 31 July Judge Clarence Mullins ruled unconstitutional the Birmingham ordinance that prevented blacks from residing in areas zoned for whites. Civil rights attorney Arthur D. Shores, the first black to practice law in Alabama, filed suit in behalf of Samuel Matthews, a black man who built a six-room house on a vacant lot he thought was zoned for blacks. While the house was located one block from a large black neighborhood and three blocks from the nearest white home, it was found to have been built on a white lot. Matthews attempted to sell the house to several whites, but was unable to do so because of its proximity to the black section. He then decided to move into the dwelling, but the city refused to issue him the required occupancy permit for a new structure, prompting the suit. Judge Mullins ruled that the ordinance—part of the city code since 1926—violated Matthews's equal rights as protected by the Fourteenth Amendment.[55]

Less than three weeks later, before Matthews could move in, a dynamite blast destroyed the unoccupied house on the night on 18 August.[56] Connor assigned two detectives to investigate the case full-time, but no arrests were ever made. The incident was the first in a series of bombings during the late 1940s and early 1950s that earned for Birmingham the nickname "Bombingham," and for which, Shores believed, the Ku Klux Klan was responsible.[57] Birmingham's racial climate grew more inhospitable during the summer of 1948, when several blacks were shot by Birmingham policemen and a group of one hundred hooded Klansmen appeared at a black Girl Scout camp to intimidate Scout leaders. Sixty-six black civic organizations formally protested the violence, but Connor promptly labeled their petition part of a communist plot.[58]

Despite Judge Mullins's ruling, few blacks were inclined to venture into the fringes of white sections during the late 1940s, and the tradition of segregated neighborhoods continued. Occasional exceptions occurred when blacks purchased homes or lots located on the line between black and white areas. Frequently, violence followed these purchases. Shores recalled that blacks "didn't attempt to go across the [zoning] lines," but that when they would "move up to the line, whites began to move out and sell to blacks" and "the house would either be dynamited or burned to the ground."[59]

Representatives of the Graymont-College Hills Civic Association appeared before the city commission in late March of 1949, protesting the issuance of building permits to blacks in "an A-1 white residential area." Commissioner James Morgan instructed a city building inspector to investigate the property sales and take the necessary steps to "enforce our laws," but admitted, "our zoning laws are both weak and illegal." Two nights later, on 25 March, three homes that had been recently purchased by blacks in the North Smithfield area were destroyed by bombs about a minute apart. Connor vowed to do "everything possible" to locate the dynamiters, but police efforts followed the pattern in the Matthews case, in which a lengthy investigation was followed by no arrests.[60]

Even though the bombings were "supposedly" investigated, the black community expected no arrests to be made by Birmingham's all-white police force.[61] Jack Warren confirmed that such episodes "would not be truly adequately investigated" because the detective division was unconcerned about crimes against black property.[62] Blacks believed that policemen were sympathetic to the bombers,[63] a feeling strengthened by such episodes as Connor's visit to a black man who had recently bought property in North Smithfield to "advise him that he felt if he did not move away his presence might lead to violence and that if he were in [the black man's] place he would move immediately."[64] Thus the blacks formed a protective association to conduct night watches on property and, according to Shores, hired a white investigator to infiltrate the Ku Klux Klan. Early in 1950, the investigator passed along information that the Klan planned to burn a house purchased recently by a black from a white. Blacks "secreted themselves across the street from this house," Shores related, "and just as they had predicted," several white men approached the unoccupied dwelling late at night. "There was a shootout" in which one white man was killed and another wounded. The incident went largely unnoticed, according to Shores, because "there was never any investigation of it" and "it was not reported to the press." But the episode had a deterring effect on those who were tempted to enforce Birmingham's zoning tradition through violence, for "there were no more bombings or burnings up there" for a period of approximately six years.[65]

Despite occasional bickering among themselves, Mayor Green and Commissioners Morgan and Connor presented a generally harmonious front to voters, and each won election to a fourth consecutive term in 1949. Green had token opposition for the first time in his career, but swept 78 percent of the vote. Morgan claimed 68 percent and Connor 56 percent against five challengers for associate commissioner spots, a higher percentage than either had collected in 1945.[66] Connor continued to project his image as the protector of Birmingham society, and his outspokenness in the area of race relations enhanced his position with the Birmingham electorate, still comprised primarily of whites.

Connor ventured into state politics during the spring of 1950, entering the Democratic primary for governor. But the fortunes of states' righters in Alabama politics had declined in the wake of the Dixiecrat debacle,[67] and despite waging a campaign based on the issues of race and communism, he finished sixth in a field of fifteen candidates. Connor polled 20,629 votes compared to 137,055 for the leader, Gordon Persons. Phillip Hamm qualified for a runoff with Persons by polling 56,395 votes, but chose not to run again, making Persons the winner.[68] The experience taught Connor that, while he continued to represent a potent force in local politics, his name as yet held no magic appeal outside the city limits of Birmingham.

Connor learned the art of headline-grabbing early and made use of the tactic at every opportunity. "He was a newshound," detective George Palmer recalled. "He always wanted to give a news release" on any big arrest.[69] Shortly after the start of the Korean War in the summer of 1950, Connor sponsored an anticommunist ordinance for Birmingham. In announcing the measure to the press on 22 August, he produced a map of the city with the steel mills and railroad yards circled in red crayon and claimed, "We took this from a Communist." Noting that communists "consider Birmingham the sixth most important target area" in the nation, he vowed to "keep them cleared out of here," and added, "I think it's a shame, in the first place, that the President and Congress have neglected to clamp all the Commies where they belong" because "we're at war with them in the Orient." Connor said Alabama had about one hundred "hard-down Communists," but added, "They've scattered out of here, and I can guarantee you that if there's one around here come Sunday, he'll be cooling off in the Southside jail."[70]

The Communist party made its Southern headquarters in Alabama as early as the 1930s, hoping to "sow seeds of revolution" in an area that had been particularly hard hit by the depression.[71] Connor monitored the activities of such party leaders as Hosea Hudson, a black union official, through the use of informants. Hudson recalled a young black man named Israel who attended meetings and asked numerous questions, claiming "he just wanted to work hisself right on up" in the Communist party. The white party members "liked him," but Hudson was suspicious of the young man. Finally, "he turned out to be what I thought he was . . . a stool pigeon for Bull Connor and the city detectives."[72]

Birmingham police relied on informants extensively, a standard law enforcement technique. "If you don't have informants," said Jack Warren, "you don't know what's going on." Generally, a detective's effectiveness could be gauged by the number or quality of "snitches" upon which he could call for information. George Palmer cultivated an informant named Lonnie who "put more people in the penitentiary than most of the detectives." Lonnie was "of the street, and he knew when something was going on and he knew that I needed to know it," said Palmer. Lonnie was not paid, but if he "got in jail for being drunk, he'd have the warden over at the City Jail call me and I'd say, 'Let Lonnie go, and if he's not in court, I'll have him there.'" Few informants were paid, although occasional exceptions occurred. Most informants were aligned through some type of favor or coercion, such as Palmer's willingness to provide verbal bail for Lonnie or an officer's decision not to arrest an individual for a minor offense.[73]

A few weeks after announcing his anticommunist ordinance, Connor was back in the headlines again for conducting a gambling raid on a local residence. The raid produced, in addition to several suspects and various gaming devices, a small red book containing the names of "big shot gamblers around the Southeast." Connor enhanced the dramatic effect by announcing that he planned to send the book to Sen. Estes Kefauver, whose Special Committee to Investigate Interstate Crime had attracted nationwide attention through its televised hearings.[74]

Gambler Sam Fiorella, called the "kingpin of the Birmingham lottery racket" by Connor, remembered how tough the commissioner was on local gambling entrepreneurs. "You couldn't take your car out of second gear if you left home," he told a 1989 interviewer. "They'd get you for vagrancy or traffic charges." Fiorella became board chairman of a holding company owned by his family to avoid vagrancy charges. During the 1950s he moved his gambling operation to a farm known as the "Kid McCoy place" in an adjacent county and operated for years outside of Connor's jurisdiction.[75]

Newspaper coverage helped Connor build his reputation as an effective police commissioner, and he was always ready with a comment on a matter of topical interest for a reporter. After the Alabama Parole Board granted 238 paroles and 112 pardons in a ten-day period shortly before Gov. James E. Folsom left office in 1951, Connor was on the front page of the *News* proclaiming his opposition to "flagrant paroling of hardened criminals" in Alabama. Not only was the practice "discouraging and sickening" to law enforcement officers and the public, it was "nothing short of outrageous," said the commissioner. "It is breaking down the morale of Birmingham police officers."[76]

Politically, Connor profited from media coverage more often than not over the years. During the winter of 1951–52, however, he made headlines of a different nature, and the episode threatened his career. On the afternoon of 21 December 1951, Birmingham detective Henry Darnell, acting on what he said was an anonymous tip, went to Room 760 of the Tutwiler Hotel and began pounding on the door. More than twenty minutes later, after Darnell attempted to force his way into the room and even removed the lock, Connor opened the door. With him was his thirty-four-year-old secretary, Miss Christina Brown. Both were fully clothed and wearing their overcoats and hats, but Darnell announced that he was arresting them for violating an ordinance that forbade members of the opposite sex to occupy a hotel room with anyone other than their spouse. The ordinance was an antiprostitution measure that had been passed with Connor's support during World War II. "You will ruin me politically," Connor told Darnell.[77]

Discussion followed, and Darnell's supervisor, Captain C. E. "Bud" Huey, was summoned by telephone. After a conversation with Huey, Darnell left without filing charges. Several days later, Connor wrote the detective that nothing wrong had been done, that he and Miss Brown had been in the room talking for five minutes when Darnell began beating on the door, and that he was the victim of "a frameup." Connor's note so angered Darnell that he changed his mind and filed charges against the commissioner and his secretary on the day after Christmas. A speedy trial was ordered, and the case was set for 4 January 1952, before Recorder's Judge Ralph E. Parker.

Testimony at the trial revealed that Darnell, a sixteen-year veteran of the police force who served on the vice squad, was unhappy with Connor for conducting several investigations into his activities. The detective claimed these investigations— which included scrutinizing several cases on which he worked as well as examining his personal income tax records—occurred only after *Birmingham News* columnist Walling Keith noted in his column that Darnell might run for the city commission. Darnell said he discovered Connor and Miss Brown were meeting at the Tutwiler from the anonymous source and went to the hotel, taking his wife and *Birmingham Post-Herald* reporter Billy Mobley as witnesses, to gain information on Connor "for his own protection." He testified that, after Captain Huey arrived, an agreement was reached by which Connor would discontinue harassing Darnell and Darnell would file no charges. But Connor's ill-advised letter negated the arrangement.[78]

Connor's attorney, John Foster, maintained that Darnell's charges were motivated by a desire for revenge against the commissioner, and that Connor—who had been at the hotel to attend a reception hosted by Tutwiler manager Ira Patton—was innocent. During the course of testimony, Foster quizzed Darnell about his feelings toward Connor. "Just like thousands of others, I'm fed

Connor, center, and Birmingham Detective Henry Darnell talk following Darnell's discovery of Connor and his secretary Christina Brown in a Tutwiler Hotel room 21 December 1951. Hotel detective H. H. Daugherty is in background. Darnell agreed to overlook the incident at first, but decided to file charges a few days later, citing Connor for violating a city ordinance prohibiting occupancy of a hotel room with a member of the opposite sex other than one's spouse. (Courtesy Birmingham Public Library)

up to here with Mr. Connor and his actions," answered Darnell. "If Judgement Day were called of killers, murderers, thieves, and they were all resurrected tomorrow, Mr. Connor would be underneath all of them."[79]

Following a two-day trial that received almost verbatim coverage in the *News*, Judge Parker found Connor guilty of disorderly conduct, joint occupancy of a room with a member of the opposite sex, and extramarital sexual intercourse. He was sentenced to 180 days in jail and a $100 fine, the maximum penalty for these convictions. Connor appealed the verdict, and the Alabama Supreme Court ultimately overturned the conviction on the basis that the laws involved were too vague.[80]

In the aftermath of the trial, and months before the Supreme

Connor's trial on charges stemming from the Tutwiler Hotel incident begins on 4 January 1952. Connor, hand in mouth, sits at left as Defense Attorney John Foster, standing left, and City Prosecutor J. Edmond Odom, standing right, exchange comments. Connor was found guilty of occupying a hotel room with his secretary, Christina Brown, but the verdict was later overturned by the Alabama Supreme Court. The aftermath of the trial, however, prompted Connor's decision not to run for re-election in 1953. (Courtesy the Birmingham News*)*

Court ruled against Connor's conviction, the city commission appointed a Citizen's Committee on the Birmingham Police Department to investigate charges of disharmony and possible corruption that surfaced in the trial testimony. After several weeks of hearings in February 1952, the committee prepared a report that praised the Police Department for keeping syndicated crime out of Birmingham but noted that department morale was low. The committee also found that Connor was "deficient in executive ability," that he "lacked an objective outlook," and that he "conducted himself in a frequently imperious manner."[81] One member of the committee, businessman H. A. Berg, went further in his criticism of the police commissioner, saying Connor had "definitely destroyed his future usefulness as head of the Police Department."[82]

Also in the wake of the trial stemming from the Tutwiler incident, a grand jury recommended impeachment of Connor on charges of moral turpitude, using city property (a load of leaf mold) at his home, making city prisoners available to work at the Federated Women's Club without charge, and general incompetence. As the impeachment trial opened on 26 March, Connor pleaded not guilty to all charges. Judge Emmett Hildreth ruled the morals counts were inadmissible as impeachment offenses, and the trial proceeded with a parade of character witnesses testifying for and against the commissioner. Connor's colleagues, Mayor Green and Commissioner Morgan, testified in his behalf. Green said Connor was "sometimes very belligerent and a hard taskmaster" but that he was "very capable" in running his department. Morgan admitted that he and Connor had occasional differences, but stressed that Connor was "a good commissioner." When the case went to the jury, a hopeless deadlock occurred, and the judge finally declared a mistrial.[83]

The entire scenario was replayed the following October, with the original charges being filed, the judge throwing out the morals counts, and the string of character witnesses (including Green and Morgan) testifying for and against Connor. Once again, after twenty-two hours, the jury reported itself deadlocked beyond hope, and another mistrial was declared.[84]

By this time, the Alabama Supreme Court had overturned Connor's conviction in the Tutwiler incident. But the aftermath of that episode—a sensational trial replete with "allegations of dishonesty and corruption in the Birmingham Police Department,"[85] the unfavorable report of the Citizen's Committee, and the negative impact of the impeachment proceedings—led to Connor's decision not to seek reelection in the Democratic primary of 1953. On 28 February 1953, the final day of qualifying for the May primary, Connor went on local television and radio to announce that he was bowing out of the city commission race.

After pointing with pride to his record of having "cleaned up crime" in the city, he said, "I feel that, due to the strong feelings which have arisen in unparallelled attacks against me, I should step aside from public office and, by doing so, offer my contribution toward a continuance of the law enforcement and law abiding record that we have now."[86]

During his thirty-minute program, Connor said hundreds of citizens had urged him to run again, but that even though it was "painful" to leave public office, "it is in the people's interest for me to take this step now." He referred to the "unfortunate episode" at the Tutwiler and the "ridiculous charges" stemming from it to remind his audience, "In all the campaign of villification that has been carried on against me in an attempt to destroy me and my family, I am glad to say that no one ever claimed that I have stolen a cent or accepted a bribe or a gift to influence me in my official duties. This is something I am proud of. Even my enemies have been willing to admit this."[87]

Connor apparently had decided not to run several weeks earlier, for he had written a confidential letter offering his services as an employee to Clark Hungerford, president of Frisco Railroad in St. Louis, Missouri, on 18 February. Hungerford answered on 2 March, saying, "It is a compliment to this Company that you would consider a return to railroad service after so many years of serving the public interest." He added, "Yet, there is also disappointment in the fact that within our organization at the present time there are no vacancies which one of your attainments could appropriately consider."[88]

Connor entered city hall as a reformer, an enthusiastic young man lamenting his lack of preparation for public office. He fought the gamblers, made life tough for the "policy boys," and built a reputation as an honest, effective police commissioner, a man of high morality. His early changes, and the positive effects of the civil service law for which he had worked, strengthened the Police Department. But his lengthy tenure, his favoritism, and the dilution of civil service that occurred while he was commissioner negated these gains, producing a stagnating effect on the department. Along the way, the power of his position became more important to Connor than the service. Four terms in office transformed the politically naive young man of the '30s—who sought to make a difference in the system—into a pragmatic politician whose primary goal became the maintenance of his own position and power.

Those who assisted him fared best, and nowhere was this more evident than in Connor's favorite area of responsibility, the Police Department. A 1977 study, *Police Revitalization,* noted that under Connor Birmingham Police Department "objectives had long been internalized" and that "every individual pursued his own personal goals in a low achievement context." The department "stifled initiative and suppressed innovations," and filled positions and assignments "randomly . . . often on a basis of favoritism."[89] Inevitably, the effectiveness of law enforcement suffered. During the last ten years of Connor's tenure, no Birmingham police officer attended the FBI Academy; instead, Birmingham policemen went to a school in Louisville, Kentucky, where they could be taught "Southern" police methods.[90] Rookies received no training other than simply observing the techniques of older policemen. The result was a poorly trained force with inadequate systems of maintaining records or internal discipline. The department kept no modus operandi file on the habits of criminals until 1954.[91] "I have seen older detectives go in a place after a robbery and get a napkin off a table and make a few notes, and that would be the report," said James Parsons, who joined the force shortly after Connor's decision not to run in 1953, then served under him later. "One time I was in the report room when an officer was calling in his report. The lady taking the report kept saying, 'Yes, yes . . . alright,' as though she were taking notes. But she was sitting there combing her hair. When he finished, she wrote down four words: 'Broke in back door.' That was the report." Discipline was inconsistent; no internal affairs division existed until the 1970s. For all of Connor's crowing over the years about keeping organized crime out of Birmingham, small-time local policy men and bootleggers still plied their trades, especially in the black community. These numbers operators and whiskey sellers paid off certain policemen to stay in business, according to Parsons, and considered the payoffs "just part of the overhead."[92]

Yet these conditions mattered not to a predominantly white electorate generally unthreatened by crime. Connor's white supporters related to his rough-hewn charisma and shared his well-publicized attitudes against public corruption, communism, and integration. As he left office after a record sixteen years as Commissioner of Public Safety, Connor smiled and spoke most directly to this audience, which held a favorable impression of the Birmingham Police Department and credited Connor with providing effective leadership. Without "your help and support," he said, "I could have done nothing."[93] It was a moment of irony, for this champion of the straight and narrow—who praised his own morality even as he abdicated—was leaving in a cloud of doubt, stirred by an episode that bespoke immorality.

4

On the
Comeback Trail

Bull Connor left the Birmingham Police Department in turmoil. Dissension was widespread in the aftermath of the various investigations surrounding the former commissioner. Allegations of dishonesty and corruption within the department filled the air. Into this cauldron stepped Robert E. Lindbergh, a quiet former chief clerk in the Jefferson County Sheriff's office who was elected in June 1953 to succeed the flamboyant Connor as Commissioner of Public Safety.

Lindbergh was a well-meaning man who had gone to school at night to earn a degree from the Birmingham School of Law. He made changes, shifting personnel and appointing a retired military officer, Col. Paul L. Singer, as director of police, a position tantamount to chief. Lindbergh's first act was to remove press "gag orders," which since 1951 had prevented all but a handful of "superior officers" from supplying information to reporters. He also announced that Birmingham police officers once again would go to the FBI Academy for training.[1] Despite this promising beginning, Lindbergh encountered problems because he "didn't understand the department," recalled James Parsons. Ultimately, "he was simply whipped by the internal machine there."[2]

Parsons joined the Police Department as a patrolman in 1954, beginning a twenty-five year career that led to the position of chief during the 1970s. Less than a year after Connor left, Parsons found a police department with "a caste system" that had been in place for years and in which corruption and brutality were common-place. The caste system divided Birmingham policemen into three groups: those receiving payoffs, those not receiving payoffs who would have been receptive to such opportunities, and those that would not accept payoffs. Parsons estimated the size of the groups to be "about 45-45-10," the ten percent representing those not interested in tainted money. "The biggest source of money at that time was bootleggers, but the second source was the policy racket that ran rampant in the black community," said Parsons.[3] The presence of corruption in the department was underscored during the summer of 1954, when twenty-three policemen were arrested for their involvement in a burglary ring that had committed forty-one robberies netting a take of $50,000.[4]

Policemen used physical intimidation "to keep people in line." The tactic was effective; resisting arrest was an infrequent occur-rence, because people understood that policemen would "rough them up." Parsons recalled asking a veteran officer about "coming down hard" on a man who had committed a minor traffic viola-tion. "You've got to come down hard on 'em, son," the officer replied, "so they won't come down hard on you."[5]

Despite the graft and "them or us" attitudes, Parsons found that he enjoyed "a lot of things" about police work. He felt that condi-tions would improve as Lindbergh grew more familiar with the workings of the department. The names changed, as the new com-missioner replaced key Connor appointees with selections of his own, but the substantive conditions remained the same. After a period of months, Parsons joined a growing number of policemen who were disillusioned with Lindbergh's leadership. During the fall of 1954, the *Birmingham News* described the police depart-ment as being "about 25 years behind time in many fields."[6]

Connor withdrew from public view in the fall of 1953 to run his service station on 41st Street and Third Avenue South in Avon-dale.[7] But the life of a small businessman removed from politics held little appeal for a man who had served four terms as police commissioner. Less than a year after leaving the commission, Con-nor jumped into the 1954 race for Jefferson County sheriff against a highly popular incumbent, Holt McDowell. "Bull was always ready to run for something," recalled James T. "Jabo" Waggoner.

"I think he enjoyed running more than he did serving. But he couldn't have beat Holt to save his life. And he didn't."[8] McDowell polled 35,880 votes to defeat both Connor (20,969 votes) and auto parts salesman Hugh Hillhouse (9,355) without a runoff.[9]

James Simpson wrote Connor a consoling letter, saying, "We timed your campaign as though you had a good field organization working for you . . . [but] overlooked the fact that you did not have the gang you had always had with you before, doing the preliminary work." Simpson added, "You will remember that this race has come less than one year after the termination of the prosecutions and impeachments against you and was, unfortunately, very present in the minds of everybody, I fear, during the campaign."[10]

Wade Bradley, a former deputy sheriff and Birmingham policeman, won a disputed race for Commissioner of Public Improvements against Waggoner in 1953. The morning following the election, the *Birmingham Post-Herald* reported that Waggoner had won a commission seat by 169 votes over Bradley, Waggoner polling 8,275 votes to Bradley's 8,106. The Jefferson County Democratic Committee discovered mistakes in the totals, however, and ordered a recount. The following day, Bradley was declared the winner with a plurality of thirty-eight votes (8,026 to 7,988).[11] "They stole that election from me," Waggoner claimed, adding that "the two men who stole it" by changing voting machine totals on two Inglenook boxes admitted their act to him in later years. Bradley was not a party to the theft and was unaware of it, according to Waggoner.[12] Early in 1956, however, Bradley decided to vacate his commission post to return to active duty with the U.S. Air Force.[13] A special election to fill the unexpired term was scheduled for 1 May.

Waggoner had been employed by the Birmingham Street and Sanitation Department since 1935 and had finished first on nine civil service examinations for the superintendency of the department. But Mayor James W. Morgan ignored the civil service procedure and appointed Lem D. Merrill as superintendent. Waggoner sued in an effort to gain the job for which he had qualified through examination, and the attendant newspaper coverage over a period of four years made his name well known to voters. That, plus his strong showing in the 1953 election, prompted Waggoner to run for Bradley's unexpired term in 1956.[14] Connor, itching to return to city hall, also entered the race, along with former commissioner Lewey Robinson (who had given Waggoner his first city job[15]), Lamar Weaver, and T. O. Ellis.

Connor conducted an aggressive campaign that included some of the first political television shows in the area. J. Morgan Smith, who handled advertising and public relations for Connor's campaign, recalled, "We developed a format of having news people interview Bull, and Bull was very impressive on television." Connor "came across very well," according to Smith, and was "quite articulate when he felt inclined to be, and he came across sincerely."[16]

Connor was also running for a delegate-at-large post to the Democratic National Convention in Chicago in August.[17] In connection with both campaigns, he scheduled appearances at segregationist White Citizens Council meetings in the Roebuck, North Birmingham, and Bayview areas of Jefferson County as well as in Jemison, Lincoln, Sylacauga, Anniston, Ashville, Vincent, and Mobile during the period January through May.[18]

Racial violence flared during the campaign when black singer Nat "King" Cole was attacked during a performance before a white audience at Municipal Auditorium on 10 April. As he performed his third song before a crowd of 3,500, four white men burst through the rear door of the auditorium. "Let's go get that coon," said one as the group rushed down the aisle and up onto the stage. Members of the audience gasped as the men knocked Cole to the floor and began beating him. Police moved in and quickly restored order, but not before Officer R. N. Higginbotham suffered a broken nose. The officers arrested four men immediately and two others later; all were from Anniston except Jesse Mabry, a Roebuck man who was associate editor of *The Southerner*, a White Citizens Council publication. After the attack, Cole returned to the stage and was applauded for ten minutes, but decided against continuing the concert. The white audience was cleared, and the singer then performed a concert for an all-black crowd without incident.[19]

A tinderbox atmosphere had prevailed prior to the performance as White Citizens Council members, with the support of Connor, staged a demonstration against "jungle music."[20] The following day, police officials identified the attackers as members of the

North Alabama Citizens Council, a radical group not recognized by the more moderate Associated Citizens Councils of Alabama. The attack had been planned four days earlier at a service station owned by one of the attackers, Kenneth Adams. Sam Englehardt, executive secretary of the Associated Citizens Councils, issued a statement deploring the violence and noted that his organization would expel any member involved in such actions. Asa E. Carter, executive secretary of the North Alabama Citizens Council, defended the action, saying the men went to the auditorium as part of his council's study of "be-bop and rock-and-roll music" and were goaded into fighting by a black who knocked one man's camera to the floor at the rear of the hall. "The incident made him mad," said Carter, "and he ran down the aisle toward Cole, who was just another Negro to him."[21]

By election day 1 May, interest in the Cole attack waned and the attention of Birmingham voters focused on the political contest. Connor led the five-man field in the first primary, polling 12,157 votes to Waggoner's 11,952 to set up a 29 May runoff between the two. Finishing far back were Weaver (who proposed employing black policemen in Birmingham), with 3,150 votes; Robinson 1,216; and Ellis, 818. Both Connor and Waggoner had stated strong prosegregation views, but Connor "hit the issue harder and his strength was reflected in areas where the Citizens Council units were most active." Connor also ran third in a field of thirty-five candidates for delegate-at-large, thus winning one of sixteen positions to the Democratic National Convention.[22]

As the runoff period drew to a close, Connor charged that Waggoner was the choice of the National Association for the Advancement of Colored People (NAACP) ticket mailed out to 7,000 black voters under the label "Jefferson County Progressive Democratic Council." Waggoner claimed he received almost no support from black voters in the first primary and that he had sought none since. Connor told prospective voters that "the tide of integration cannot be stopped if you put on guard men who just believe in segregation during campaigns."

Waggoner countered by saying that the NAACP thrived on turmoil and that the organization preferred the election of a candidate "whose record is that of creating turmoil and agitation." Declaring himself a segregationist "right down the line," Waggoner added, "I do not stand with the race haters and race baiters. I don't believe any right thinking Southern citizen believes in creating an agitation between the races. I'm happy the Citizens' Councils are weeding out those who try only to create trouble."[23]

Waggoner then accused Connor of being "closely allied with this radical element in the Citizens' Council Movement," noting that Connor spoke from the same platform as North Alabama Citizens Council executive secretary Asa Carter and was endorsed by Carter's group. Waggoner also accused his opponent of avoiding the issue of Connor's inexperience in matters relating to the public improvements post, reminding voters that all of his sixteen years prior service on the commission was in public safety.[24]

Waggoner won the runoff, receiving 17,396 votes to Connor's 14,868,[25] and he believed Connor's lack of knowledge in the area of public improvements was the deciding factor. "He didn't know anything about how to fix a street," Waggoner said. "He didn't know asphalt from a scuttle of coal. And the public recognized that."[26] J. Morgan Smith agreed: "People thought of Bull as a police commissioner, and they couldn't make the transition."[27] Waggoner took office immediately after the special election. Connor congratulated his opponent and thanked his own supporters, adding, "I would like to remind them that though I have been defeated in this race, I am still ready to carry on the fight in their interest and for their protection whenever I am needed."[28] He then turned his thoughts to another campaign, the upcoming Democratic National Convention in Chicago in August.

Not surprisingly, Connor opposed the nomination of Sen. Adlai E. Stevenson of Illinois as the Democratic presidential candidate. Stevenson advocated a platform approving the 1954 *Brown* decision against segregated schools. Connor hoped a Southerner might be nominated. Another delegate, Major W. Espy, Jr., of Headland, Alabama, also opposed Stevenson, saying he would vote against any platform that included a civil rights plank. But some Alabama delegates seemed willing to support a platform carrying a civil rights plank if the platform also included a statement prohibiting infringement upon states' rights.[29]

Connor sought to put the Alabama delegation on record as refus-

ing "to yield to anybody," should the Illinois delegation request
such a move to nominate Stevenson first. The Alabama group,
caucusing in the LaSalle Hotel on 12 August, decided to withhold
commitment to any candidate until after the platform was drafted
and adopted. The Arkansas and Mississippi delegations took similar actions. Judge George C. Wallace of Clayton, one of Alabama's
two platform committee members, encouraged his fellow delegates, saying, "I feel we have a chance of getting a platform that
will have no mention of the Supreme Court anti-segregation decision." Sen. John Sparkman, chairman of the Alabama delegation,
told his group that delaying tactics might help Averell Harriman
of New York claim the nomination and suggested that "certainly,
Stevenson would be preferred so far as the South is concerned."
Connor disagreed, saying, "I can't see one iota of difference between Stevenson and Harriman."[30]

To maintain party unity, the Democrats adopted a civil rights
plank that Wallace described as "palatable" to the South, but a
group desiring a stronger civil rights stand offered a substitute from
the floor of the convention. Massachusetts Cong. John McCormack, who chaired the platform committee, spoke immediately
in favor of the milder version. Following McCormack's plea, former Pres. Harry S. Truman also made a personal appeal for the
milder platform, prompting a standing ovation from the Alabama
delegation—with one exception. Bull Connor sat on his hands
scowling. "I don't like that guy and he'll get no applause from
me," said Connor, adding that he opposed "the civil rights plank
he's speaking for."[31]

The Democrats nominated Stevenson on the first ballot. Connor
made a motion that the Alabama delegation commend Senator
Sparkman "for his fairness" as chairman, and the entire delegation
stood and gave Sparkman prolonged applause. Delegate Gene
Starnes provoked laughter when he said, "This is the first time
I've agreed with Connor on anything."[32] For his part, Connor
agreed to support the Democratic ticket of Stevenson and Sen.
Estes Kefauver of Tennessee, the vice presidential nominee, even
though Kefauver was unpopular with many Alabamians for saying
in Birmingham that the Supreme Court's desegregation decision
was law and must be obeyed.[33] With the hullaballoo of the conven-

tion over, Connor returned to quieter pursuits, operating his service station and selling radio advertising. But politics remained his consuming priority, especially with the Birmingham city elections less than nine months away.

Bull Connor, once highly popular with Birmingham voters, faced the 1957 election with uncertainty. After leaving the city commission in a cloud of discord in 1953, he had run unsuccessful races in 1954 and 1956. Nevertheless, he joined the fray eagerly, to the surprise of no one, seeking to dislodge incumbent Commissioner of Public Safety Robert Lindbergh. Former Commissioner Wade Bradley, Citizens Council leader Asa Carter, and union official Joe Captain also announced their candidacies.

"I'll enforce the law 24 hours a day throughout my term," Connor told the Young Men's Business Club at the Redmont Hotel on 9 April 1957. He then hit the theme that would recur through the remainder of his political life, saying he would not permit "professional agitators and radicals to come into Birmingham and stir up racial strife." Connor's candidacy was endorsed as "acceptable" by the Birmingham Federation of Labor on 16 April, along with those of Bradley and Captain. The endorsements followed a daylong meeting of area American Federation of Labor, Congress of Industrial Organizations, Railroad Brotherhood, and United Mine Workers locals, at which candidates were quizzed by union leaders.[34]

The following Sunday, 21 April, the *Birmingham News* endorsed the three incumbent commissioners for reelection—Mayor James Morgan, Commissioner of Public Improvements Jabo Waggoner, and Lindbergh—noting that, "Individually, they are handling their heavy responsibilities well," and adding, "Their cooperation is in happy contrast to the costly wrangling that too often has been known at City Hall in the past." Of the incumbent commissioner of public safety, the *News* added, "Mr. Lindbergh has proved himself an official of sincerity, courage and competence. He has faced some difficult conditions in striving to increase the efficiency and morale of the Department of Public Safety itself, in dealing with the many complex police problems of this growing and far-spread city. . . . He has made progress in building up a police department that had been subject to demoralizing conditions."[35]

Connor continued to emphasize such positions as no city tax increases without voter approval, continued maintenance of the city reserve fund, credit spending or issuance of city bonds only within the limit of the city's income, sound management-employee policies such as those used in private enterprise, and impartial but positive law enforcement. Most of these were vintage Connor promises, but with Jim Simpson's help, the former commissioner updated his program to keep in step with the times. To the point regarding impartial but positive law enforcement, he added the phrase, "based on the law as written for the South and Alabama." Further along the list, he became more specific, promising "strict enforcement of segregation of the races." He was also for progressive recreation programs for teen-agers, modern traffic lighting systems to alleviate bottlenecks, and a "high standard of honest, decent and economical government."[36] Summing up his candidacy before the Birmingham Chamber of Commerce on 23 April, Connor said, "I have more experience running these departments than all the other candidates in the race combined."[37]

Several days later, Connor ran an advertisement in the *News* reminding the voters, "I'm no yes man." The ad quoted Connor further: "I don't think the people of Birmingham want a Casper Milktoast [sic] as head of their police department, especially in this time of serious unrest. I am definitely not a 'yes man.' . . . This does not mean, of course, that I could not get along with my fellow commissioners."[38]

The *News* lauded Lindbergh again in a 1 May editorial. The "sincerity, fairness, balance and common sense with which Lindbergh served warrants a high degree of confidence," the newspaper stated, adding, "He well deserves renomination . . . and re-election next Fall." In his campaign statements, Lindbergh underscored his common-sense approach and the harmony of his tenure in city hall. "The internal politics, strife and discord prevalent when I took office in November, 1953, have been eliminated," he claimed. Lindbergh reminded voters of his commitment to open city government, saying, "My first official act as the elected head of the Police Department was to remove the press gag that had heretofore clothed the activities of this department in a veil of secrecy, through which the truth was shining only dimly and sometimes not at all."[39]

The *News* restated its belief in the Lindbergh candidacy—and in those of the other two incumbents—again on the Sunday prior to election day Tuesday, 7 May. Connor said without exaggeration that he had "worked harder and shaken more hands with more people" in the 1957 campaign than in any of his previous races. Lindbergh thanked his supporters for "the hard work that is being done to assure my renomination." *News* political reporter Fred Taylor summed up the race as "a quiet campaign" that would produce a light turnout and a Lindbergh-Connor runoff.[40]

Generally, the election went as expected. Morgan was reelected mayor and Waggoner won his first full term as commissioner of public improvements. Lindbergh, with 14,238 votes, and Connor, with 11,938, led their race, but Lindbergh fell short of gaining a majority, necessitating the anticipated runoff. The size of the turnout proved mildly surprising, for a total of 31,775 went to the polls, approximately 45 percent of the city's 70,000 registered voters. The *News* had predicted a turnout of less than 25,000.[41]

Although Lindbergh led the ticket, coming within 1,560 votes of winning, Connor's strength was unmistakable, especially in the heavily industrialized areas of western Birmingham. Lindbergh had not straddled the segregation issue, but his references to the race question were often couched in vague terms. He called "sensible and sane law enforcement without bombast and bluster" a major need, "especially in these troublous times."[42] Already, the Montgomery bus boycott led by Martin Luther King, Jr., had ended segregated bus service in the Alabama capital[43] and a young black woman, Autherine Lucy, had enrolled briefly at The University of Alabama, only to be expelled for accusing university officials of conspiring with rioters opposed to her acceptance.[44] The white South was bracing for a frontal judicial assault on its way of life, and for those concerned with this threat to the dual society, Connor had a quick and forceful answer. He stated, simply and unequivocably, that he was "for strict enforcement of segregation of the races."[45]

Lindbergh grew more pointed in his references to racial matters as the 4 June runoff approached. A Lindbergh advertisement in the *News* on 27 May proclaimed, "It doesn't take AGITATION to maintain SEGREGATION." The ad said, "No city in the entire South has maintained segregation more firmly and effectively on every front than Birmingham" and credited Lindbergh's "intelligent and common sense handling of race relations" for such an "outstanding record." The message asserted further, "Bob Lindbergh has always stood and will continue to stand foursquare for segregation down the line."[46]

The *News* endorsed Lindbergh twice more during the four days leading up to the runoff. On 31 May the newspaper said the incumbent was well qualified "for upholding the deep traditions of the community, for fairness to all groups, for keeping down extremism, violence and bitterness." On 2 June the state's largest daily added, "The problem of law enforcement is particularly complex in these disturbed times. Effective dealing with racial and other tensions requires good judgement, firmness, balance, courage, intelligent insight into difficult problems." The paper stressed that voters should go to the polls because the election was "of high importance."[47]

Although the *News* carried little coverage of Connor activity during the final week of the campaign,[48] the former commissioner was carrying on his usual aggressive technique. Connor was "a good politician," Waggoner recalled, noting that he "remembered names well" and that he "got around and saw people," especially "key people around the community." Waggoner believed that Connor was "dollars-and-cents as honest as a person could be," but that he was prone to saying "things he didn't mean in order to get some group for him."[49] In addition to his personal contacts and appearances before groups, Connor continued to use the half-hour interview television shows that he and J. Morgan Smith developed during the 1956 campaign against Waggoner.

Lindbergh had been an employee of the Street and Sanitation Department for a time prior to his election to the commission in 1953 and thus was acquainted with Waggoner even before their service together on the city commission. Several weeks before the 1957 election, Waggoner offered to take Lindbergh to the Ensley section of Birmingham, where Waggoner lived, and introduce him to prospective voters. Connor traditionally ran well in labor areas, and Ensley, situated within the shadows of U.S. Steel's massive plant, was heavily unionized. Lindbergh never got around to accepting Waggoner's offer.

Another opportunity came Lindbergh's way a week prior to the 2 June runoff when Waggoner invited him to ride in a Shrine parade through downtown Birmingham on Saturday, 30 May. Waggoner and Mayor Morgan—both Shriners—planned to be in a car bearing a city commission banner. "There will be a gang of folks downtown," Waggoner reminded Lindbergh. "You can ride in the car with City Commission on the side of it and wave at an awful lot of people, if you want to." Connor had been a Shriner, but had left the Masonic order, and the Saturday opportunity was thus unavailable to him. But Lindbergh neglected to join the parade; Waggoner and Morgan rode unaccompanied in the city commission auto.[50]

"Smitty, I think we have just lost this race," Connor confided to his campaign manager while following election returns at his Crestwood home. The mood was subdued as Connor, his family, J. Morgan Smith, and a few friends listened to reports. Early returns favored Lindbergh overwhelmingly, and even though Connor's total began to lessen the gap, Lindbergh continued to lead as the night wore on.

"Now, wait a minute, Bull," Smith said. "The race isn't over yet. You still have some of the eastern section to come in."

A few minutes later, Connor's telephone rang. A *News* reporter said, "Bull, you have won the race." Eight years had elapsed since Connor had heard those gratifying words. It was an exhilarating moment. As Smith remembered, "He exploded."[51]

By the narrow margin of 103 votes among a total of 31,674 cast, the predominantly white electorate of Birmingham returned Eugene "Bull" Connor to the city commission on which he had served from 1937 until 1953. Another large turnout gave Connor 15,891 votes and Lindbergh 15,788.[52]

"Bob Lindbergh was just overconfident in that race," said Jabo Waggoner. "He wasn't there [at the Shrine parade], and he got beat by just a handful of votes."[53] Jamie Moore, who had been appointed police chief by Lindbergh in 1956, recalled that Lindbergh was "a good man" but an inept politician. "His wife would pick him up for lunch every day," said Moore. "If I had been running for office, I would have eaten in North Birmingham one day and Pratt City one day and somewhere like that every day."[54] Smith said, "That campaign, I believe, was won by Bull's stronghold . . . people who felt that he had been a good police commissioner, that he was a protective person. Lindbergh, too, had been soft on speaking out on certain issues."[55]

Connor talked himself hoarse during the latter stages of the campaign, but he beamed as his three-year-old grandson dusted off the nameplate that had stood on his desk during his first four commission terms. A *News* photographer recorded the moment. In his prepared statement, Connor "humbly" thanked the people of Birmingham for their confidence in him, noted that the voters had given him "a mandate to uphold our laws," which he said he would do, and promised to "cooperate with my colleagues to the fullest."[56] Its candidate beaten, the *News* wished Connor well in his victory and added editorially, "We are especially pleased by Mr. Connor's statement that he intends 'to cooperate with my colleagues to the fullest' and that 'any differences and bygones will be forgotten for the good of the city.'"[57]

Meanwhile, the civil rights issue was growing in importance on the national scene. Later that summer, under the leadership of majority leader Lyndon B. Johnson of Texas, the United States Senate passed the first civil rights law in eighty-two years. The Civil Rights Act of 1957, passed on 9 September, established a six-member Civil Rights Commission and a Civil Rights Division within the Department of Justice. The law provided federal protection for blacks who wished to register to vote.[58]

That same September, in Little Rock, Arkansas, federal troops were used to integrate all-white Central High School. Court-ordered integration had been scheduled to start with the opening of school 2 September, but Arkansas governor Orval E. Faubus called out the state National Guard to prevent nine black students from attending classes. On 24 September Pres. Dwight D. Eisenhower dispatched 1,000 U.S. paratroops to Little Rock and placed the National Guard under federal command. The black students entered Central High the next day.

Despite allowing the Little Rock situation to fester for three weeks before acting, Eisenhower finally abandoned his policy of drift in the area of civil rights. For the moment, Little Rock was the hub of Southern resistance to racial desegregation.[59] But the federal intervention, ordered by an administration that had not been at the forefront of the civil rights movement, was viewed with alarm by segregationists across the South, and especially in Birmingham, Alabama.

Connor expected to face Republican opposition in the general election of 1957, but none materialized, and he, Morgan, and Waggoner were sworn in on 4 November 1957. In his inaugural remarks, Connor noted that the principle of segregation was law in Birmingham and Alabama. "At the time those principles were written into our ordinances and statutes, they were constitutional ... because the Supreme Court of the United States said they were," he said. "The only way you can change the Constitution of the United States, as provided by the instrument itself," said Connor, "is by a vote of the Legislatures or conventions of the people of three-fourths of the states. I know that such a change has not been made since the Supreme Court said these laws of ours were constitutional. Therefore, these laws are still constitutional and I promise you that until they are removed from the ordinance books of Birmingham and the statute books of Alabama they will be enforced in Birmingham to the utmost of my ability and by all lawful means."[60]

Connor criticized President Eisenhower for his use of troops in the Little Rock desegregation case, noting that four years previously, segregation was the "law of the land" according to then-current Supreme Court rulings and that no troops were used to enforce that law. Connor said, "It is clear to me that he [Eisenhower] is wrong, and I am one of those who believe that right will triumph." He called on "all people of Birmingham, both white and colored," to be calm, cool, and considerate of the rights of others. "Since we are right—both morally and legally—in this matter, let's be stout-hearted and firm in the defense of the laws of Alabama and the ordinances of the City of Birmingham," he added, "and ultimately, there will enlist under our banner all good thoughtful people, both white and colored, everywhere."[61]

Connor reiterated his promise to "work in harmony" with his fellow commission members, thanked the voters who "generously forgot and forgave all my many former mistakes and shortcomings," and said his narrow victory over Lindbergh made him "more grateful for my election and more determined not to disappoint the people who placed confidence in me."[62]

Jim Simpson wasted little time in complimenting Connor on his remarks. "As I read the speech," he wrote to Connor on 12 November, "it sounded like a pretty common sense exposition of the legal theory of stare decisis. Your doctrine that when it is written into the Constitution it stays written there until it is taken out by an amendment, sounds like good law to me."[63]

Connor began inspecting the Police Department immediately after his inauguration with the idea of switching personnel. "The people wouldn't have elected me if they were satisfied with the operation of the police department," he said. His first week back in office, he ordered crackdowns on downtown parking violations and the drinking of alcoholic beverages at football games and began a drive to collect delinquent traffic fines.[64] These moves reflected high Connor priorities, according to Jamie Moore, who was still serving as the Lindbergh-appointed Police Chief.

"Bull was especially interested in some areas, such as traffic," Moore recalled. "He got upset if there was congestion, or if we didn't solve a hit-and-run. He gave us hell if we didn't get traffic moved out quick after a football game."[65] Although Connor usually voted wet in any wet-dry referendum,[66] he was "strictly in favor of enforcing alcohol laws [against] selling to minors, selling on Sunday, and so forth," said Moore.[67]

Connor's proposed changes involved more than procedures and priorities. He told the *Birmingham News* on 10 November that veteran police captain Ben F. Walker would be returned to actual police work from a Civil Defense post to which he had been assigned under Lindbergh. "I'm not underestimating the value of Civil Defense," said Connor, "but Walker is too valuable a man to the department. We need him."[68] Three days later, Connor placed Walker in charge of all police personnel, "effective immediately," and shifted Capt. Glenn V. Evans, who had been responsible for all uniformed officers, to Walker's Civil Defense post. Walker had held the police personnel position previously and had done "a wonderful job," according to Connor. The commissioner added that other changes were forthcoming because "the people expect changes."[69] By the end of his first ten days back in office, Connor had announced thirty shifts in police responsibility.[70]

Police Chief Jamie Moore felt uneasy. Moore had joined the Police Department as a beat patrolman on 21 October 1936 and progressed upward through the ranks. By 1955 he was assistant chief. Commissioner Lindbergh appointed him temporary chief in late 1955, and he was named chief on 6 May 1956, after posting the highest score on a competitive exam. Following the successful completion of the required one-year probationary period in 1957, Moore became Birmingham's first permanent chief in seven years.[71] But with Bull Connor once again calling the shots as Commissioner of Public Safety, not even a permanent chief was safe.

"You don't fit into the picture as my chief of police," Connor told Moore several days after the inauguration. Connor suggested that Moore voluntarily vacate the chief's post and take a demotion to captain.

"I hear you have not been enforcing the law," the commissioner said, adding that he had reports that liquor was sold after the legal closing time at the Angus Club in downtown Birmingham. Moore asked Connor if he had "heard anything bad about me, whether he doubted my integrity," and Connor answered no to both points.[72]

Connor had made a practice of moving temporary police chiefs in and out of the post to maintain firm control of the department, and Moore believed that he "just wanted to put his own man in."[73] The commissioner suggested that Moore take over direction of the police training program and added, "I would hate to see you lose your pension."[74] But Moore, who was protected by the civil service law that Connor helped pass during his younger days in the Alabama legislature, refused the suggestion.

Determined to name his own chief, Connor decided to seek Moore's ouster "on charges of political activity and waste of city property." He filed suit against Moore with the Jefferson County Personnel Board as a private citizen, charging the chief with a total of forty-eight counts of political activity in behalf of former Commissioner Robert Lindbergh prior to the 1957 primary, allowing illegal liquor sales, and misuse of city vehicles. A hearing was set to begin on 16 January 1958, before the three-member board of Chairman Howard Yielding, Charles A. Long, and Dan Hudson.[75]

"We don't want that loudmouth talking up and down the halls," Moore was quoted as saying prior to the 1957 primary. The term "loudmouth" referred to Connor, according to Patrolman C. H. Rushing, one of twenty-four witnesses called by Kingman Shelburne, Connor's attorney. Moore not only denied having made the statement, but all the charges brought against him by the Commissioner.[76]

The three-day hearing attracted wide interest, bringing near-capacity crowds to the largest courtroom in the courthouse. Moore's attorney, Roderick Beddow, relied on a parade of character witnesses and Moore's own testimony for his defense. Midway through the trial, Connor dropped the charges relating to political activity and misuse of vehicles. The remaining illegal liquor sale charges stemmed from alleged after-hours activity at the Angus Club. Patrolman R. N. Higginbotham testified he saw liquor sales made past the legal Saturday night closing time of midnight while he worked at the club from mid-September until 1 December.[77] Two other witnesses said they saw drinks served at the Angus, but Moore testified that he had not heard that the club was selling liquor late. He added that the Police Department followed the wishes of the city commission on illegal liquor sales, rather than strict enforcement of the law.[78]

After little more than an hour of deliberation behind closed doors on the afternoon of 21 January, the personnel board returned its findings, acquitting Moore by a two-to-one vote. While Moore restated his belief in "the system which created civil service" and claimed "no malice toward any man," Connor sputtered that the personnel board had failed to perform its duty. "The people who sent me back to City Hall want law enforcement," Connor fumed. "They do not want law enforcement through a police chief who is known to eleven men in his department to have openly violated the law against political activity and to have winked at illegal sale of whiskey." Moore pledged continued loyalty to his superiors, and

Connor lamented the damage that "this failure of enforcement" had done to civil service.[79]

"For a few months, Bull was poison to me," Moore recalled. "Then he called me one day and wanted to go to lunch at Joy Young's. I went with him. That really made my wife mad." During the next few months, Connor began to give Moore some control over police administration. "He treated me better after that," Moore said wryly. "He didn't tell me everything to do."[80]

But the presence of an unwanted chief continued to irritate Connor, so he began simply to bypass Moore and run the department "through some crony down within the ranks," according to James Parsons. "Sometimes, the lowest patrolman ran it," Parsons asserted, referring to Connor's executive secretary, John W. Preddy, a uniform policeman who ferried orders from the commissioner. "I can assure you that Chief Moore under no circumstances ran that department," said Parsons.[81]

After the Personnel Board decision for Moore, Connor began another practice that enabled him to exert even greater control over the Police Department. In 1958 the Personnel Board approved an arrangement allowing the city to assign patrolmen as plainclothesmen with a twenty dollar per month clothing allowance.[82] This enabled patrolmen to be assigned "temporarily" as detectives, whether or not they had taken the detective examination, and to draw detective pay while on the assignment. The underlying idea was to provide new faces to work such areas as vice and stakeout and to offer less experienced officers on-the-job training working with veteran detectives. Connor not only endorsed the arrangement but made it work in his favor. Whenever a detective resigned or retired, Connor simply assigned one of his favorites "temporarily" to the plainclothes position, which carried more prestige, the use of an automobile, and greater work freedom. Such temporary assignments might continue indefinitely, because nothing in the civil service law required Connor to fill these vacancies with permanent appointments.

"Bull didn't have enough places to put all his cronies, and give them any status, unless he had the detective division he could use," recalled Parsons. "Once that change was made, all those people that were in his clique or on the fringe of his clique were made detectives. It shut out that rank."[83]

Parsons was part of a group of younger officers—all disillusioned with Lindbergh's administration—that supported Connor's reelection bid. These half-dozen or so upwardly mobile patrolmen were not well known by Connor and were included in neither the Connor clique nor the fringe group. Connor's use of the detective rank to reward favorites "shut the door in all our faces," leaving Parsons and the others with a sense of having been betrayed. They arranged a meeting with Connor to protest the change.

"Son, you're going to have to understand something," Connor told Parsons. "I am the man that runs this thing. If you don't like the way I run it, you're going to have to leave."

Parsons reminded the commissioner that the detective rank was covered by the merit system.

"Merit," said Connor, "is what I say it is."

Parsons and the others complained about their low salaries, and Connor said, "Well, the salaries may be low, but I know what you people are making." He "implied that he was aware of the corruption in the department and that that was part of the pay . . . your salary was simply a base income."

"Some of us are trying to live on the base salary," said Parsons. Connor laughed and said, "Well, that's your problem."

Some departments—such as vice—had frequent opportunities for payoffs whereas others—like traffic—had few. Connor controlled the department by approving assignments, said Parsons. "It was a masterful way of controlling the department. There's forty-five percent that's not going to say anything because they're getting it [payoffs], and there's forty-five percent that's going to be quiet hoping to get in there. He probably first went in [as commissioner] hoping to make a difference, and the system was just impossible to control. So he went with the flow and ran it the best he could. And he figured out these ingenious ways of control."[84]

Bull Connor felt like a winner again, for he was back at City Hall, back in the public eye, and back in control. Gone were the uncertainties of his years away from the commission, and the nagging fear that he might never serve again. Because his political life was at stake, the 1957 election was a highly significant point in Connor's lengthy career. Victory by Robert Lindbergh would have dimmed Connor's hope of ever regaining a city commission post. Such a loss would have been his third consecutive defeat in the wake of the embarrassing Tutwiler Hotel incident of 1951, and even for Connor—called "the consummate optimist" by J. Morgan Smith[85]—a difficult obstacle to overcome.

The election held equal significance for the city of Birmingham. Twice during the late 1940s and early 1950s, attempts had been made to establish and maintain communication that would lead to harmonious relations between blacks and whites in the city. After World War II, blacks and moderate white businessmen tried to create a local chapter of the National Urban League, but the effort failed in 1949 in the aftermath of the Dixiecrat movement and the emergence of race as an issue in the 1948 presidential campaign.[86] In 1950 white leaders formed the Interracial Committee as a division of the Community Chest's administrative agency, the Jefferson County Coordinating Council on Social Forces. The Interracial Committee organized subcommittees to tackle such issues as hospitals, day care, housing, recreation, transportation, and black police. Its most visible project was a highly publicized campaign to persuade the city to hire black policemen, a measure that Connor staunchly opposed. "You can rest assured that as long as I am head of the Police Department, I'll never vote for negro [sic] policemen," Connor wrote Jim Simpson on 9 October 1952. He had investigated the use of black policemen in other cities, he told Simpson, and found that "officials of the Police Department as well as the policemen say that a negro [sic] policeman is not worth a damn."[87] After the 1954 *Brown* decision, Birmingham's racial climate worsened, and in 1956 the Community Chest withdrew its support from the Interracial Committee out of fear that segregationists would boycott the Chest's fund-raising drive. The committee was forced to disband, thus closing the one avenue of communication between the races.[88] Bull Connor's victory the following year, by no means sweeping, nevertheless signalled the beginning of massive, stubborn resistance to desegregation and a period during which the voices of racial moderation were silent in Birmingham.

5

"That Bomb Had My Name on It"

On Christmas night of 1956, the Reverend Fred L. Shuttlesworth, Jr., pastor of Bethel Baptist Church in North Birmingham, relaxed in the bedroom of his home next to the church, chatting with Bethel deacon Charley Robinson. About 10 P.M., Shuttlesworth's daughter Ruby heard something hit the front porch of their home. Moments later, an explosion ripped through the dwelling, destroying the house and damaging a portion of the church.

Within minutes, a crowd of some five hundred blacks gathered at the scene, fearful that Shuttlesworth and his family had been killed. The appearance of two white police officers, W. E. Howse and C. L. Crutchfield, sparked angry murmurs. As Howse and Crutchfield approached the shattered parsonage, the crowd surrounded them, blocking their way. But Shuttlesworth and the others had survived. Hearing that policemen were on the scene, the pastor emerged from a neighbor's home and told the crowd, "The Lord has protected me. I'm not injured."[1]

Fred Shuttlesworth, then thirty-four years old, had been at Bethel Baptist since 1953. A native of Mt. Meigs, Alabama, but reared in the Birmingham area at Rosedale, Shuttlesworth held degrees from Selma University and Alabama State College. He represented a new breed of black preacher that emerged after World War II, the social activist. These men believed in working to improve conditions on earth rather than in being totally concerned with saving souls for the hereafter.[2]

Shuttlesworth had been at the forefront of the civil rights movement in Birmingham throughout much of his tenure at Bethel Baptist Church. He had served as membership chairman of the National Association for the Advancement of Colored People (NAACP) since 1955, helping to lead efforts to secure paved streets, covered ditches, street lights, and better police protection for black areas. He had appeared before the Birmingham City Commission in 1955 petitioning for black policemen "in Negro areas, not to arrest white people," but the attempt failed.[3]

Shuttlesworth's experience with the NAACP was frustrating, partially because the local chapter was dominated by members of the black business elite. To Shuttlesworth, this group seemed out of step with the majority of the black community and more concerned with building on its own business and professional success. Many local blacks considered the organization elitist, and membership of the Birmingham chapter had fallen off dramatically.[4]

Early in 1956, Alabama's segregationist attorney general, John Patterson, launched an attack against the NAACP. Labeling it a foreign corporation, Patterson charged the organization with encouraging the Montgomery bus boycott and an attempt by Autherine Lucy and Polly Hudson to desegregate the University of Alabama. He sought an injunction, which Circuit Judge Walter B. Jones issued on 1 June 1956. Judge Jones ordered a halt to all NAACP activities and required the organization to turn over all records and membership lists. When it refused, Jones held the NAACP in contempt of court and fined it $100,000.[5] More important than the fine, however, the action effectively closed down the civil rights organization in Alabama for years.

With the NAACP thus throttled, Shuttlesworth and others held a strategy session at the Smith and Gaston Funeral Home on 4 June, where they planned a mass gathering for the following night to form a new organization. Several elderly members counselled against a new body led by "hotheaded" activists such as Shuttlesworth and fellow pastors R. L. Alford and Nelson H. Smith, Jr.[6]

Undaunted, the activists scheduled a 5 June meeting at Sardis Baptist Church. The next night, more than 1,000 people[7] attended the session at which the Alabama Christian Movement for Human Rights (ACMHR) was founded; the organization was dedicated to "press forward for the removal from our society of any forms of second class citizenship."[8] Shuttlesworth was elected president by acclamation following an impassioned speech in which he declared that black citizens were "restive under the yoke of segregation."[9]

Shuttlesworth had been present at the birth of Martin Luther King's organization, the Southern Christian Leadership Conference, in New Orleans on 10 February 1956[10] and was closely identified with activists in that body. After the NAACP was enjoined, the ACMHR became "the leading organization" for civil rights in Alabama. A consensus existed among Birmingham blacks active in the civil rights movement to follow Shuttlesworth's lead, according to attorney Arthur Shores, who described the pastor as an activist "who surrounded himself with similar persons."[11] Not everyone in the black community agreed with Shuttlesworth's approach, however. Conservative pastors such as G. W. McMurry and J. L. Ware did not support ACMHR, nor did members of the black upper class such as former NAACP chapter president John Drew and attorneys Shores and Orzell Billingsley, Jr. Both groups opposed the use of direct action[12] and both were offended by Shuttlesworth's autocratic nature.[13] Lower-class blacks, the great majority of Birmingham's black population, also chose not to participate in ACMHR activity but for different reasons. They feared reprisal and shared a sense of frustration that efforts to change segregation were foredoomed.[14]

A year after the Montgomery bus boycott began in late 1955, the Supreme Court issued its findings in the case of *Gayle* v. *Browder*, striking down on grounds of equal protection the ordinance requiring segregated buses.[15] On the night the decision was announced over the national wire services, Shuttlesworth and Smith, who was pastor of New Pilgrim Baptist Church, were visiting the newsroom of a local television station watching "the ticker tape." They decided to request the city commission "to voluntarily desegregate" Birmingham buses "in light of the Supreme Court decision." Shuttlesworth recalled that they "coupled it with the implied threat" that if Birmingham did not rescind its bus segregation ordinance, the blacks "were going to ride anyway."

The ACMHR made its announcement on Christmas Eve, and as Shuttlesworth remembered, "the Ku Klux Klan didn't intend for me to be around to ride, so that night, December 25, Christmas night, they placed this sixteen sticks of dynamite at the corner of my house and the church and blew the house down."[16]

Earlier the day of the bombing, in his Christmas sermon, Shuttlesworth told his congregation, "If it takes being killed to get integration—I'll do just that thing, for God is with me all the way." After surviving the destructive blast, he credited God with saving him to lead the fight against segregation, saying, "One reason I was sure God wanted them [the buses] unsegregated is because I came through this alive.

"That bomb had my name on it, but God erased it off."[17]

The Christmas tree lights still burned in the rubble,[18] but little else remained intact in the parsonage. Shuttlesworth recalled that "the wall was shattered, the roof was gone, the floor was gone from under the bed," and the bed springs were nowhere to be found. The frame house bore the brunt of the force rather than the brick church, "and I didn't get a scratch, so I knew God saved me to lead the fight."

Shortly after the blast, at the rear of the house, Shuttlesworth encountered a policeman examining the scene. "Reverend, I know these people," said the officer, "and they mean business. If I were you, I would get out of town as quickly as possible."

"If God could save me through this," replied Shuttlesworth, "then I think he could save me in something else. Tell your Klan brothers that they missed me this time, and they will have to go a little deeper than this. I'm here for the duration."[19]

The following day, Shuttlesworth and his group held a meeting at the Smith and Gaston Funeral Home to discuss plans for desegregating local buses. Some ACMHR board members had been unnerved by the blast of the previous night, but Shuttlesworth refused to waver. "We said we were going to ride," he reminded the group in his opening remarks, "and I have to be a person of my word."

Shuttlesworth's strategy was for blacks to ride from the heart of downtown Birmingham, where bus routes intersected, to outlying areas, in order to achieve maximum coverage. The meeting was covered by the local press, but reporters were not permitted to sit in on the actual sessions and thus were unaware of the specific plan. Shuttlesworth had promised an announcement after the meeting, and the reporters anticipated learning the date on which blacks would ride in sections reserved for whites. Rather than making an announcement, Shuttlesworth strode out of the meeting and led more than two hundred black people toward downtown Birmingham. The ride was on at that moment.

"I don't want three or four black people sitting together," Shuttlesworth told his followers. "Divide out. And don't all sit in one spot. Spread out all over the white area, but leave space for your white brother. If they choose to stand up, then let's let them stand, but you sit down, and don't sit together.

"And don't say anything to anybody that says anything to you. If somebody strikes you, remember that we are here to prove a cause, not to fight."[20]

The sudden maneuver caught the press—and the police—by surprise. More than two hundred fifty blacks rode buses in disregard of the ordinance requiring that they sit behind signs marked "Colored Only." Shuttlesworth rode from the downtown area to University Hospital, a distance of some ten blocks, to visit his daughter Patricia, who was recovering from burns she had suffered in a small kitchen fire a few days earlier. He offered his seat to "a young white lady" as a courtesy en route. The blacks rode the buses "all over town," the ACMHR leader recalled, but the suddenness of the action prevented all but a few "who loved integrated riding so, they rode two and three times" from being arrested.[21]

Birmingham police arrested a total of twenty-one blacks for violating the city bus ordinance. Commissioner of Public Safety Robert E. Lindbergh stated that the Montgomery bus desegregation ruling did not apply to Birmingham and added, "We are not going to stall around on this."[22] One additional black was arrested for sitting in the white section the following day. At that point, ACMHR leaders instructed their members to return to segregated riding while the organization prepared to take the case to federal court.[23] The Shuttlesworth strategy was to violate the city's segregation ordinance, then to use the subsequent conviction to test the validity of the local law in federal court.[24] The ACMHR leader employed this technique frequently throughout the civil rights struggle; by 1971 Shuttlesworth had become the most litigious individual in the history of the U.S. Supreme Court, having appeared before the body eleven times in civil rights-related cases.[25]

His actions petitioning for black policemen in 1955 and leading the bus desegregation effort in 1956 identified Shuttlesworth as Birmingham's leading civil rights activist. This position was underscored in September 1957—after Bull Connor had been reelected but before his return to office—by Shuttlesworth's attempt to integrate Birmingham public schools. Alabama's Pupil Placement Act gave local authorities broad discretion in the placing of students in schools; the Alabama legislature passed the measure in 1955 to maintain segregated schools. As the 1957 school year approached, Shuttlesworth and eight other black families petitioned the Birmingham Board of Education for permission to send their children to white schools. School Superintendent Frazer Banks replied that the school board would discuss the matter at a 6 September meeting.

While Shuttlesworth and the others awaited the decision, white extremists decided to send the black community a message. On Labor Day, 2 September, four white men kidnapped, stabbed, and emasculated a black man named Judge Aaron on a road near Tarrant, an industrial community bordering northeast Birmingham. Picked at random because of his color, Aaron neither knew Shuttlesworth nor had been involved in any civil rights activity. His attackers warned Aaron that if Shuttlesworth did not stop his integration attempts, he would face the same fate.[26] They then poured turpentine into Aaron's wound to increase the pain; ironically, this action cauterized the wound and probably prevented Aaron from bleeding to death.[27] He was found on a roadside by two police officers and hospitalized. The same night, crosses were burned at ten public schools in the Bessemer and west Jefferson County area.[28]

Later that week, on Friday 6 September, the school board met to discuss the petitions of the black families, but failed to take action. The following Monday, 9 September, after informing television stations, the police department, and the board of education of his intentions, Shuttlesworth and his wife drove three children to Phillips High School to enroll. With the couple were their daughter Patricia and two other black students, Nathaniel Lee and Walter Wilson.

A crowd of toughs awaited. As the minister's car rolled to a stop, "15 or 20 white men" gathered around the vehicle and knocked out the windows. Shuttlesworth tried to escape, but the attackers chased him and beat him "with brass knuckles and a large link chain about a foot long and wooden clubs." Birmingham police arrested three of the attackers—W. H. "Jack" Cash, I. F. Gauldin, and J. E. Breckinridge—and charged them with assault with intent to murder.[29] Shuttlesworth was confined to bed after the attack with a sprained arm, cuts, and bruises; Gauldin was identified as having inflicted some of the wounds with a bicycle chain.[30] A grand jury later dropped the charges against the three, however, when police officers failed to identify the suspects.[31]

Bull Connor rode back into office in 1957 on a promise to maintain Birmingham's strict segregation ordinances. His inaugural address criticizing President Eisenhower's use of federal troops in Little Rock set the tone for his intransigent approach to matters of race. Connor had won his first term on the city commission in 1937 at a time when segregation was the unquestioned way of life in the South. While the two decades between 1937 and 1957 wrought tremendous changes nationally in the area of racial accommodation, Connor returned to office espousing the same strongly racist views that had been so widely accepted twenty years earlier, and which had characterized his first sixteen years in the post of commissioner of public safety. Connor assigned only the basest motive to any attempt on the part of blacks to climb above the status of second-class citizen. He typically referred to civil rights activists as "outside agitators coming into our city and dabbling into our affairs";[32] attorneys engaged in defending civil rights suits, Connor said, were primarily interested in "financial benefits."[33]

Connor was still preoccupied with reorganizing the Police Department and trying to rid himself of Chief Jamie Moore when, during the early morning hours of 7 December 1957, another bomb blast shattered the quiet of a Birmingham night. The explosion destroyed a home purchased a short time earlier by a black in the formerly all-white section of Fountain Heights. It was the fourth such bombing within a year in Fountain Heights, earning the north Birmingham area the dubious nickname of "Dynamite Hill." Connor condemned the bombing as "a terrible thing" and reassured the public that the Police Department would "do all we can to find the person or persons who did this and send them to the penitentiary." Fire Marshal Aaron Rosenfeld termed the blast the worst of the recent Fountain Heights incidents, indicating that dynamite had been placed at each end of the unoccupied dwelling and the bombing had been carried out "more skillfully than previous explosions."[34]

The following day, after reiterating the Police Department's commitment to ending such blasts, Connor placed the blame not on the bombers, but on the real estate agents who sold the homes and the blacks who bought them. He proposed that the Real Estate Board void the licenses of agents who sold homes to blacks in white areas, saying, "They know when they sell those houses that it is liable to cause trouble, and the Negroes themselves should know not to buy those homes." The commissioner of public safety called for the "full cooperation of the board, the white and the colored, and the police department" to stop the bombings "before somebody gets killed." While Connor was prompt to voice his official concern, and the usual flurry of investigative activity followed, no arrest was made in connection with the incident—the typical pattern. Police spokesmen explained that detection of dynamiting was difficult because any person could purchase the explosive legally and a large amount was sold for construction purposes.[35] But an informant for the Federal Bureau of Investigation added this footnote to the incident: "Connor did not intend to attempt to solve this bombing."[36]

During the spring of 1958, Shuttlesworth appeared before the city commission once more to petition for the hiring of black policemen. A 1953 survey conducted by the Birmingham Interracial Committee indicated that eighty-two Southern cities had integrated police forces and that Birmingham was the only city with a population of more than 50,000 to have an all-white police department.[37] Now, five years later, the all-white policy continued and, with Bull Connor back in office, was likely to remain in effect. Shuttlesworth believed that not only would having black policemen "cut down on crime in black areas," it would also "bring this city forward," points he attempted to make before the city commission.

Connor, facing Shuttlesworth for the first time in the commission setting, chastized the ACMHR leader for doing "more to set your people back than any man in the history of this city." Shuttlesworth, accompanied by a delegation of forty-two blacks, retorted that "history will have to decide whether I have done more to set them back or bring them forward," and added, "You have done some to set them back."

Shuttlesworth reminded Connor that the issue was the need for black policemen, to which Connor replied, "Well, I wouldn't vote for nothing for you." Mayor James Morgan interrupted saying, "We aren't going to argue," and told the Shuttlesworth group— which had not been recognized until the close of the agenda—that the commission would "take it [the petition] under advisement."[38]

Following the meeting, Connor accused Shuttlesworth in the local press of "doing this for publicity" and of "taking money from the north to pad" his own pockets. He challenged the ACMHR head to take a lie detector test about the events surrounding the bombing of his home on Christmas night of 1956. Shuttlesworth volunteered to take such a test if Connor would do the same and answer questions about his Ku Klux Klan sympathies, police corruption, the bombing of churches and homes, and police brutality.

Despite Shuttlesworth's chiding that if the commissioner had nothing to hide, "let's quit talking and get on with the test," Connor declined to be tested.[39] Declaring that he found it difficult to believe that anyone would say he was a member of the Ku Klux Klan, Connor said, "I am not and never have been."[40] He then dropped the public debate with Shuttlesworth. The city commission took no action to hire black policemen, Shuttlesworth feels, because "they didn't want to do anything to look as if they were giving in to the black community."[41]

During the late 1940s, the black community had taken steps to protect property against Ku Klux Klan bombings by establishing night watches at suspected target sites. Following the 1950 episode in which blacks surprised a group of whites about to bomb a home, no bombings occurred for a period of six years. The blasts resumed in April 1956, when a North Birmingham home was bombed, and continued with the destruction of the Shuttlesworth residence in December of the same year. Members of the ACMHR began holding night watches immediately after the Shuttlesworth home was bombed, with volunteers taking turns watching for marauders.

Between April 1956 and December 1957, seven bombings of black homes occurred in North Birmingham.[42] Although such incidents were "supposedly" investigated by the Birmingham Police Department, the failure of the police to make even one arrest in the bombings fueled persistent suspicion among blacks that the investigations were half-hearted, said civil rights attorney Arthur Shores. Blacks were convinced that Birmingham police were indifferent to Klan activity and that certain policemen were sympathetic to and even members of the KKK.[43] In a 1988 interview, former acting chief Jack Warren confirmed black suspicions, saying that "one or two policemen" were members of a Klan klavern in Fairfield, an industrial area adjoining Birmingham's western boundary, and that the Klan "had many other sympathizers" on the police force. "Not all of them" were sympathizers, said Warren, "but the majority."

"Now, of course, Bull, I don't think he ever joined the Klan or nothing," Warren continued, "but he certainly concurred in their efforts."[44]

At various times during 1957 and 1958, members of the Birmingham Police Department appeared without warrants at black churches and homes, confiscating weapons that the blacks used on their night watches. On 29 June 1958, Birmingham policemen visited Bethel Baptist Church and confiscated four guns from church members.[45] That night Will Hall, a retired coal miner and a deacon standing guard at Shuttlesworth's church, discovered a paint bucket with a lit fuse at the side of the structure. He grabbed the bucket, raced thirty feet to the middle of the street, dropped it, and scurried away with just enough time to avoid a blast that blew out the church windows and shook plaster loose. Shuttlesworth said the church would have been demolished had it not been for Hall's quick action.[46] The following day, the guns were returned to the church members after Hall and five others in or near the church at the time of the blast took lie detector tests at the suggestion of Shuttlesworth to prove that they were "victims only—not plotters or conspirators."[47]

Smarting from the second bomb attack against Bethel Baptist Church within eighteen months and a series of police actions against church guards which he considered harassment and intimidation, Shuttlesworth wrote Connor a letter requesting for blacks "that protection due us as American Citizens and law abiding residents of Birmingham, Alabama." Shuttlesworth argued that the Police Department offered no protection against the threat of bombers, and that it continued "to needlessly harass us and interfere as we try to prevent our Church and Parsonage from being bombed a third time." The letter detailed six occasions of such harassment, including confiscation of guns prior to the 29 June bombing and another occasion on which Assistant Chief J. C. Lance took four guns from Bethel, one of which still bore the tag of release from a prior confiscation by police. The actions left blacks "utterly helpless and at the mercy of bombers," Shuttlesworth wrote, and added, "the fact that high officials are leading these excursions lead us to believe them the acts of high policy."[48]

Shuttlesworth's real purpose in writing was revealed in the final paragraph, in which he told Connor, "In light of the extreme dangers and officials [sic] provocation we have no recourse but to seek aid of other and higher enforcement agencies of the State and Nation."[49] Toward that end, Shuttlesworth sent a registered copy of his letter to the Birmingham office of the Federal Bureau of Investigation, along with a note to the FBI to "at least look into this problem of improper protection and other problems mentioned in this letter." Shuttlesworth felt the moment was significant; as he dispatched the envelope to the FBI, he remarked: "Bull Connor finally made the mistake we have been waiting for. We've got him where we want him now."[50]

In a sense, Shuttlesworth was correct, because the FBI already had begun to grow suspicious of Connor's activity in the area of race relations. After the unsuccessful bombing attempt of a Jewish synagogue on Birmingham's Southside in the spring of 1958, Connor had called on the FBI to investigate, a request that the Bureau viewed as an attempt "to unload his investigative responsibilities, in connection with the bombings."[51]

A bomb consisting of fifty-four sticks of dynamite was discovered undetonated in a basement window of Temple Beth-El on 28 April 1958. This attempt—which had been timed to coincide with the bombing of a synagogue in Jacksonville, Florida—apparently failed when a twenty-one foot fuse fizzled less than two minutes before triggering the explosion. Connor called the attempt part of an "interstate conspiracy."[52] Substantiating this claim were the simultaneous bombings of synagogues in Nashville, Tennessee, and Miami, Florida, on 16 March with circumstances similar to the Jacksonville-Birmingham cases, and a telephone call to officials from a member of the Confederate Underground taking credit for the Jacksonville blast. The caller identified himself as "General Ponce de Leon" and told Jacksonville officials: "We have just blown up a Jewish center of integration. Every segregationist in the South must go free. All integration must stop."[53]

Still, the FBI declined to enter the Birmingham case, calling it a matter for local police. Mayors and police officials of twenty Southern cities met in Jacksonville on 3 May to consider evidence in these and more than forty other bombings that had occurred across the South since 1 January 1958, seeking a way to end the violence. Connor represented Birmingham at the two-day gathering. During the meeting, a representative of the Anti-Defamation League, former FBI agent Milton Ellerin, provided a long list of known anti-Semites who might be suspected of such activity as violence against synagogues.[54] Connor discovered his own name on the list.[55]

Later that summer, on 24 July, FBI headquarters instructed its Birmingham office "to hold contacts with Connor to a minimum in view of his unsavory background."[56] Connor's decision the following 12 September to refuse police cooperation with federal civil rights investigators and U.S. marshals involved in integration incidents did nothing to improve relations between the commissioner and the Bureau.[57]

As the 1958 school year approached, Shuttlesworth announced that no enrollment attempt would be made, but the Ku Klux Klan marked the anniversary of the pastor's attempt to integrate Phillips High School with a series of cross burnings. On Sunday night 31 August Klansmen lit eighteen crosses at various points across Jefferson County—all at 8 P.M. Fourteen crosses burned on or near schoolyards, underscoring the Klan's commitment to segregated education. The practice continued for the next several years.[58]

During the fall of 1958, the bus desegregation matter flared again when the city commission replaced Birmingham's old ordinance—still under attack in the courts—with a new law that left seating of passengers up to the transit company. The new ordinance removed the segregation signs from the buses, but gave bus drivers the right to request that whites seat themselves from the front of the bus and blacks from the rear. Failure to comply with a driver's "reasonable request" would constitute breach of peace, a misdemeanor, under the new ordinance. John S. Jemison, Jr., president of the Birmingham Transit Company, hailed the measure as a "forward step in race relations in Birmingham."[59]

But Shuttlesworth and members of his organization "immediately rejected that and rode again the next day,"[60] seating themselves at the front of the bus. The driver of one bus carrying thirteen blacks who had refused to sit from the back drove his vehicle to the transit garage, where the blacks were met and arrested by police. Shuttlesworth, who had directed the riding effort, was not on the bus, but Connor ordered his arrest after learning that the pastor instructed riders in a downtown office prior to the 20 October episode.[61]

The fourteen defendants were found guilty of breach of peace by Recorder's Court Judge William C. Conway on Thursday 24 October.[62] Rather than allowing them to post bond and remain free over the weekend while awaiting sentencing the following Tuesday, Judge Conway forced the blacks to remain in jail. Their incensed attorney, Orzell Billingsley, lashed out at the action, saying, "The arbitrary, unconstitutional and high-handed methods of the City of Birmingham in confining respectable Negro citizens in the City Jail certainly will not stop or deter their efforts to secure first class citizenship," but would accelerate such efforts.[63]

On Monday 27 October, the Reverend Martin Luther King, Jr., of Montgomery dispatched three of his colleagues—the ministers

S. S. Seay, H. H. Hubbard, and A. W. Wilson—to visit Shuttlesworth's wife to see "if she needed anything" or "if they could help
out" while the ACMHR leader was in jail. A short time after they
arrived at the Shuttlesworth residence, the three ministers were
arrested by Birmingham police and "held without charges" until
later in the day, when they were released.[64]

The court rendered its verdict the following day. Twelve of the
riders were given suspended sentences of 180 days in jail. Shuttlesworth and another rider, ACMHR vice president J. S. Phifer, were
fined $100 each; Shuttlesworth was sentenced to ninety days in
jail and Phifer, a pastor who often accompanied the ACMHR leader
on direct action projects, to sixty days. The two were released
under $300 bond pending appeal of the case. Connor issued one
of his periodic warnings against "out-of-towners coming to Birmingham and agitating our people." Specifically, the police commissioner stated, "We don't intend to let them come to Birmingham if they are from Montgomery, Alabama, or New York City
or any other place and let them agitate like they have in Montgomery the last two or three years."[65]

Mayor James W. Morgan blamed the bus disturbance on "these
unholy forces attempting to move in and replace peace with unrest, and joy with unhappiness." In Morgan's view, the white and
black races had coexisted "for generations," and "except for the
few occasions on the part of hot-heads, nothing had occurred to
unduly disturb our happy existence in this beautiful valley of
ours."[66] Shuttlesworth saw no such idyllic place as Morgan described, but rather a city in which "black folks had no rights,"
a city in which blacks "were confronted everywhere by a law that
said, 'You can't do, you can't be, you can't do.'"[67]

The symbol of that law, Bull Connor, had been back in office
for only one year, yet his hard-line policies in matters of race
clearly had been reestablished. Mindful of his promise to voters
to maintain strict segregation, Connor fought the civil rights
movement fiercely and self-righteously, using the tactics of harassment, intimidation, and bellicosity to remain on the offensive.

When the Civil Rights Division of the Justice Department began
looking into the detainment of the three Montgomery ministers,[68]
Connor ordered his policemen to give the FBI no information on

the case.[69] The United States attorney general William P. Rogers requested an immediate probe into the matter, but U.S. District Judge Seybourn H. Lynne of Birmingham "respectfully declined," preferring to delay consideration of the case until the next regularly scheduled federal grand jury to be convened on 16 February 1959. W. Wilson White, assistant attorney general in charge of the Civil Rights Division, protested that the two and one-half month delay "would seriously impair the possibility of obtaining the true facts and might well have the result of permitting an open defiance of federal law enforcement in a miscarriage of justice."

Birmingham officialdom treated the entire matter with a general lack of concern. Judge Lynne justified the delay, citing the court's already heavy calendar and his personal conviction that a federal grand jury needs a federal judge available at all times during its session. This condition could not be met until the session scheduled for February 1959, according to Judge Lynne. Connor dismissed the episode, saying he had no apology to make for checking on "outsiders" who might stir up racial trouble in Birmingham. "I haven't got any damn apology to make to the FBI or anybody else," said Connor. "Maybe I just didn't tell the FBI what Rogers wanted me to tell them. Maybe that's why that jackass is yapping his brains out."[70] Local U.S. attorney William L. Longshore seemed primarily concerned that his cosignature appeared at the end of White's letter protesting the delay; Longshore's signature had been affixed "most reluctantly," possibly to avoid being fired, according to *Birmingham News* Washington correspondent James Free.[71]

Finally, in Judge Lynne's own good time, the grand jury convened, but took no action in the detainment. This well may have disappointed Connor, as the local FBI office reported to its headquarters in Washington,[72] for a federal case would have afforded the police commissioner yet another opportunity to underscore the depth of his commitment to enforcing Birmingham's segregation ordinances.

As the decade of the 1960s opened, civil rights activists in the South began widespread use of another tactic aimed at focusing attention on their fight against segregation—the lunch counter sit-in. On 1 February 1960 a group of young black college students in Greensboro, North Carolina, began a series of sit-ins at downtown department store lunch counters. Within a few days, the sit-ins spread to Charlotte, Durham, and Winston-Salem. Custom was the only thing that prevented waitresses from serving the black students, for these cities had no segregation ordinances covering lunch counters. But custom was enough, and the blacks were ignored. By mid-February, sit-ins had been reported in eight North Carolina cities and Rock Hill, South Carolina, Hampton, Virginia, and DeLand, Florida.[73]

On 25 February 1960 the sit-in came to Alabama as thirty-five young blacks staged a brief demonstration in the grill of the new Montgomery County Courthouse in Montgomery. The grill was closed immediately, although no arrests were made. John Patterson, Alabama's segregationist governor, suspected that students at a nearby black college, Alabama State, had been involved. Patterson told Alabama State president H. C. Trenholm to expel any student who had participated in the sit-in, adding that he would have the State Board of Education take such action if the college failed to do so.[74]

Birmingham newspapers gave scant coverage to the lunch counter sit-ins in North Carolina, carrying only brief wire service articles. Bull Connor made bigger news locally when he suggested that the new city zoo be named in honor of Mayor James Morgan, when he endorsed a $3 million bond issue to build a University of Alabama psychiatric hospital in Birmingham, and when he attempted to improve community relations by sending forty-five Birmingham police officers at city expense to a Dale Carnegie course entitled "How to Win Friends and Influence People."[75]

When the lunch counter demonstrations reached Montgomery, however, the sit-ins became front-page fare in Birmingham. Connor forgot Dale Carnegie and refocused his attention on civil rights activity. On the day following the Montgomery courthouse incident, Connor warned against "food counter sitdown demonstrations" in Birmingham. His statement, carried on the front page of the *News*, notified "all citizens, white and Negro, that the City of Birmingham will not tolerate activity on the part of anyone or group that will breach the peace or infringe on the rights of others."[76]

Birmingham blacks were not particularly interested in staging lunch counter demonstrations until Connor "assured the people of Birmingham that there would not be sit-ins" in their city, according to Shuttlesworth. Blacks "thought it was an insult to the black community to say we couldn't sit in or didn't have the courage," the ACMHR leader recalled. Given that impetus, Shuttlesworth and a group that included ten students from Miles College and Daniel Payne College planned a lunch counter demonstration for Birmingham.

The plan called for the students to meet at Shuttlesworth's home, from which they would be driven in pairs to five downtown department stores. The students synchronized their movements so that they would be one floor above the store counters by 10:25 A.M. and within fifty feet of the lunch counters by 10:27 A.M. Promptly at 10:30 A.M., each pair of students would sit down at the counter. Such precision was necessary because Birmingham police were paying close attention to any potential demonstrator.[77]

On 31 March 1960, the students executed the plan to perfection, staging sit-ins at Loveman's, Pizitz, Newberry's, Woolworth's, and Kress department stores. As in North Carolina, they were refused service. Within minutes, Birmingham police moved in to arrest the ten, charging them with "trespass after warning." Connor and other top-ranking police officers went to the area immediately and posted themselves near the patrol wagons to which the youths were escorted.

"That was quick, wasn't it," Connor noted, adding, "It looks like I've been police commissioner long enough for the Negroes to have learned that I'm not going to put up with this kind of carrying on."[78]

Shuttlesworth recalled that the sit-in demonstration was carried out "with precision" and that Connor's action "was done with precision also. But we proved that we would sit-in," the minister added.[79]

Shuttlesworth's activism hastened the widespread identification of Bull Connor as the major obstacle to civil rights progress in the Birmingham of the late 1950s. The pastor's continuing attempts to knock down the city's segregation ordinances caused Connor to redouble his efforts to enforce the laws of the dual society. As the 1950s drew to a close, the adversarial relationship between the police commissioner and the ACMHR leader came to epitomize the struggle between the races in Birmingham. Their actions moved the city toward the spotlight of national media attention. Both men enjoyed the limelight; each was convinced of the righteousness of his cause.

Massive resistance was faltering by 1960, but Connor remained firmly opposed even to token integration and believed that white Birmingham shared his conviction totally. The police commissioner thought Birmingham so independent that "it didn't have to have the world," nor even did it "have to recognize that it was part of the world," said Fred Shuttlesworth.[80] For his part, the ACMHR leader believed with equal fervor that God had saved him from the 1956 bomb blast so that he could lead the civil rights cause in his city. According to one fellow activist, "Shuttlesworth sees himself as taking orders only from God who speaks to him and through him."[81] Like Connor, Shuttlesworth ran his organization with an iron hand. "It was Fred all the way . . . a one-man show," recalled John Porter, pastor of Sixth Avenue Baptist Church.[82] If his dictatorial leadership style offended the black elite and middle classes, it nevertheless mobilized the ACMHR into an effective civil rights organization. "I lived through that," he told the frightened ACMHR members in 1956, "and if I lived through that, you don't have anything to think over. God was there. Let's commit ourselves further."[83] Not everyone liked Fred Shuttlesworth, but nobody including Bull Connor questioned the commitment of the man whose name had been on the bomb.

6

Violent Sunday

Massive resistance to desegregation was the prevailing mood of the South during the middle and late 1950s. In Alabama, Attorney General John Patterson fanned the flame of defiance with his attacks on the NAACP in 1956 and his racist campaign for governor in 1958. While running for governor, Patterson boasted that he had "run the NAACP out of the state" and chided his opponents for not taking a more definite stand against the organization. George Wallace, Patterson's chief foe, claimed, "I was fighting against civil rights 10 years ago, before many knew what civil rights were."[1] In the gubernatorial runoff election between the two, Patterson adopted a much more inflammatory style and defeated Wallace handily. The race signalled the beginning of a period in Alabama politics during which the most militant segregationist candidate had the best chance of becoming governor. And according to Alabama political lore, it prompted Wallace to say, "No one is ever going to out-nigger me again."[2]

Through a policy known as "interposition," Alabama and five other states sought to avoid integration legally by nullifying the Supreme Court decision in the *Brown* v. *Board of Education* case. The doctrine of interposition simply meant "states' rights." Its genealogy could be traced through the 1948 Dixiecrat movement to the Civil War and ultimately back to the Kentucky and Virginia Resolutions of Thomas Jefferson and James Madison. In his resolution—written in response to the Alien and Sedition Acts of 1798—Jefferson stated that whenever Congress overstepped its powers in the passage of an act, each state had equal right to declare the act void and to unite with other states in asking appeal. Madison's resolution—in response to the same acts—included the doctrine of interposition, that is, "interposing" of state authority between a citizen and the federal government.

During the spring of 1956, the Alabama legislature nullified the Supreme Court desegregation rulings, passed various segregation measures, and proposed two constitutional amendments related to the fight against desegregation. The first proposed amendment provided white parents with "freedom of choice" in choosing schools for their children; the second gave municipalities the right to sell, lease, or simply give away public housing, parks, and playgrounds to prevent racial mixing. Alabama voters approved both amendments in August 1956.[3]

By 1960 the popularity of interposition as a means of resisting desegregation had declined. In the fall of that year, a three-judge federal panel ruled directly on interposition, saying, "The conclusion is clear that interposition is not a constitutional doctrine. If taken seriously, it is illegal defiance of constitutional authority."[4] With the opening of the 1960s, some Southerners who had been staunch advocates of segregation began to question the practicality of all-out opposition to the civil rights movement. The feeling grew that such opposition "posed a far more serious danger to social stability than did token change, and, increasingly, it threatened the region's economic progress." Thus the threat to the pocketbook began to turn the South's established order away from massive resistance fanaticism.[5] Yet the trend was seen more quickly in some areas than others. In Birmingham, elected leaders continued to find the prospect of even token integration repugnant. Their refusal to yield, coupled with unwillingness of the city's economic leaders to assert their influence in behalf of moderation, led Birmingham ever more quickly down the path of hardline resistance to change.

White Birmingham professed shock in April 1960 when the *New York Times* described the city as a community in which blacks lived in fear of police brutality. Reporter Harrison Salisbury, a Pu-

litzer Prize winner, wrote that "every inch of middle ground has
been fragmented by the emotional dynamite of racism, enforced
by the whip, the razor, the gun, the bomb, the torch, the club,
the knife, the mob, the police and many branches of the state's
apparatus."[6] Led by public officials, the two daily newspapers, and
the Chamber of Commerce, Birmingham reacted angrily. Bull Connor called the two-part series "a cheap attempt to smear our city
and state."[7] Congressman George Huddleston, Jr., labeled it "an
example of the most severe type of irresponsible journalism . . .
one of the most vicious slanders" in his memory.[8] The *Birmingham News* called it "an amazing recital of untruths and semi-
truths" that provided a "maliciously bigoted, noxiously false, viciously distorted" picture of Birmingham.[9] The Chamber of
Commerce passed a resolution calling on the *Times* to print "the
true facts" about Birmingham in the interest of "fairness and unbi-
ased reporting."[10]

White Birmingham felt besieged by an unfriendly Northern press,
especially after the *Washington Post* printed an article several days
later under the headline "Birmingham Brims with Race Bias." *Post*
Editor Alfred Friendly told *News* Washington correspondent James
Free that Salisbury's articles had prompted the follow-up. *Post*
writer Elsie Carper reported the reaction of Birmingham whites
to the *Times* articles as "one of disbelief."[11] The Birmingham paper
reflected this attitude in editorials appearing over the next several
weeks. "There is little race hatred here—indeed, far less than there
is in New York or Washington," said the *News* on 20 April.[12] The
next week, it added, "This Birmingham of ours is a lovely place.
It is a city in which fear does not abide. What Harrison Salisbury
reported, we all should know, is in substance untrue."[13]

Yet despite this outcry of self-righteousness, Birmingham remained a city with a violent history of bombings, cross burnings,
and physical abuse of blacks. It also remained, in the words of
the *News*, a city in which the "vast majority" of whites "are
fiercely opposed to any integration," and a city in which "the police at times have been ineffective in digging up tangible evidence
of such as dynamiting."[14] And it remained a city in which Bull
Connor, who had returned to office on a platform to uphold segregation at all costs, was the guardian and protector of public safety.

Although much of the force had ebbed from massive resistance by 1960, Connor remained firm in his stance. Efforts to desegregate buses, schools, and lunch counters only intensified his dogmatic opposition to integration. Connor blamed the South's racial strife on "Northern Democrats, the NAACP, and Communist-inspired front organizations" led by "fanatical leaders who will not stop at bloodshed in their fight to mix the races." Addressing a Selma Citizens Council meeting a few days after the appearance of the Salisbury articles, Connor said, "I'll tell you right now, unless the South makes up its mind to stand up and fight this plague—and it is a plague—we are going to find Negroes who can't read or write . . . enforcing our laws." He told his audience that blacks did not seek equality, but black supremacy. "Yes, we are on the one-yard line," he bellowed to a cheering crowd of several hundred. "Our backs are to the wall. Do we let them go over for a touchdown, or do we raise the Confederate flag as did our forefathers and tell them . . . 'You shall not pass!' "[15]

Connor also discussed at Selma his monitoring of "Negro mass meetings."[16] Since his return to office in 1957, the police commissioner had expanded his surveillance tactics to include the weekly Monday night meetings of the ACMHR, sending either sergeant Thomas H. Cook or detective Marcus Jones to sit in on the sessions and relay information to a nearby police car. Written reports of such proceedings were forwarded to Connor. "You could sit there in a police car and hear everything that was going on," said former acting chief Jack Warren. There was nothing secretive about a white detective surveilling a black church meeting, however. "Knowing that you were listening to everything they said, they were selective," said Warren. "That's what tickled the hell out of me." He called it "the damndest joke I've ever seen," but stressed that those directly involved took the surveillance system very seriously.[17]

Shuttlesworth confirmed that the systematic surveillance occurred, describing it as "a tactic to harass the harassers."[18] Yet when Harrison Salisbury wrote in April 1960 that "the eavesdropper, the informer, the spy have become a fact of life" in Birmingham, Connor cried foul. "There are always representatives of the Northern press, radio and television who, through ignorance or evil intent, forsake the principle of responsible journalism to cry havoc over victims and situations that don't exist," said the police commissioner.[19] Adding to the furor created by the *Times* articles, Connor sued the newspaper for "false and malicious reporting of racial tensions," saying it was "high time someone put a stop to irresponsible Yankee journalism."[20] The case eventually reached the U.S. Supreme Court, which upheld the *Times* on freedom-of-the-press grounds.[21] Ironically, the written reports of Connor's ACMHR surveillance were discovered among discarded files in a fire station about to be demolished several years after Connor's death, and they serve as a valuable historical document of the civil rights movement.[22]

Most Birmingham whites likely would have accepted Connor's surveillance of ACMHR as necessary to effective law enforcement. Over the years, he had established an image with the city's white electorate as an efficient, affable, and honest commissioner of public safety, and he received wide support. Connor was, first and foremost, a "police commissioner." Under the commission form of government, he was responsible for the Fire Department, Health Department, Public Library, Board of Education, and several other areas. But he enjoyed the authority and attention that accompanied police work and placed his greatest energies there. Firemen referred to their department as Bull's "stepchild." The community thought of Connor as a police commissioner, which proved to be one of his problems in his unsuccessful 1956 race for commissioner of public improvements. His supporters believed Connor enforced the law impartially, "on black and white alike, and it didn't matter whether you were a United States Senator or Mrs. Franklin Roosevelt," said former commissioner James T. "Jabo" Waggoner. "Bull never did let the gamblers and mob folks get a hold in the City of Birmingham," he added.[23] Connor's former campaign manager, J. Morgan Smith, characterized the police commissioner as "a good vote-getter with a dedicated following of people who thought he was a protective person."[24] Jack Warren felt that "not only the police department, but the community, in the majority, backed Bull Connor."[25]

Birmingham blacks failed to share the view of Connor as an affable and protective public official. Blacks were "politically impotent," however, and could do little to register their objections at the polls, recalled civil rights attorney Arthur Shores. Blacks longed for "a new civic tradition" that offered something more than simply being "Southern." The *Birmingham World*, a black newspaper, pointed up this need in a 1961 editorial, saying, "The Birmingham 'Southern way of life' which excludes a vital segment of the population from the meanful [sic] benefits of this city's life needs correction."[26] But "whites and conservatives and Klansmen" continued to elect Connor, "and he saw to it that, so far as he was concerned, blacks would not integrate or associate," said Shores. Connor's political success was indicative of the void in Birmingham leadership, according to Shores and civil rights activist Fred L. Shuttlesworth.[27]

As the Democratic primary of 1961 approached, attention focused on the contest for mayor. Incumbent Jimmy Morgan announced that he would retire rather than run for reelection, throwing the field wide open. Seven candidates qualified for the 2 May primary. To a lesser degree, interest centered on the race for commissioner of public improvements, where incumbent Jabo Waggoner hoped to fend off seven aspirants. Connor faced three challengers for commissioner of public safety.

Throughout the campaign, the mayor's race received the lion's share of coverage. Attorneys Art Hanes, a former FBI agent, and Tom King, who had served six years as Congressman Huddleston's administrative assistant, emerged as the leaders. Waggoner's opponents attacked the incumbent's voting record on the commission, but Connor's foes were hard-pressed to find any issue more significant than the city's new traffic patterns and the courtesy of its policemen. One Connor opponent dwelt at length on his own segregationist beliefs, but Connor's position on that question was hardly suspect. Safety commissioner hopeful Richard R. Andrews blamed Connor for turning Fifth Avenue downtown, where small shops once thrived, into a "dormant and deserted" area because of his parking ban. Candidate T. E. Lindsey, a former Birmingham policeman, promised to restore parking on Fifth Avenue.[28] Lindsey also claimed, "I am a full-time segregationist," saying he had worked on "these problems" during his twenty-six years "as an officer of the Birmingham Police Department."[29] Another Connor

foe, Alvin A. Billingsley, promised to make policemen more cour-
teous, especially in their treatment of minor offenders. "A person
committing a minor traffic violation should not be treated as
though they had just robbed the first national bank," said Billingsley.[30]

At the outset of the race, Connor campaigned hard, reminding
voters of such recent accomplishments as improved police and fire
training academies, jail expansion, increases in the number of and
salaries for policemen, and institution of the K-9 police dog corps.[31]
By 19 April he had the *Birmingham News* endorsement locked
up. Although the commissioner "has not always handled himself
well . . . and has been irritating to some citizens," he had shown
"a tangible maturity, a mellowness" during his most recent term,
the *News* editorialized. Connor "has consistently warred on
crime," said the paper, and added, "This newspaper has full confidence that not only will Mr. Connor serve well in preventing outsiders from using our city for agitating purposes, but that he will
continue his determination to see that law and order prevail and
that riot or other outbreak will be suppressed with dispatch regardless of who initiates it."[32] On election eve, the *News* reported "little activity" in the safety commissioner race and "considerable
speculation that Connor would be reelected without a runoff."[33]

Election day 2 May proved the accuracy of the speculation. Carrying a whopping forty-two of fifty-one boxes, Connor won by a
landslide over his three opponents, amassing 25,104 of the 41,106
votes cast—the biggest sweep (61 percent) of his career. "By golly,
we swamped 'em this time," he exulted. Flanked by family and
friends in his city hall office, he repeated the count over and over:
"Just think of it, 25,000 votes."[34]

King, the candidate with Washington connections, surprised
many by leading the mayor's race over Hanes, who had received
the *News* endorsement on 23 April. The two prepared to face each
other in a 30 May runoff. Waggoner led his race, but also faced
runoff opposition from Earl Bruner.

Connor, meanwhile, enjoyed the largest vote of confidence in
his career. His official victory statement noted, "It is comforting
to know that a majority of the people of Birmingham approved
the policies I have endeavored to follow in the conduct of this

office." Connor believed his stand against integration had resulted in Birmingham being one of the few cities in the nation to have been free of major race riots and violence. "I am grateful for the fact that, whatever the cost, Birmingham has not suffered the anxiety and violence other Southern Cities have suffered due to the integration movement," he said. "I hope the same policies which have protected us so far will continue to protect us during the next four years."[35] The *News* noted in an editorial that Connor's "conduct in office the past four years, his firmness in striving for law and order in potentially troublous times, earned him a considerable vote of confidence."[36]

After Connor's resounding victory, some of Tom King's supporters suggested the mayoral candidate visit the commissioner of public safety "to pay his respects." Connor was known to support Hanes, but King hoped to neutralize the commissioner's impact on the runoff campaign. "I knew there was no way that I could get him to support me, but we hoped at least to get him not to come out for my opponent," King recalled.[37] On Monday 8 May, King telephoned Connor for an appointment and Connor suggested meeting in his office at 10 A.M. the following day.

"He was very cordial in the meeting," said King. "We shook hands, I told him I thought we could work together cooperatively, and he said he felt sure we could. I visited with him about fifteen minutes."

As King prepared to leave, Connor brought up the subject of the Freedom Riders,[38] an integrated group that had left Washington, D.C., by bus on 3 May "to assert constitutional rights in southern bus stations." Such rights were the result of a Supreme Court decision in December 1960 outlawing segregation in terminals and aboard trains and buses used in interstate commerce.[39] Connor told King that the Freedom Riders—sponsored by the Congress of Racial Equality (CORE)—would arrive in Birmingham on the following Sunday, Mother's Day. King acted surprised.

"We will be ready for them, too," Connor said with a smile.

"I bet you will, Commissioner," answered King, turning to leave.[40]

The mayoral candidate walked down the steps of city hall and headed for the Jefferson County Courthouse across Woodrow Wilson Park. As he neared the curb, a voice called, "Mr. King, Mr. King." He turned with his hand out, almost a reflex after weeks of campaigning. A large black man grabbed his hand and shook it firmly, refusing to let go. Finally, the man released King's hand and walked quickly away. The significance of the act was not apparent until three days later, when King discovered copies of a photograph were being distributed to discredit him. The photo showed King shaking hands with the black man, a political faux pas in early 1960s Birmingham. King blamed Connor for setting up the photo, which was to play a major role in the runoff campaign. "Nobody knew I was going to be at City Hall except Commissioner Connor," he said.[41] The following Sunday, the *News* switched candidates and endorsed King for the runoff, saying he was the man to lead Birmingham forward. Noting that Hanes had implied that King was "the Negroes' candidate," the paper said it believed "the vast majority of Birmingham voters will not be sent astray by raising of this scarecrow."[42]

That same Mother's Day morning, the Freedom Riders divided into two groups in Atlanta for their bus trip to Birmingham—one riding on Greyhound and the other on Trailways. The Riders had encountered only minor trouble through Virginia, the Carolinas, and Georgia, but that changed when they reached Alabama. As the Greyhound bus rolled to a stop in Anniston, about sixty miles east of Birmingham, a menacing crowd of more than one hundred white men—many of them armed—surrounded the vehicle, shouting epithets and striking the bus exterior. The mob surged toward the bus door, but plain clothes Highway Patrol investigator Ell Dowling—who had ridden from Atlanta—stood in the doorway and prevented the men from boarding. During the brief stop, someone slashed two bus tires. When the Greyhound left for Birmingham, groups of whites followed in a caravan of some forty cars. West of Anniston, the damaged tires went flat and the bus stopped. As the mob surrounded the vehicle, Dowling once again posted himself in the doorway. The driver attempted to make repairs, but the mob chased him away and set the bus afire by shooting an incendiary bomb through a rear window. As the passengers scurried off the burning Greyhound, a Highway Patrolman arrived on

*A Greyhound Bus burns beside a highway west of Anniston, Alabama,
14 May 1961, set afire by a mob protesting the arrival in Alabama of
an integrated group of "Freedom Riders" sponsored by the Congress of
Racial Equality. The twelve passengers, some of them Freedom Riders,
required treatment for smoke inhalation after escaping the fire. A Trailways Bus carrying another group of Freedom Riders continued on to
Birmingham, where another mob attacked some of its passengers. (Courtesy Birmingham Public Library)*

the scene and dispersed the crowd by firing his pistol into the
air. The bus was destroyed and twelve passengers required treatment for smoke inhalation.[43]

When the Trailways bus, traveling on a later schedule, made
its stop in Anniston, violence erupted again. Another group of
white men met the bus, and eight boarded the vehicle and beat
several of the Freedom Riders, including the group's white leader,
James Peck of New York City, and a white college professor, Dr.

A mob attacks Freedom Riders in the Birmingham Trailways Bus Station on Mother's Day 14 May 1961. Moments later, the mob attacked Birmingham Post-Herald *photographer Tom Langston, who shot the photograph. Birmingham police were faulted for delaying their response to the violent incident. The episode, coming two weeks after Bull Connor's landslide re-election to a sixth term, marked a turning point in the support of the police commissioner by Birmingham economic leaders. (Courtesy the* Birmingham Post-Herald/*Tom Langston)*

Walter Bergman of Detroit. Finally, with order restored but with the eight attackers remaining on board, the Trailways bus headed for Birmingham.

At the Greyhound Bus Station in Birmingham, located directly across the street from the city hall, a crowd of white men and several reporters waited. According to Columbia Broadcasting System producer David Lowe, in Birmingham with CBS News correspondent Howard K. Smith to prepare a program on Birmingham race relations, the men around the bus station "by dress and demeanor, did not appear to be travellers." They stood in groups of twos and threes; Lowe counted fifty-eight inside the terminal and estimated another fifty outside. Several men appeared to be leaders and walked about conversing with the groups inside the station.

At about four o'clock, the most active leader, "a heavy-set man wearing a T-shirt," began going from group to group "with some sort of information." As he did so, the men began to leave the Greyhound terminal and walk in the direction of the Trailways Bus Station three blocks away. Lowe and Howard K. Smith followed in their car. The Trailways bus had made its way safely to Birmingham, but an angry mob waited to greet some of its occupants.

"I got to the door of the Trailways Terminal and saw a tall man there twirling a handkerchief," Lowe recalled. "Thereupon, a group of men ran over to the terminal. At this moment, I heard women screaming."[44]

As the bus rolled to a stop, the whites who had beaten Peck and the others in Anniston left the bus. Members of the mob then attacked the other passengers with heavy weapons. Peck and black Charles Parsons were beaten, along with several blacks not a part of the CORE group. *Birmingham Post-Herald* photographer Tom Langston was one of several reporters on the scene:

> I shot a picture with a Rolleiflex camera that required a flash, because it was fairly dark inside the bus station. They saw the flash go off, and that's when they came after me. They said something like, "Get him."
>
> I had a 35-millimeter camera around my neck, and they were pulling it and choking me. I finally got it off, and I never saw it again.
>
> They began hitting me with chains and iron pipes, and I threw my hands up to protect myself. My watch was torn off. I had a lot of cuts and bruises, but no broken bones.
>
> They destroyed the Rollei, and one of the idiots started trying to take the strobe [light] pack apart. I knew if he did, it would give him a hell of a shock. He got it opened and it knocked him for a loop. That gave me some satisfaction.[45]

After the attack, nine passengers were taken to local hospitals for treatment. During the Anniston and Birmingham attacks, Peck suffered a rib injury and head cuts requiring fifty stitches.[46]

Langston—his face bleeding and his clothing torn—returned to his newspaper office three blocks away, then went to a hospital for treatment. A reporter who had accompanied Langston retrieved the damaged Rolleiflex—the film still intact—and returned it to the paper.

"Joe Chapman [another *Post-Herald* photographer] called me at the hospital and told me the film was not fogged," said Langston. Mindful that those in the photograph might seek retribution, Chapman asked Langston if he should "fog it or print it." "I told him to go ahead and print it," Langston said. "Nobody ever knew that."[47]

Langston's photograph told a graphic story of racial violence in Birmingham. It ran in both the *Post-Herald* and *News*—an unusual occurrence, since the two were competitors—and in newspapers around the world, courtesy of Associated Press. No policemen are visible in Langston's photograph, for throughout the brief melee, Birmingham police were conspicuously absent. No arrests were made at the scene, even though the police knew well in advance that the Freedom Riders would arrive on Sunday. Their progress south had been covered by the press and followed by the Federal Bureau of Investigation, which had relayed information to Police Chief Jamie Moore. Connor certainly expected the Riders, based on his comment earlier in the week to Tom King. The *Post-Herald* "had gotten information that they were coming in," Langston recalled, which explained his presence at the station.[48]

One of the men at the Greyhound station before the attack was Gary Thomas Rowe, Jr., a Klan member who led a double life as an informer for the FBI. Rowe told the Bureau several days before the attack that Klansmen planned a hostile reception for the Freedom Riders in Birmingham. He also said Klansmen were told that no Birmingham police would appear for fifteen minutes after the attack began[49] and that any Klansman arrested would receive a light sentence.[50] While the FBI suspected Connor of being sympathetic to the Klan, if not an active Klansman, the Bureau seemed confident that Chief Moore, a graduate of the FBI Academy, would safeguard the Freedom Riders.[51] Moore, however, spent Mother's Day in the north Alabama town of Albertville, his hometown where he annually attended Decoration Day at Alder Springs Cemetery. Realizing that the Freedom Riders were headed in a direction that would bring them through Birmingham, Moore checked with Connor before deciding to go to Albertville. "Go ahead and be with your people," Connor told him.[52]

In his 1976 book *My Undercover Years with the Ku Klux Klan*, Rowe reiterated that the men at Greyhound were Klansmen involved in a conspiracy to greet the Freedom Riders with a violent "welcome party." He maintained that, as part of the conspiracy, Birmingham police would give the Klan fifteen minutes to beat the Riders before they intervened. Rowe's assignment at Greyhound was to monitor the progress of the Riders. He accomplished this by telephoning the Police Department every fifteen minutes for information from a policeman sympathetic to the Klan. Late in the afternoon, Rowe's contact—who was assigned a fictitious name in his book—told Rowe to get every Klansman he could find and rush to the Trailways station three blocks away. "There's been a foul-up; they're not coming where you are," Rowe quoted his police contact.[53]

Rowe reported his information to a Klan leader. Word was passed and the men left the Greyhound station and rushed to the Trailways depot. Three buses were pulling in about that time. A white man who had been beaten and a large black man stood in the doorway of one bus. Rowe recalled hearing someone shout, "Kill the black bastard; he's hurt the white man!" But the white man [Peck] held up his hand and said, "Stop. We've had enough. You'll have to kill me before you hurt him." The mob then attacked both men and the other passengers.[54] Large numbers of police arrived at the Trailways station "about 15 minutes later," the *Birmingham News* reported, but by this time, the attackers had fled.[55]

Connor spent Mother's Day at city hall, at one point receiving a telegram from Fred L. Shuttlesworth urging that the Freedom Riders be given the protection to which they were entitled as citizens.[56] Sgt. Thomas H. Cook, Connor's civil rights monitor, made "a number of trips back and forth" between city hall and the Greyhound Bus Station during the course of the day. He also checked the Trailways station, according to *Birmingham News* managing editor John Bloomer, who spent the minutes preceding the attack riding with Cook through the downtown area.[57]

Cook reported later that, after the burning of the Greyhound bus west of Anniston, he received information that "all 22 of the so-called 'Riders' were hospitalized." As a precaution, he checked the Trailways station shortly before 4:00 P.M. for a bus scheduled to arrive at 4:05 from Atlanta. He found "no indication of any crowd either inside or outside of the Terminal and nothing whatsoever to cause me to believe that any incident of any kind might occur there." When the bus failed to appear at 4:05, he returned to city hall four blocks away. Arriving back at city hall, he was told "a fight was in progress at the Trailways Bus Station." He returned to the Trailways station "immediately," and "it could not have been more than three or four minutes from the time the call was received until I was back at the bus terminal." By that time, the incident had ended and "all persons who had participated in any sort of fight at that place were gone," said Cook.[58]

The day following the episode, in a front-page banner editorial, the *Birmingham News* demanded to know, "Where were the police?" In light of the *News'* reaction to the Harrison Salisbury articles in the *Times* the year before and its strong endorsement of Connor three weeks earlier, this stance represented a significant break with the past. Written by Assistant to the Publisher S. Vincent Townsend, the editorial noted that the police knew the Freedom Riders were en route, police cars roamed the downtown area, uniformed policemen were visible at various points, a national network television news crew was on hand at the Greyhound Bus Station to film any outbreak of violence, and Commissioner Connor knew the situation existed and was on duty in his office. Despite these circumstances, the *News* continued, the police did not stop the beatings at the Trailways Bus Station nor an attack on WAPI Television newsman Clancy Lake in his car near the station.

"Fear and hatred did stalk Birmingham streets yesterday," the newspaper said in obvious reference to the Salisbury article in the *Times* a year earlier. The *News* added:

The Birmingham Police Department did not do what could have been done Sunday. . . . The people—and the police—permitted that fear and hate to ride our streets. It was a rotten day for Birmingham and Alabama. The thugs did what they had come to do—up to now they have gotten away with it. Today many are asking "Where were the police?" The *News* asks that, too, but the *News* also asks: When will the people demand that fear and hatred be driven from the streets?[59]

The *Birmingham World* noted editorially that, "Customs, no matter how cherished and venerated, are no substitutes for the law," and added, "There is something equally as bad as the mob. That is the mob spirit. The mob spirit is as detestable and as loathsome as the mob itself. For it is the mob spirit which refines itself into the spirit of defiance of the law of the land and of the natural law of change."[60]

Connor blamed the violence on "out-of-town meddlers" and noted that both sides were from other places, "the ones who got whipped and the ones who did the whipping." He pointed out that the episode happened on Mother's Day, "when we try to let off as many of our policemen as possible so they can spend Mother's Day at home with their families." He added, "We got to the bus station as quick as we possibly could."

Connor then issued a warning. "As I have said on numerous occasions, we are not going to stand for this in Birmingham. And if necessary we will fill the jail full—and we don't care whose toes we step on. I am saying now to these meddlers from out of our city the best thing for them to do is stay out if they don't want to get slapped in jail. Our people of Birmingham are a peaceful people and we never have any trouble here unless some people come into our city looking for trouble. And I've never seen anyone yet look for trouble who wasn't able to find it."[61]

Attorney General Robert F. Kennedy dispatched Justice Department representative John Siegenthaler to Birmingham to investigate. He found the Freedom Riders with their heads bandaged still in the bus terminal, although they had spent some of the hours since the attack at the Shuttlesworth residence. The injured Freedom Riders were flown to New Orleans, Louisiana, on the Monday following the attack.

On Wednesday 17 May a group of ten students from Nashville, Tennessee, boarded a bus for Birmingham to continue the Freedom Ride to New Orleans via Montgomery and Jackson, Mississippi.

The students, two white and eight black, were members of the
Nashville Non-Violent Movement. As their bus crossed the Birmingham city limits, a police car forced it to stop. Birmingham
police had received word that the second group of Freedom Riders
was en route from Nashville, and the department seemed determined to avoid a replay of the Mother's Day violence. A detective
boarded the bus and made an announcement.

"The police officer said that we were not going to get off the
bus in Birmingham but were going straight on through," recalled
James William Zwerg, a white member of the student group.[62]

By the time the bus reached the Greyhound station, a large
crowd had gathered. A number of traffic division police officers
and several members of the K-9 police dog corps were on hand
for crowd control. The plan for the bus to go straight through hit
a snag, however; the driver from Nashville had ended his shift,
and his relief driver refused to leave with the Freedom Riders
aboard.

With the crowd becoming unruly, Chief Moore and Connor decided to place the students under protective custody. Moore
walked over to the bus station, introduced himself to the Riders,
and said, "In view of the circumstances surrounding you here, it
is my opinion and the opinion of other superior officers . . . that
it is dangerous for you and others for you to stay here. I am therefore
taking you into protective custody of the city of Birmingham to
remove you from these premises."[63]

The students were taken to the city jail for safekeeping. The
police treated them "very, very nice," recalled John Lewis, a black
member of the group. "They didn't rough us up or anything like
that, just very nice," he said.[64] Sometime during the night of Thursday 18 May Connor and several detectives appeared at the jail,
told the students they were taking them back to Nashville, and
loaded them into cars. Connor rode in the car with Lewis and
several others.

"He was really funny," said Lewis, "he was really joking with
us, saying he was gonna take us back to Nashville, and we told
him we would invite him to the campus, and he could have break-
fast with us and that type of thing. He said he would like that."[65]

Instead of Nashville, Connor and his lieutenants transported the students to Ardmore, a small town straddling the Alabama-Tennessee border, and dropped them there during the early morning hours.[66] The students went to the home of a local black family and telephoned friends in Nashville. The friends drove to Ardmore, met the students, and returned them to Birmingham, where they reappeared at the Greyhound Bus Station Friday afternoon.[67] As word of their return spread, a crowd began to gather once again. The police reestablished their vigil, limiting access to the station and even refusing admittance to persons with tickets until five minutes before their bus was scheduled to depart.[68]

Greyhound officials once again found it difficult to locate a driver willing to transport the Freedom Riders, but finally, on Saturday morning, 20 May, a bus carrying the students left for Montgomery. Birmingham police escorted the bus to the city limits and Alabama highway patrolmen continued the escort to the city limits of Montgomery. No Montgomery police met the bus, however, and the mob gathered at the Montgomery bus terminal attacked the Riders.[69] "Oh, there are fists, punching," exclaimed Justice Department official John Doar, speaking to Robert Kennedy via telephone from the terminal. "A bunch of men led by a guy with a bleeding face are beating them. There are no cops. It's terrible. It's terrible. There's not a cop in sight. People are yelling, 'Get 'em, get 'em.' It's awful."[70]

Student James Zwerg recalled that there were "more than fifty" in the crowd of attackers, including one man with a pipe in his hand. "I realized I would probably be next so I started praying," said Zwerg, a pre-seminary student who planned to become a minister. "I was jolted from my prayers when I heard someone curse me and call me a nigger lover. I opened my eyes and saw they were almost on top of me. The crowd grabbed me and pushed me down and then they kicked and hit me. The last thing I remember was rolling over and this foot coming down in my face."[71]

John Siegenthaler jumped out of his car to aid a Freedom Rider, a young white girl under attack, and was hit from behind and knocked unconscious. He awoke with a concussion in a Montgomery hospital. The next day, this second group of Freedom Riders—with their wounds bandaged—continued by bus to Jackson, Mississippi, with the National Guard accompanying them.[72]

In the wake of the Freedom Rider attacks in Birmingham and Montgomery, Attorney General Kennedy sued the Montgomery Police Department, the Ku Klux Klan, and various individuals associated with each for violation of the civil rights of the Riders. Kennedy quickly amended the suit to include Bull Connor and Jamie Moore. In a case tried before Federal Judge Frank M. Johnson in Montgomery, the prosecution attempted to show that the Birmingham Police Department "allowed the beatings on the Freedom Riders." Police time records disputed the charge, however, as did testimony at the hearing.

According to affidavits taken for the trial before Judge Johnson, Birmingham police patrolmen F. C. Garrett and A. Y. Parker were assigned to patrol the area around the Greyhound station on the evening shift beginning at 3 P.M. on Mother's Day, 14 May. About 4:10 or 4:15 P.M., the two were engaged in arresting an intoxicated man carrying a pistol who was attempting to enter the Greyhound station.[73] At about 4:15 or 4:20 P.M., a call came to Sgt. T. E. Sellers, the police department radio dispatcher, that a "fight was in progress" at the Trailways station three blocks away. Cars 25 and 13 normally would have answered a call in that area, but both "were tied up," according to Sellers. Car 25 was dealing with the drunk carrying the pistol at the Greyhound station, but Car 13's whereabouts were not noted. Sellers dispatched Car 37, the nearest available, "two minutes after the call was received," a fact borne out by the time stamp on the rear of the radio dispatch record. Car 13 checked in several minutes later and was also dispatched to the Trailways station.[74]

Birmingham News reporter Tom E. Lankford witnessed the attack and photographed the beating of *Post-Herald* photographer Tom Langston. The attackers then forced Lankford to turn his film over to them. In the hearing before Judge Johnson, Lankford testified that police arrived at the Trailways station no more than five or six minutes after the trouble started,[75] although his bylined coverage in the *News* the day after the attack said police arrived "about 15 minutes later."[76]

Paul G. Sutter, manager of the Trailways station, was on duty at the time of the attack and made the call to the police department for help. "In my judgment not more than five, six, or seven

Connor, right, and Police Chief Jamie Moore, second from right, were
included in a suit brought by Attorney General Robert Kennedy after
the Freedom Riders were attacked at bus stations in Birmingham and
Montgomery. Attorney Jim Simpson, second from left, Connor's longtime
counsel and political confidant, defended the two before Federal Judge
Frank Johnson in Montgomery. After testimony and police dispatch re-
cords indicated that Birmingham police answered calls for help without
undue delay, Simpson moved successfully to have Connor and Moore
dismissed from the suit. Here, the trio leaves the Federal Courthouse
with Birmingham City Detective Vernon Hart on 4 June 1961. (Courtesy
the Birmingham News*)*

minutes had transpired between my first call and my walking out
to the rear and finding the police cars standing there," Sutter said
in an affidavit for the hearing before Judge Johnson. "I do not know
how long the police cars had been there before I went out and
saw them."[77]

After two days of testimony in the case, Judge Johnson granted
a motion by defense attorney Jim Simpson—Connor's longtime
confidant—discharging Connor and Moore from consideration in
the suit.[78] Johnson continued to hear evidence against the Mont-

gomery Police Department for another two days, after which he faulted the department for failure to take precautions against a possible attack and enjoined it to provide such protection in the future.

"Through various sources, [Montgomery Commissioner of Public Service L. B.] Sullivan and the Montgomery Police Department were aware of the explosive situation that existed in this area with reference to the riders," said Johnson, "and with knowledge did not take any of the usual precautionary measures to keep down violence in the city of Montgomery upon arrival of this bus." Johnson also pointed out that a Montgomery newspaper reporter testified that a city detective told him Montgomery police "would not lift a finger to protect" the Freedom Riders.[79]

Jamie Moore defended his dismissal and that of Connor, saying, "There was no prearrangement [to delay responding to the Birmingham attack] that I know of. Bull was certainly not in sympathy with those people [the Freedom Riders], but he wouldn't shirk his duty" by holding up on a call for help, said the man Connor tried to replace as chief.[80]

Yet the belief persisted that Connor did have a hand in delaying the police's response to the Freedom Rider attack. In 1983 former Freedom Rider Walter Bergman brought a suit against the FBI for not protecting the CORE group despite its knowledge of the Klan's planned attack. Federal Judge Richard A. Enslen of the Western District of Michigan noted that the Riders encountered a "statewide conspiracy and official involvement" during their violence-marred stops in Anniston and Birmingham. Without naming Connor, Judge Enslen said Bergman was the victim of "a violent mob purposely unrestrained by local law enforcement, coupled with lack of protection or intervention from the federal government."[81]

The slow response "could have happened with Bull fully knowing it," said James Parsons. "You've got to remember that he's made all the assignments. They're not going to tell everybody in the department about all that. It's going to be a very small group to handle that. One of his closest friends was in charge of the intelligence at that time, the intelligence division . . . Tom Cook, one of the few bright people that Commissioner Connor had around him. These people were loyal to Bull only, not to the department and not to the city. To Bull only."[82]

James Peck, who refused to provide Cook with any information on his attackers in the hospital following the 1961 assault,[83] also filed suit against the FBI in 1983, claiming the Bureau was at fault for not protecting the Riders when it had advance information of the impending attack. Testimony in the Peck case indicated the FBI was so leery of Connor's Klan sympathies that it ordered local agents to "use care in furnishing racial information to the Birmingham Police Department" and to be especially discreet in contacts with Connor and Cook. In a memo written on 19 April 1961, Thomas J. Jenkins, special agent in charge of the Birmingham FBI office, noted that while Connor "has been outspoken to agents of this office as being against the Klan," it must be realized that "he is an extremely strong segregationist, is an opportunist, and it is not believed that he would pass up any opportunity to become re-elected as commissioner of public safety."[84]

FBI informant Rowe reported to Bureau agents on Friday 12 May—two days before the attack—that a Klan leader told fellow Klansmen that Connor would delay police response fifteen or twenty minutes. Rowe also testified that, prior to the attack, an unnamed Birmingham police lieutenant told him he wanted the Klan to "beat, kill, whatever, I don't give a damn," and added, "I don't want those freedom riders ever to come to Alabama again." Rowe said the lieutenant promised, "No Klansmen will be arrested in 15 minutes."[85]

Rowe's credibility has diminished in recent years following revelations that he was present when Detroit civil rights worker Viola Liuzzo was killed near Selma, Alabama, on 25 March 1965.[86] Testimony in two suits filed during the 1980s against the FBI—the Peck case and one brought by the family of Viola Liuzzo—placed Rowe at the scene of both the Freedom Rider attack and the Liuzzo murder. According to testimony in the Liuzzo case, Rowe had been photographed beating a Freedom Rider and was subsequently ordered by his FBI liaison to disclaim participation. In a deposition for the Liuzzo trial (Rowe enjoys government immunity from prosecution and lives under an assumed name at an undisclosed location), Rowe said the FBI agent told him, "That's Arny Kagle. As long as you live, that's Arny Kagle or we're all in trouble."[87]

FBI agents who served as Rowe's contacts during the mid-1960s characterized him as an effective agent sometimes given to embellishment of the facts to gain attention for himself. In the Liuzzo trial, former agent Byron McFall, who handled contact with Rowe from June 1961 until January 1964, said Rowe was reliable and "pretty productive," but that he suspected the informant of "embellishing things." Former FBI agent Barrett G. Kemp, Rowe's contact from April 1960 until June 1961, said Rowe was an effective informant, but that the book Rowe authored about his undercover work contained many inaccuracies. When Kemp was asked during the Liuzzo trial if he believed Rowe were a braggart, he answered, "I never felt that until I read his book."[88]

The courts have disagreed on whether Connor had a hand in delaying police response to the Freedom Rider attack. The 1961 trial before Federal Judge Frank Johnson exonerated Connor, Jamie Moore, and the Birmingham police. But that trial, held only three weeks after the Mother's Day attack, included no testimony from Rowe, who continued as an FBI informant until 1965. In 1975 Rowe—wearing a hood to cover his face—testified before the Senate Select Committee on Intelligence about his undercover days in the Klan. He reported that two Birmingham police detectives arranged the fifteen-minute delay and that four FBI agents filmed the attack but made no attempt to interfere with the beatings.[89] Rowe's book about his undercover days appeared in 1976. Following these public disclosures, Rowe's testimony figured prominently in the Peck and Bergman trials of 1983 and contributed to Judge Enslen's conclusion in the Bergman trial that local law officers "purposely" failed to protect the Freedom Riders in Birmingham.

The posting of minimal security at each bus station—one across the street from city hall, and the other only three blocks removed—would seem to have been a very basic precaution. While plainclothes detective L. J. Wilson was stationed at the Greyhound station "to keep an eye open for any persons who appeared to be in and around the bus station without a proper reason,"[90] no officer was posted at the Trailways station. Car 25 patrolled the street around the Greyhound station, but except for an occasional check by Sergeant Cook and Detective J. E. Allbritton, the Trailways station was ignored. Allbritton recalled that the police department "had been specifically informed that the trouble, if it came, would come at the Greyhound Bus Terminal," and the random checks at the Trailways station were simply "an added precaution" against "the outside possibility" that the Freedom Riders might arrive there.[91]

Why was the Birmingham police force so inconspicuous? According to police Lt. George Wall, who was in charge of the evening shift on Mother's Day 14 May, the department had a policy of not stationing "a large number of uniform officers on any detail likely to draw public attention, because the very fact of the presence of a number of officers at any particular point tends to draw a large crowd of people." His men were available, said Wall, "but not in the public view unless it became necessary."[92] Attorney Jim Simpson cited this policy during the hearing before Judge Johnson to explain the absence of officers at the two bus stations.[93] The use of such a policy—perhaps meritorious in some situations—certainly left the way clear for the attackers to stage their brief but vicious assault on the Freedom Riders, undeterred by official presence. The same policy left Connor open to the charge of a slow response by the police.

Whether he was part of a planned delay or not, the Freedom Riders episode affected Connor in two important ways. First, the international coverage underscored his reputation as a symbol for racial brutality, making him a prime target for later forays by civil rights groups seeking to dramatize their movement. Second, the episode shocked white moderates in Birmingham to the extent that they began actively to withdraw support from Connor. A telling example of this occurred in Tokyo, Japan, where incoming Birmingham Chamber of Commerce president Sidney Smyer was attending the Rotary International meeting. Smyer winced as he encountered a wirephoto of the attack in a newspaper, shook his head and muttered, "Something's got to give."[94] During his tenure as a chamber leader, Smyer became a prime mover of the Senior

Citizens Committee, an organization of leading Birmingham business executives who sought a solution to racial problems so that the city might move forward economically.

The Freedom Riders episode also had a sobering effect on those who felt that, with Bull ensconced as the commissioner of public safety, Birmingham somehow might avoid a major civil rights confrontation. As the scene of the Freedom Riders saga shifted first to Montgomery and then to Jackson, where the Riders were arrested by Mississippi authorities, Birmingham sought to forget the furious Trailways Bus Station attack that had shattered a peaceful spring Sunday. Yet Tom Langston's photograph of angry white toughs pummelling defenseless citizens provided a vivid reminder—the hate-filled faces of the attackers contorted with physical effort, cigarettes dangling from their lips, weapons raining blows upon bloodied victims whose upstretched hands offered scant protection. It was little wonder that Langston hid in Shelby County for six weeks, fearful that those pictured would seek retribution against him. He felt safe only after he had testified in court that he "couldn't identify anyone in the attack."[95] Never again would Bull Connor be able to say, as he had in the flush of political victory less than two weeks before the Freedom Riders attack, that Birmingham had not suffered the anxiety and violence of other Southern cities during the integration movement.

While the Freedom Riders episode underscored Connor's racist image and shocked white moderates, it had an immediate effect on Birmingham's mayoral runoff. After Tom King led the first primary with the help of Birmingham's black voting districts, Art Hanes intensified the racist nature of his campaign, painting his opponent as the candidate of the blacks. The photo of King shaking hands with the black man was a key element in this effort. Anti-King circulars and advertisements showed a black hand placing a ballot in a box under the headline "Defeat the NAACP Bloc Vote."[96] As the 30 May runoff approached, Hanes and King grew more and more strident in their attacks. Hanes hammered at King's Washington connections and charged that his opponent had the support of the black "bloc vote," which did not come "without promises, pledges or price." In his final speech before the runoff, he told voters that Bull Connor would vote for him.[97] "You may be assured," said Hanes on election eve, "if my opponent is elected tomorrow that this will be hailed as the fall of the South's greatest segregation stronghold." King responded by calling Hanes a "race-baiting coat-tail rider" in obvious reference to Connor.[98] Maintaining that he was a strong segregationist, King accused Hanes of "hate-mongering, deceit and untruths" throughout the runoff campaign. *News* political writer Eddie Badger summed up the runoff as "one of the hardest fought and most bitter campaigns in the city's history."[99]

Despite his contention that the damning photograph was set up by Connor, King saw his 1,500-vote lead of 2 May evaporate in the runoff election. Hanes was elected mayor by 21,133 votes to 17,364, and Jabo Waggoner retained his public improvements seat, 19,753 to 18,051 over Earl Bruner.[100] The segregation issue had been downplayed during the first primary; after stating they would maintain segregation, the candidates had emphasized other issues. King offered a forward-looking program such as airport expansion and metropolitan merger, which appealed to the city's more progressive elements, but his support in the black community proved his downfall.[101] Hanes's reversion to "black hand" politics in the runoff became all the more effective after the Freedom Riders incident, which King believes was calculated by Connor "to fan further the fires of racial prejudice" and to ensure a Hanes victory.[102] Birmingham was jarred by the violent Mother's Day outburst at the bus station, but subsequent national coverage—such as the CBS program "Who Speaks for Birmingham?" four days later—pushed the city back into its familiar defensive stance. Nowhere was this more graphically reflected than in the election two weeks later of segregationist Art Hanes as mayor. The election assured that Birmingham would continue its pattern of official intransigence in race relations, for if Hanes, Waggoner, and Connor shared one philosophy, it was their bitter opposition to integration. A year earlier, Harrison Salisbury had ended the second of his two Birmingham articles with a quote from an unnamed Alabamian: "Things will get better some day. But first, I'm afraid they will get a lot worse."[103] As far as prospects for racial harmony were concerned, the 1961 primary lent credence to that dire prediction.

7

This Park Is Closed

he Reverend Fred L. Shuttlesworth accepted a pastorate in Cincinnati, Ohio, in August 1961, leaving the Bethel Baptist Church post he had held since 1953. If Bull Connor cheered the departure of his adversary, the celebration was brief. Shuttlesworth had the city of Birmingham back in court less than two months later, suing to desegregate its parks and other recreational facilities. Some facilities, such as golf courses, swimming pools, and parks, were completely segregated; others, such as the zoo and art museum, were "semi-segregated," with separate restrooms, drinking fountains, and concessions. On 24 October U.S. District Judge H. Hobart Grooms ruled unconstitutional Section 850 of the Birmingham code, which provided for segregation in public places. The outcry from Birmingham officials was immediate.[1]

Mayor James W. Morgan (in his final week in office before retirement) and Connor gave notice that the city would appeal. They requested a stay until a higher court could hear the case. Connor said that the commission hoped Judge Grooms would delay the order and added, "if not, we will close the parks immediately, including Legion Field [football stadium], swimming pools, golf links, and all other facilities affected by this decision yesterday," and offer them for sale to private concerns. "The great majority in Birmingham do not want integration," Connor added. "It will cause nothing but chaos and bad relations between the two races.

Birmingham has been fortunate in having good relations, until now, between Negroes and whites. We have given our Negroes public parks, swimming pools, community centers and golf links."[2]

Connor blamed the situation on black attorney Ernest Jackson, Sr., of Jacksonville, Florida, and Shuttlesworth, maintaining that the two were "pushing this for financial benefits." Morgan, concurring with Connor, noted that Birmingham had provided golf courses and other recreational facilities for blacks prior to the landmark 1954 Supreme Court decision, and that these facilities also would close. Mayor-elect Arthur J. Hanes, who would shortly become Morgan's successor, said simply, "Everybody lost."[3]

Hanes, Connor, and Commissioner of Public Improvements James T. "Jabo" Waggoner were inaugurated on 6 November 1961. In their inaugural remarks, Hanes called for Birmingham's merger with surrounding bedroom communities to boost economic growth; Waggoner said city officials "must contribute something more to their jobs than broad smiles, firm handshakes, and modest talents," suggesting they should also possess courage and vision; and Connor dusted off one of his time-worn themes. "Let me tell you again what I told you during the campaign," said Bull. "I owe no political debts. I have made no private promises. I have no political tie-ups. I am free to devote my efforts and energy to the interest of Birmingham without any entangling alliance of any kind, shape or character."[4]

Connor had used these exact words during inaugural remarks following his first election to the city commission in 1937.[5] During his 1961 inaugural, he promised to do his best, praised Birmingham police and fire departments as "the finest," and said he would enforce the laws impartially. "If you don't like our present laws, you have the power to change them," he said, "but so long as they exist, I propose to enforce them."[6]

Because he had received the highest number of votes, Connor was designated to serve as Mayor Pro-Tem during the Hanes administration.[7]

Two days after the inauguration, on 8 November, Judge Grooms set 15 January 1962, as the date after which segregation of Birmingham public facilities would no longer be legal. In formally issuing the ruling he had made in the suit brought by Shuttlesworth, Judge Grooms noted that segregation would be illegal in any public theater, auditorium, ball park, playground, or at "all types of entertainment, games, sports, amusement or recreation therein to which the public is admitted."[8] City attorney J. M. Breckinridge said the city would "definitely appeal."[9]

The city commission held little actual hope that its appeal would reverse the Grooms decision. Similar rulings had already been upheld at the next level of the federal judiciary, the U.S. Fifth Circuit Court of Appeals in New Orleans, Louisiana. Thus the commission set machinery in motion to follow through on its threat to close the parks. The Park and Recreation Board had requested a budget of $1.5 million for fiscal 1962 to operate sixty-eight parks, fourteen community centers, eight swimming pools, four golf courses, a hobby house at Highland Park, and a greenhouse on Green Springs Road. The commission pared that request to $295,000 for the operation of a skeleton program only through 31 August 1962. In early December Mayor Hanes instructed City Parks Superintendent Frank Wagner to give notice to all employees that they would be dismissed on 1 January 1962, and told them to prepare signs to read THIS PARK IS CLOSED . . . NO TRESPASSING.[10]

Opposition to the measure was widespread and immediate. Already on 28 November Birmingham had lost its professional baseball team, a member of the Southern Association minor league since 1901. Albert Belcher, owner of the Birmingham Barons, announced at the annual meeting of professional minor leagues in Tampa, Florida, that he would not operate his team in 1962 because some teams in the previously all-white league might use black players. That would violate Birmingham's ordinance against whites and blacks playing together.[11] Now, with the commission's decision, Birmingham faced the loss of its neighborhood parks, where children had chased pop flies, long passes, and each other since the boyhood days of the commissioners and before.

Although former Mayor James Morgan had echoed Bull Connor's statement about closing the parks while still in office in October, he now labeled the action "grossly unfair." Mrs. J. H. Berry, a member of the Park and Recreation Board, voted for the reduced budget, along with fellow members Hanes and Dan Gaylord, but

THIS PARK IS CLOSED

she stated, "I think it's a shame that this should happen to such a fine segment of our city, and I think the blame should be placed right where it belongs—on the City Commission."[12]

The Birmingham Jaycees voted unanimously to oppose the parks closing and marched to city hall from their Redmont Hotel meeting to deliver personally their resolution to Mayor Hanes. Jaycees president Bob Hart said the real issues were "the impact it would have on our economy and the precedent established by closing the parks," adding that public schools were next in the integration picture and "we've got to take a stand whether three people have the right to say whether your child or mine gets an education."[13] Joining in opposition to the closing were the Birmingham Committee of 100, Birmingham Chamber of Commerce, Downtown Improvement Association, Young Men's Business Club, and various church organizations.[14]

The *Birmingham News* urged citizens to voice their opinions on the parks issue to the city commission. A front-page editorial stated that a negative decision on the parks could hurt Birmingham's economic future, discouraging businesses and industries seeking expansion sites from considering the city. The *News* pointed out that firms make relocation decisions not only on the availability of recreation and other physical factors, but "on the approach of a city in facing such a problem as now stands on our doorstep." The newspaper promised, "If they [the citizens] speak, City Commission will listen."[15]

Mayor Hanes gave no indication that listening would make him change his decision. He regretted the parks action, he said, but blamed the federal courts. "I personally resent the federal courts telling us we've got to integrate our parks," said the Mayor. "I think the U.S. Supreme Court has gone far afield in not interpreting our constitution but in making special laws."[16]

Hanes responded to a People's Park Committee headed by two West End citizens, Carl Miller and Ferman Kelly, by saying, "The City Commission is not going to appropriate any more money for the park board—and that's it."[17] The mayor told an open meeting at city hall that he had watched integration in Washington, D.C., where the whites moved out of neighborhoods when blacks moved in. "If you integrate these parks, and roll over and play dead, you hasten integration in the schools," he said. Someone asked Hanes if he would also close schools and libraries to avoid integration. "If they integrate, it will be at gunpoint," said Birmingham's leader.[18]

Commissioner Jabo Waggoner recalled that, during this period, the city of Birmingham received orders from the Justice Department "almost daily about what we were going to have to do . . . integrate the swimming pools and the parks and the golf courses and schools and everything else." Waggoner and Connor developed a standard procedure for accepting the orders, which were delivered by local federal bailiffs. "We just wadded it up while the bailiff was there and threw it in the waste basket, " Waggoner said. "They [sic] would just laugh. They [sic] didn't care. [We] might take it out later and read it after he was gone."[19]

After Birmingham received an order from Attorney General Robert Kennedy to integrate its swimming pools, Hanes and Waggoner decided to seek relief from Kennedy in person. Connor declined to travel to Washington with his fellow commissioners, suggesting that the attorney general "wouldn't let me in his office."

Kennedy "left us cooling our heels in this anteroom for about an hour after our appointment time," Waggoner recalled, "and he sat there with his feet up on his desk in my face" throughout the meeting. The Birmingham officials told Kennedy that integration would "fill those pools with blood." They requested that he remove the order and promised, "otherwise, we are going to fill them up with dirt." The attorney general refused to consider the request, saying, "You folks down South are going to have to learn that you can't just rule blacks down there like you want to and treat them like you do." Despite this lecture, Waggoner left Washington convinced that Kennedy was more interested in black votes than in black rights. "He didn't give a darn about the kids in Birmingham having a place to swim," Waggoner averred.[20]

Albert Belcher's decision not to operate his baseball team in 1962 doubtless saddened Bull Connor. A lifelong sports fan who particularly loved baseball, he would miss the Barons keenly. Connor had gained his large radio following as the voice of the team during the 1920s and '30s, and this name identification had led to his first political success. Yet Bull never wavered on the issue of closing the parks. He had campaigned over the years on the necessity of maintaining strict segregation and had demonstrated the depth of his belief numerous times, such as in 1948 when he stormed out of the Democratic National Convention in protest of the party's civil rights plank. Connor contended that much civil rights activism was inspired by communists and other "outside agitators" who stood to gain from the exploitation of the race issue in the South. Conversely, the commissioner of public safety, as a sixty-four-year old white Southerner steeped in the traditions of the dual society, viewed segregation as the legitimate heritage of his region. His views were reflected in the composition of the police department that he headed; no black had ever served on the force of the South's fourth largest city, nor would one do so until after his retirement as commissioner. Clearly, Connor surprised no one when he stood foursquare with Hanes on the parks issue.

Connor vowed that "no trespassing" would mean exactly that, and said if he saw any children in the parks after the closing date, he would have his police officers "run 'em out." In response to a Chamber of Commerce resolution urging another solution to the parks quandary, Connor said, "I'll never vote to integrate our parks, our swimming pools, our community centers, golf links or Legion Field." After assailing the "yapping" being done by protest groups, he asserted, "This is my final statement on the parks."[21]

Golfers played their final rounds on Birmingham greens on 31 December 1961. As the new year opened, the holes on the links were filled with concrete and Birmingham golf courses were closed, along with all other park facilities.

"Change which takes us backward, which boards up recreational buildings, puts up closed-to-all signs on the parks, and packs the cups on golf links—adds nothing to progress," observed the black *Birmingham World*. "Change which turns out mean words from the lips of public officials is not good for either Birmingham or democracy. Birmingham needs the kind of change which transforms customs to harmonize with the American credo and the Golden Rule."[22]

Robert Kennedy confided in 1961: "I won't say I stayed awake nights worrying about civil rights before I became Attorney General." Nor had his brother John. But the need to win black votes in the 1960 presidential election had forced John Kennedy to think intensely about civil rights, and during the campaign, he promised to fight vigorously for equal rights if elected. While both Kennedy brothers were abstractly in favor of equal opportunity, the narrowness of the Kennedy victory in 1960 suggested that the best immediate route to achieving that goal was through executive order rather than through civil rights legislation.[23]

Prior to the Freedom Rides of 1961, civil rights leader Martin Luther King, Jr., had suggested to Robert Kennedy that the president have the Interstate Commerce Commission (ICC) act against segregation in terminals. Kennedy answered that the ICC was an independent commission not subject to presidential order. Following the violent reception accorded the Freedom Riders in Alabama and Mississippi, however, the attorney general formally petitioned the ICC to issue regulations that would end segregation in the terminals. As the result of this "quite novel administrative step," such an order was issued on 22 September 1961.[24]

Section 369 of the Birmingham city code prohibited serving "white and colored people" in the same room unless a partition seven feet high and separate entrances were provided. On 3 November 1961, Ralph R. Sizemore, the thirty-four-year-old manager of the Greyhound Bus Station Restaurant in Birmingham, permitted whites and blacks to be served in the same cafeteria. Connor promptly ordered his arrest. Sizemore claimed that he was simply carrying out the orders of his company's central office in Chicago, which had come as a result of the ICC ruling the previous September. Connor replied that Section 369 was still part of the local code, and although it well might be branded unconstitutional, he planned to enforce it "as long as this ordinance is on the books" of Birmingham. "As long as I can keep segregation in effect in Birmingham I'm going to do it," said Connor, "regardless of U.S. attorney general Bobby Kennedy. I'm going to enforce segregation of the races here just as long as I can find a law on which to act. . . . Kennedy and the other meddlers up North are behind all our trouble here," he continued. "They tried the so-called 'freedom riders' move and it failed, so they turned to the Interstate Commerce project."[25]

Connor instructed Police Chief Jamie Moore to arrest anyone attempting to violate the ordinance, which was punishable by a maximum fine of $100 and six months in jail. He said each violation would be considered a separate offense.[26]

Four days later, on Inauguration Day for the city commission, Connor underscored his intention to enforce local segregation laws by having Sizemore arrested a second time for the same offense. In Washington, a Justice Department official accused the commissioner of trying to "stir up racial trouble," and added, "The courts certainly will force Connor to stop such illegal arrests."[27]

U.S. Attorney Macon Weaver of Birmingham sought a compromise. He requested and received approval from the Justice Department to withhold filing an injunction against Connor provided the commissioner would discontinue the arrests of bus station employees. Connor offered to stop the arrests if the Justice Department would reinstate segregation in the bus station until the matter could be resolved in the courts. Weaver said "the quiet and orderly settlement of the issue in the court" was the Justice Department goal as well, but that the Department was not sure Connor would permit this.

"For the life of me, I can't see where the ICC has the authority to make the laws of this country contrary to those of a sovereign state," said Connor, "and then have the nerve to try and enforce it. The ICC is a rule-making body and not a law-passing body." The commissioner added that the Tenth Amendment to the U.S. Constitution gave the states or the people "the powers not delegated to the United States by the Constitution, nor prohibited by it in the states." He predicted "if the Supreme Court handles it [Ordinance 369] like they have all other laws of the South regarding racial issues, I am afraid they will find it unconstitutional regardless of the Constitution of the United States." He indicated he had reached a tacit understanding with Weaver to discontinue the arrests. "I want it strictly understood," he added quickly, "that Bobby Kennedy or no one else from the federal government has contacted me or anyone in our legal department about those arrests at the bus station."[28]

The following day, Sizemore was found guilty in Recorder's Court of two charges of allowing blacks and whites to eat together in the Greyhound Bus Station Restaurant. He was fined $25 on each count and given a thirty-day suspended sentence in one of the two cases. Defense attorney William H. Cole filed notice of appeal.

In a front-page editorial calling for a "sensible solution" to the "bus cafe dilemma," the *Birmingham News* urged the Justice Department to bring to an end "at least temporarily" the mixed eating attempts and to allow the Sizemore case to proceed through the courts. The *News* also suggested that the city commission meet the problem by removing Ordinance 369 from the city code. "Birmingham needs a constructive, positive decision on the part of members of the City Commission," said the *News*. "Commission members do not have much time. They should act immediately."[29]

Connor discontinued the arrests, but shortly thereafter, he introduced a resolution that the city commission adopted ordering the Greyhound Bus Station operators to show cause why its restaurant license should not be revoked. The order charged bus officials and employees with violation of Ordinance 369 relative to "separation of the races" and ordered them to appear before the city commission on 19 December.[30]

A week prior to the scheduled hearing, however, Weaver filed a suit enjoining the city commission from interfering with the operation of the bus station. Weaver said he "regretted" that the question could not be settled in the courts, but that if the city "insists on closing down the Greyhound Restaurant on the basis that Greyhound was violating a city ordinance," he had no alternative but to request federal intervention.[31]

Connor's handling of the simultaneous issues of the parks and the bus station restaurant reflected his intransigence in racial matters, and it was this inflexibility that continued to erode his support in the business community. By 1962 a spirit of moderation had begun to envelop the race issue in the South. It was not so much the federal court's direct ruling against interposition in the case of *Orleans Parish School Board* v. *Bush* that sounded the death knell of massive resistance. Rather, it was the realization on the part of Southern community leaders that the struggle against desegregation threatened the region's economic progress.

More and more through the early 1960s, Southern leaders came to accept the inevitability of token integration.[32]

While the Hanes administration's outcries of "Never!" indicated otherwise, proponents of moderation could be found even in Birmingham. Following the closing of the parks, which proved unpopular with a wide cross section of people, several members of the progressive Young Men's Business Club (YMBC) formed an organization called Citizens for Progress. Its purpose was clearly stated: to campaign for a change in Birmingham's form of government. YMBC members were concerned about the impasse in resolving racial matters and about business stagnation. Moderates especially disliked Connor and the old-line politics for which he stood; they credited Connor's extreme policies with strangling business growth and expansion.[33]

Birmingham voters had endorsed intransigence in 1961 when they swept Connor back into office, along with his ardently segregationist colleagues, Hanes and Waggoner. But a series of negative developments—the Freedom Riders incident, closing of the parks, the Greyhound bus cafe imbroglio, a black boycott of downtown stores organized by Miles College students in 1961–62, and a generally declining economy—pointed up the need for more flexible leadership.

During the spring of 1962 Birmingham blacks, led by students from Miles, launched a selective buying campaign against downtown stores. Frank Dukes, the thirty-one-year-old president of the Miles student body, organized the campaign with the blessing of Miles president Lucius Pitts. Miles students had formed the Anti-Injustice Committee in January to press for an end to segregation and had carried on negotiations with white merchants. But when six weeks of talk produced no results, the students met with Shuttlesworth to discuss a possible boycott. On 6 March Dukes sent merchants a letter requesting the desegregation of stores and hiring of black sales clerks. After the merchants refused to concede these points, Dukes called a meeting and the students approved a boycott.[34]

Adopting the slogan "Wear Old Clothes for Freedom," blacks systematically curtailed their shopping at downtown stores. "Let's walk together and decide to be free by not buying at stores which uphold segregation, discrimination and inequality," urged a boy-cott leaflet.[35] By late March, merchants felt the impact of the cam-paign; one store owner admitted the effort had been 80–85 percent effective in stopping trade by blacks, and others conceded privately that their stores were suffering noticeably.[36]

The early success of the boycott brought retaliation by the city commission. At the 3 April meeting of the body, Connor moved that the city cut off appropriations to Jefferson County for the sur-plus food program for needy families, almost all of which were black. "A boycott can work both ways," said Connor. "I don't in-tend to sit here and take this with a smile." Mayor Hanes sug-gested that if blacks were going to heed "irresponsible and militant advice" from the NAACP, the organization could feed them as well.[37]

Pitts and other members of Birmingham's black upper class had opposed the student involvement with Shuttlesworth and ACMHR, but the action of the city commission overcame this objection and drew the black community together. The boycott continued to be effective through April and May; Easter sales dropped 12 percent below the previous year and some stores lost 90 percent of their black trade. Along the way, the effort received unwitting help from the white community, such as when two stores, Woolworth and Newberry, fired their black employees and when Connor announced he would "sic the dogs" on any black entering a downtown store unless black leaders ended the boy-cott.[38] By the time the effort ran out of steam in mid-June, Birming-ham blacks had become more united in their quest for equal rights than ever before. At the same time, Birmingham's white mer-chants and Chamber of Commerce leaders seemed more willing to discuss changes in public accommodations than before; in Au-gust, the chamber created the biracial Senior Citizens Committee, which began a series of closed-door meetings to discuss solutions to Birmingham's racial problems.

Connor's response to the boycott illustrated once again his heavy-handed and inflexible leadership style. If there were any doubts about his unwillingness to adopt a moderate stance, he erased it during a 1962 run for governor of Alabama. His old politi-cal confidant, Jim Simpson, had cautioned Connor about making the statewide race the previous fall. "You know how happy it would make me to see you Governor and I know you don't mind taking a political licking; neither do I," Simpson wrote Connor in September 1961. "I think, however, I would ride a little while longer before making up my mind."[39] Despite this cogent advice and the memory of his lack of success in a statewide campaign twelve years earlier, Connor jumped into the gubernatorial race the following spring against such formidable opposition as George C. Wallace, Ryan deGraffenreid, and James E. "Big Jim" Folsom, as well as several lesser-known opponents.

In the Alabama of the early 1960s, Bull Connor had a built-in issue: race. "A weak-kneed and feather-legged crowd on integration is taking over in some of the Southern cities and States," Connor bellowed in a campaign speech. "Alabama, fortunately, is among those states still standing firm. She needs a Governor in the coming four years whom the people can trust on this issue."[40]

In another speech, Connor shared insight into his attitudes on race:

Our people in the South want to see him [the Negro] rise and we want to see him go just as high as he can and as fast as he can. He must realize, however, that no man can instill manhood and character into another. He must do that for himself. We want the white race in the South to progress, just as we want the black race in the South to progress. We want them to go parallel and side by side, but not intermixed, intermarried and integrated.[41]

In a campaign letter, Connor extolled the virtues of segregation, saying, "It will keep our nation from becoming another Brazil, where the intermingling of the races, I am told, has produced a hapless, helpless nation."[42]

Wallace had run a close race for governor with John Patterson four years earlier, losing out in a bitterly contested runoff session in which Wallace credited Patterson with "outsegging" him. The little judge from Clayton had vowed that he never again would be defeated by the segregation issue. During the spring of 1962, Wallace fired the Alabama crowds with his branding of federal Judge Frank M. Johnson as "a low-down, carpet-baggin', scalawag-

Connor, second from right, acknowledges cheers at a Connor for Governor rally 20 April 1962, flanked by fellow Commissioners Art Hanes, left, and Jabo Waggoner. As in 1950, when he finished sixth in a field of 15, Connor was no factor in the gubernatorial contest, coming in fifth among seven candidates. He supported George Wallace—making his first successful race for governor—in the runoff. (Courtesy the Birmingham News*)*

gin', race-mixin' liar."[43] He led the pack with 207,062 votes to de-Graffenreid's 160,704 and Folsom's 159,640.[44] Folsom—who had been governor twice—hurt his cause with an election eve television appearance in which he appeared to be drunk; at one point he was unable to remember the names of his children as he attempted to introduce them.[45] MacDonald Gallion ran fourth with 80,374 votes and far back in fifth place was Connor, whose total of 23,019 ballots confirmed once more that his appeal was largely local.[46]

Thus the 1962 Democratic gubernatorial runoff—tantamount to election—pitted the moderate deGraffenreid against the avowed and highly vocal segregationist Wallace. Connor, no great factor in the first primary, nevertheless chose to endorse a runoff candidate. "The filthy hands of the NAACP and CORE are spreading over this great State like a black cloud," Connor said in a 17 May press release. "I think I know which candidate for Governor will secure the block of Negro votes around Legion Field here in Birmingham and in other such areas. I don't want to see Alabama taken over by them." Surprising few people, if any, Connor supported Wallace, whom he claimed to have known since Wallace "came as a ragged country boy in knee britches to the Legislature" as a page during the 1930s. "Let us unite behind this great son of Alabama and have four years of peace, progress and segregation," Connor urged voters.[47]

Although Connor's endorsement meant little, Wallace swept to victory in the runoff, polling 340,730 votes to deGraffenreid's 269,122.[48] Thus began the Wallace era, which would become the most dominant political reign in Alabama history.

Alabama law provided that a petition bearing the signatures of 7,000 registered voters was needed to call an election. The Citizens for Progress—led by attorneys David Vann, George Peach Taylor, Charles Morgan, Vernon Patrick, and Erskine Smith[49]—decided to use the law to change Birmingham's form of government. Such a change would be a convenient method of removing Connor and his fellow commissioners from office prior to the next scheduled election in 1965.[50]

During the spring of 1962 the Alabama legislature passed reapportionment legislation that necessitated special elections to choose the new members of the lawmaking body. Jefferson County's election was set for 29 August. In Birmingham, change-of-government had been a topic of conversation since the unpopular decision to close the parks. As David Vann drove to his office one morning in mid-August, he listened as local radio commentator Dave Campbell suggested that "either somebody ought to get a petition and have an election or we ought to get behind the government we have."

"Listening to his editorial," recalled Vann, "the idea hit me that if I set up a petition booth across the street from each election place, and had a petition drive on the same day as the special election, that I would have all these people and would know they were registered voters because they were coming to vote. We could check their names off the voter lists in the newspaper and know that every signature we were getting was valid."[51]

Reaching his office, Vann telephoned his friend Abe Berkowitz, an attorney who had made speeches calling for a change of government. "Abe, if you really want to change the city government, I've figured out how to do it," said Vann.

Berkowitz listened to Vann's proposal and arranged a meeting that afternoon with a group of businessmen. They met in the office of real estate executive Sidney Smyer, the Chamber of Commerce president. After Vann outlined his plan, Smyer called it "a practical, workable idea." Don Stafford, president of the Birmingham Labor Council, said he "had been sitting there wondering not whether we should do it, but why in the hell we hadn't already done it." There was, however, one problem: the special election was scheduled to be held in only ten days.

To test whether there was sufficient interest in mounting a change-of-government campaign, the Vann group first decided to try to collect the signatures of 500 interested persons in three days. "If we couldn't get 500 names in three days, our advice would be to drop it," said Vann.

Three days later, the group met at the Bankhead Hotel with "well over 500 names" and decided to organize its campaign to collect the signatures of 7,500 people interested in holding a change-of-government election for Birmingham. During the next week, Citizens for Progress volunteers spent long hours preparing packets with instructions and petition forms. Plans were made to distribute the packets at all predominantly white polling places for the 29 August legislative election; no packets would be placed at black polling places, to avoid a white backlash against change-of-government, should the petition drive prove successful.

"But on Tuesday morning, election day, it turned out that about half of all the people that had volunteered to take our packets had taken them to kill our campaign," said Vann. "We had to get volunteers to make up new packets. We hired Kelly Girls. By mid-afternoon, we had about two-thirds of the places covered. The Klan beat up one of our people."[52]

Despite these problems, the campaign was a resounding success, far exceeding the goal. More than 11,000 of 28,000 participating voters signed the petition, even though the campaign had moved into high gear only five days prior to the election and signatures were collected at only thirty of Birmingham's fifty-two polling places.[53]

Probate Judge J. Paul Meeks certified the petition on 20 September after an exhaustive check—required by the 1955 law providing for such measures—to ascertain that all signers were registered voters.[54] Mayor Hanes, who had stated that he would call an election if the petition were successful, thus was thrust into the position of having to call for a vote which might turn him out of office. He wrestled with the problem as the prescribed ten-day deadline drew near. With Connor and Waggoner out of town, Hanes telephoned Police Chief Jamie Moore to discuss the matter. Moore was away from his office, but returned Hanes's call later in the day. Hanes "said he had wanted to ask me something, but had already made the decision himself," Moore recalled. The mayor "had decided not to call the election himself, to let the courts call for it."[55] Hanes justified his decision by saying, "I think we would be going backward. The present form is best, so why should I call an election on it?"[56]

Judge Meeks thus called the election, as required by law in the event the mayor failed to do so, and set the date for 6 November 1962.[57] Moore felt Hanes's refusal was a mistake: "I don't think there is any doubt that it would have been better politically, for him and for Bull, if he had called the election."[58] Vann told Hanes, "If you're for us, I think you can probably be mayor of this city for the next 20 years. If you're against us, I think it's a dangerous position to take."[59]

During the days leading to the vote, Connor urged voters to maintain the commission form. "Do you burn down your barn if there are rats in it?" he asked the Ensley Chamber of Commerce. "If you don't like what I am doing, impeach me, but don't change your form of government." He suggested, "You don't have to go to New York to see about the council form of government. Go to Homewood [a suburb]. They argue for weeks about something and put it off."[60]

The city commission also offered city employees pay raises in return for support on election day. But a secret meeting that the commission held with the firefighters backfired when a tape of the proceedings fell into the hands of the Citizens for Progress. Vann's group then prepared some radio advertising spots detailing "what really happened at the meeting with the city's firefighters."

Vann laughingly re-created one of the spots two decades later:

ANNOUNCER: Listen as the honest firefighter asks the city commission how much is this promised pay raise going to cost.
FIREFIGHTER: How much is it going to cost?
COMMISSIONER JABO WAGGONER: Let me answer that. I'll tell you. It's going to cost one million dollars.
ANNOUNCER: Stop corruption in city hall. Vote for the mayor-council government.
FIREFIGHTER: Where's the money coming from?
MAYOR ART HANES: What do you care where the money's coming from? We're here to talk about raises, not taxes.
ANNOUNCER: Stop corruption in city hall. Vote for the mayor-council government.
FIREFIGHTER: Do we get the raise regardless of how the election comes out?
MAYOR HANES: Absolutely not. You don't get the raise unless we're here to give it to you.[61]

"It was the funniest political ad ever run by anybody," Vann felt, "because you had the actual, recognizable voices. Now, Bull had the good sense not to say anything. We didn't have Bull's voice."[62]

On election day, Birmingham voters made the decision that Hanes had feared, calling for an end to the city commission format instituted in 1911 and choosing the mayor-council form as their government for the future. By a margin of 18,068 votes to 16,415, the citizens of Birmingham rejected the politics of the past, symbolized more by Connor than by either of his colleagues, neither of whom had served lengthy tenures. Connor was philosophical about the outcome, saying, "I have but one thing to say, the people have voted, and if they want a council, that's democracy."[63] Birmingham thus took a stand in favor of moderation, but those who felt that the vote signalled an end to hard-line resistance in Bull Connor's city deluded themselves.

8

Two Mayors
and a King

T he Southern Christian Leadership Conference attempted to break down the walls of segregation in Albany, Georgia, during 1961–62 through a series of massive nonviolent protests. But Albany repelled the efforts of SCLC leader Martin Luther King, Jr., using the same nonviolent approach that King had adopted from India's independence leader, Mohandas K. Gandhi. King hoped to bring Albany's white leaders to the bargaining table by filling the jails with demonstrators and overextending the city's capacity to deal with the protests, much as Gandhi had used massive peaceful demonstrations against the British in India. However, Albany's police chief, Laurie Pritchett, researched King prior to his arrival in the south Georgia city and made plans to cope with such tactics. Rather than filling—and ultimately overtaxing—jails in Albany, Pritchett arranged to house demonstrators in jails in neighboring cities and counties, so that the buildup in Albany never occurred. The chief coupled this strategy with a policy of protecting the arrested demonstrators to ensure that they were treated courteously. The confrontation with which the SCLC sought to dramatize its movement failed to materialize, and King left Albany in frustration.[1] Not long thereafter, the civil rights champion cast his eyes in the direction of Birmingham, Alabama.

The Alabama Christian Movement for Human Rights became one of eighty-five affiliates of SCLC soon after its founding. SCLC leaders were impressed with the efforts of ACMHR head Fred L. Shuttlesworth, Jr., who continued to fight vigorously for civil rights causes despite bombings of his home and church and periodic arrests. King acknowledged Shuttlesworth's value to the civil rights cause, saying, "This courageous minister's audacious public defiance of Bull Connor had become a source of inspiration and encouragement to Negroes throughout the South."[2]

Following the unsuccessful attempt to desegregate Albany, SCLC—at the invitation of Shuttlesworth—scheduled its annual convention for September 1962 in Birmingham. Rumors swept through the business community that King's organization had targeted Birmingham as the site of its next major protest action. Hoping to forestall large-scale demonstrations like those in Albany, the Birmingham Chamber of Commerce in August 1962 organized the biracial Senior Citizens Committee. Real estate executive Sidney W. Smyer, the former chamber president, headed the eighty-nine-member group, which included such representatives of the black upper class as A. G. Gaston, a wealthy businessman, and Dr. Lucius H. Pitts, president of Miles College. Committee members were concerned that such disruption not only would hurt downtown business, but also would undermine the upcoming change-of-government election, thus thwarting their hope of removing Connor from office. Pitts, serving as negotiator, conferred with Attorney General Robert Kennedy and with local black leaders before reporting to Smyer that demonstrations could be avoided if downtown merchants gave some indication they would desegregate stores. Shortly before the SCLC convention, Smyer and several white merchants set up a meeting with Pitts, Gaston, and other black leaders.[3] Gaston suggested the meeting include Shuttlesworth, describing the pastor as "the man with the soldiers."[4]

Shuttlesworth's ACMHR organization was comprised of approximately six hundred followers who generally were better educated than the black populace as a whole; more than two-thirds could vote at a time when only six percent of Birmingham blacks were registered.[5] "One of our chief works was encouraging, and even pressuring, people to vote," recalled Shuttlesworth. "For instance, in my church, Bethel, we got everybody who was qualified to vote registered, and we tried to do the same in all the other churches.

I said I didn't want any deacon wearing out the carpet on the floor praying to the Lord who wouldn't get up and walk to the polls."[6]

Shuttlesworth had not met previously with the white leaders, who traditionally limited their contact to members of the black elite. At the meeting, he recalled, "All of a sudden, I became a Doctor overnight. So I told them I didn't need the friendly polemic, because I had been there, there had been bombings, and I had never heard nothing from the civic leaders, or the preachers.'"[7]

Shuttlesworth requested that the merchants discontinue segregated drinking fountains and restrooms, points that the whites showed little interest in granting. The pastor underscored his commitment by telling department store owner Isadore Pizitz that, should demonstrations occur, he and King would "make your store the cause celebre" by being arrested there. "When we go to jail," he added, "we're going to stay in there and fast. You'll be out of business."[8]

After further negotiating, the groups reached an agreement under which the merchants would paint over the segregation signs in their stores and the Senior Citizens Committee would work with blacks to end lunch counter segregation. In return, Shuttlesworth announced that SCLC's upcoming convention would not be marked by demonstrations.[9]

SCLC held its meeting on 25–28 September in the Louis Richard Hall Auditorium of the A. G. Gaston Building. Congressman Adam Clayton Powell of New York and Jackie Robinson, the first black man to play organized professional baseball, addressed the gathering, along with representatives of such organizations as the NAACP, the Urban League, Congress of Racial Equality, and Student Non-violent Coordinating Committee (SNCC). The theme of the sixth annual meeting of the body was "Diversified Attack on Bias."[10] King addressed the gathering's final session; as he spoke, a man came to the podium and suddenly began punching the SCLC leader in the face. Several men pulled the attacker off King, and Birmingham police arrived shortly to arrest the man, a twenty-four-year old member of the Nazi party from Arlington, Virginia, named Roy James. King refused to press charges, but the city took the man before a local judge immediately, convicted him of assault, and sentenced him to thirty days in jail and a twenty-five dollar fine. Mayor Art Hanes came to the courtroom to tell the man never to set foot in Birmingham again.[11] Connor had taken the precaution of roping off the area around the meeting site,[12] and other than the brief commotion caused by the attack, the sessions were orderly and uneventful. As SCLC left town, members of the Senior Citizens Committee breathed a collective sigh of relief.

Then Connor struck again, reminding store owners that the segregation ordinances were still on the books and threatening those who refused to obey them with the loss of their business licenses. Attorney David Vann recalled that "the threat was made very clear that [the city] would arrest Mr. Pizitz and whoever else and put them in jail and hold them up to public ridicule and ruin their business."[13] The signs went back up.[14]

While the Senior Citizens Committee was comprised of prominent local individuals who were clearly Birmingham's business and economic leaders, it could implement those agreements only with the cooperation of the city commission, which was empowered to enact and repeal ordinances. And the commission—comprised of segregationists and dominated by Connor—was not disposed to accommodate civil rights activists such as King and Shuttlesworth. Connor's quick action forcing restoration of the signs indicated clearly the commission's total disregard of any accords that might have been reached by Smyer's group and the blacks. Although the Senior Citizens Committee had made its concessions in good faith, Connor's forceful response filled some committee members with a sense of futility, and they reassessed their "tacit commitment" to seek further progress in desegregating Birmingham facilities.[15]

SCLC members also sensed the futility of the Birmingham situation and redoubled their efforts to end segregation in the city. Following restoration of the Jim Crow signs, SCLC decided to make Birmingham the site of a massive nonviolent direct action campaign. Bull Connor's city had been "the country's chief symbol of racial intolerance," said King, and if the SCLC campaign were successful, it could "break the back of segregation all over the nation." Thus planning began for Project C—confrontation in Birmingham, Alabama.[16]

Connor expended much of his energy during the fall of 1962 campaigning for the commission form of government. Following the 6 November vote in favor of a mayor-council format, Connor issued his "That's democracy" statement and said he was relieved the issue had been decided. The commissioner of public safety stressed prior to the election that he would have no part of a mayor-council government, should the voters decide in that direction. Once again, however, his compulsion to run for office prevailed. Stating that the men who administer government "make the real difference" and not the format, Connor qualified on 18 January 1963 to run for mayor under the new system. He reminded the people of Birmingham that they knew what he stood for and if not, they only had to ask him: "They know I don't spin off a lot of high sounding words and in the end, straddle the fence and not take a stand on anything."[17]

Connor traditionally emphasized fiscal responsibility, and a move to increase the mayor's annual salary from $15,000 to $25,000 gave him a chance to underscore his opposition to unnecessary expenditures. "The people of Birmingham haven't even had a chance to vote on who will be the new mayor, and here they are talking about raising his pay and giving him a $15,000-a-year assistant," he said. "I want to say I'm running for the $15,000 job of mayor, not the $25,000 job. I'll never approve such a change unless they let the people vote on it." He also opposed a one-cent gasoline tax to help finance interstate highways.[18]

Connor told the voters he would work for equal enforcement of the law, the suppression of crime and maintenance of peace and order, continued improvement of schools and "their preservation from the Washington blight," and "equal treatment for all, rich and poor, black and white, strong and weak," with no special favors for "the high and mighty."[19] Speaking before the Downtown Action Committee on 22 January, he said he was running on his record of honesty and twenty-seven years of experience and shared a bit of political philosophy: "The only way to run for office is to tell them the cockeyed truth and then let them vote how they please."[20]

While Connor happily immersed himself in running for mayor under the new system of government, he continued to serve—

along with Mayor Art Hanes and Commissioner Jabo Waggoner—as a member of the city commission, Birmingham's government of the moment. Despite his easy dismissal of the November vote as "democracy," he had no intention of relinquishing his police commissioner's post without a fight. On 1 February 1963, attorney Jim Simpson—Connor's longtime political ally—filed an appeal with the Alabama Supreme Court contesting the law under which Birmingham voted to change its form of government. Simpson argued that the 1955 and 1959 legislatures passed conflicting laws regarding methods of change; he further asserted that, should the legality of the November 1962 election be upheld, the new mayor-council government should not take office until 1 October 1965, at the expiration of the four-year terms of the city commission members.[21]

Joining Connor in the mayoral race were Alabama's lieutenant governor, Albert Boutwell, along with Commissioner Waggoner and attorney Tom King. Boutwell and Waggoner were segregationists, whereas King continued as a voice of moderation. Boutwell, described by Shuttlesworth as "just a dignified Bull Connor,"[22] had been the chief sponsor of Alabama's Pupil Placement Act and "freedom of choice" amendment, measures aimed at ensuring segregated public schools.[23] He promised to repel "within the fabric of law and maintenance of order" every attack on Birmingham's "long-standing habits of tradition in the matter of race." Boutwell wished to "unify the people and the government into a single force with which to build a great city and move it forward." A polite segregationist, he believed, "It is the sheerest folly to resort to panic and pure defiance. Our resources lie not in disorder but in firm legal resistance."[24] Shuttlesworth's description of the lieutenant governor was probably unfair, for the highly educated Boutwell stopped short of the extremism reached by his rougher-edged opponent, Connor.

Election day, 5 March, dawned dark with rain and a tornado darted across Jefferson County at one point, but the Birmingham voters turned out in record numbers to elect their first mayor under the new system. Boutwell led the ticket with 17,437 votes, or 39 percent of the 44,736 ballots cast. Connor polled 13,778 votes, or 30 percent, to gain a runoff spot opposite Boutwell. Tom King, twenty-one months removed from his ill-fated 1961 mayoral race, received 11,639 votes for 26 percent. Waggoner finished far back with 1,872 votes and four percent. The runoff was set for 2 April, and Connor noted that the race "has become a showdown of whether two foreign-owned newspapers, one owned by Newhouse in New York and the other by Scripps-Howard in Cleveland, Ohio, and the bloc vote are going to rule Birmingham or whether the people of Birmingham are going to rule themselves."[25]

Weeks before the election, SCLC had targeted the Birmingham business community for its planned series of demonstrations aimed at ridding the city of its sytematic segregation. Stores with lunch counters were to be the first targets because blacks felt "a special humiliation" at being refused food service. SCLC decided to mount its campaign around the Easter season, the second largest shopping period of the year. Easter would fall on 14 April, meaning the campaign would start in early March, about the time of the mayoral election.

Wyatt Tee Walker, an aide to Martin Luther King, Jr., began visiting the city in January and laying some groundwork for the campaign—familiarizing himself with city picketing codes and bail bond situations and scheduling workshops on nonviolence and direct action. By 1 March the project was "in high gear" and SCLC had the names of 250 persons who volunteered to participate in initial demonstrations and pledged to stay in jail at least five days.[26] Although King and Shuttlesworth had been working on plans since shortly after the first of the year, they agreed to postpone demonstrations until after the mayoral runoff in deference to the pleas of A. G. Gaston and Dr. Lucius Pitts. Gaston and Pitts convinced the SCLC group that demonstrations at that crucial point would help elect Connor,[27] and King agreed that "our presence" would have provided the police commissioner "an emotion-charged issue" with which to "persuade the white community that he, and he alone, could defend the city's official policies of segregation." King left Birmingham during the runoff interim to build support for the upcoming campaign, concentrating in two areas— informing the leaders of such organizations as the NAACP, CORE,

SNCC, and the Southern Regional Council of plans for Birmingham, and raising the thousands of dollars that would be needed for bail bond money once Project C began.[28]

Albert Boutwell was the early mayoral choice of Birmingham business community moderates, who accepted the inevitability of desegregation of some aspects of Southern society. While Boutwell proclaimed the segregationist cause, his utterances were far less strident than those of Connor, and his statements gave promise of his willingness to negotiate. "I am determined that we are going to defend, I hope maintain, segregation," he said, "but we are not going to be a city of unrestrained and unhampered mockery of the law."[29]

During the runoff period, political smear sheets linking Boutwell with the black vote and "printed suggestively in red" began to appear in the Birmingham area. Boutwell reminded voters that he wrote "the laws which today successfully maintain our traditional segregation in Birmingham public schools" and charged that Connor, "faced by certain defeat," had "stooped to a new low" in his "panic."[30] Connor disclaimed any knowledge of the sheets and suggested that Boutwell "got them out" in order to "have something to cry about." Connor called Boutwell an ineffective lieutenant governor who had "an open breech" with Gov. George Wallace and who had been unable to gain a single block of interstate highway for the Birmingham area.[31]

Connor told a political gathering in Roebuck that he resigned from "the Mountain Brook-controlled Birmingham Chamber of Commerce because they tried to brainwash Ol' Bull about integration."[32] Jabo Waggoner recalled that he and Connor had attended a chamber of commerce meeting during the summer of 1962 at which "the burden of the whole meeting was that we were just going to have to change our attitude" and "allow blacks to become foremen and superintendents" and to make other concessions. "Bull and I got up and left the meeting, and told them they could do what they wanted to," Waggoner said, "and that was the beginning of the effort" of businessmen to negotiate independently with black leadership.[33]

Connor's consistent refusal to discuss the possibility of changes in the segregation ordinances prompted moderates, as well as the city's two daily newspapers, to support the change-of-government move and Boutwell's candidacy. Boutwell voiced the feeling of these groups when he described Connor as the head of "the old political order" that held Birmingham in a vise, restraining municipal and individual expansion. In endorsing Boutwell two days prior to the runoff, the *Birmingham News* called for "fresh new leadership in a government without hangovers from old, often bitter disputes and an atmosphere of distrust and squabbling." The newspaper urged voters to "cut away the old political vines which tangled our city's life" by voting Boutwell into office.[34] The *Birmingham World* said, "Birmingham has too much at stake to flirt with negativism," and added, "Standstillism is a kind of civic fatalism. Government by stalemate is akin to political frustration."[35] The black newspaper avoided endorsing a candidate but simply urged eligible voters to go to the polls on election day—its usual practice.

A note in Connor's FBI file suggests that, as the runoff neared, he considered a vote-winning ploy of arresting persons to be identified as the bombers of Bethel Baptist Church.[36] No such arrests occurred, however, and Connor based the windup of his campaign on his familiar railings against "foreign-owned" newspapers, the "Mountain Brook-controlled" Chamber of Commerce, and the black vote attempting to "take over" and "integrate Birmingham." (Not until 26 September 1977 did a Jefferson County grand jury indict Georgia segregationist J. B. Stoner for bombing Shuttlesworth's church; Stoner was convicted of the crime on 14 May 1980 and began serving a ten-year sentence on 2 June 1983, after two unsuccessful appeals.[37])

Boutwell and Connor voted early on 2 April, each smiling confidently for newspaper photographers. They joined another record turnout of 51,278 voters (75 percent of the electorate) who went to the polls on a bright, sunny day to elect a new mayor and nine city council members. Boutwell, who enjoyed the support of the affluent and middle-class whites as well as almost all blacks who could vote, received 29,630 votes to Connor's 21,648. As expected, Connor's strength came from predominantly blue-collar areas, Ensley and East Lake. Boutwell interpreted the result, "not as a personal victory, but as a victory for unity and harmony."

Connor, saying he would leave office "with a treasure of happy memories," extended Boutwell his "heartiest congratulations," but warned the people of Birmingham to be watchful of "government by remote control from newspaper offices and from the Chamber of Commerce and from the leaders of the minority group of 10,000 votes, none of whom are [sic] under oath as public servants."[38]

Presiding Circuit Judge J. Edgar Bowron had upheld the legality of Birmingham's change-of-government election in January, and all seven Alabama Supreme Court members agreed with that ruling. The 1955 acts dealing with changes of government provided that newly elected bodies would take office on the second Monday after the election in which full membership was determined, in this case on 15 April. However, the 1959 act relating to changes of government stated that incumbents would be permitted to serve out their terms of office, in which case the Birmingham City Commission would remain the government of record until 1 October 1965. This was the basis of attorney Jim Simpson's suit in behalf of the commission. Three members of the Alabama Supreme Court stated that, in their opinion, the new form of government should commence on 15 April, but the remaining four members, constituting a majority, declined to rule until a suit was filed seeking clarification.[39] Thus Bull Connor and his colleagues continued to serve as Birmingham's official government as SCLC began its campaign with a series of low-key lunch counter sit-ins on 3 April, the day following the runoff election. When the demonstrators were asked to leave and refused to do so, they were arrested under Birmingham's "trespass after warning" ordinance, and Project C was under way.[40]

Martin Luther King, Jr., had been a student at Crozer Theological Seminary in Chester, Pennsylvania, when he first encountered a detailed analysis of Gandhi's philosophy of nonviolence.[41] The Montgomery bus boycott in which King rose to prominence was marked by its commitment to nonviolent demonstrations, as was the unsuccessful effort in Albany. At the start of the Birmingham campaign, King underscored his commitment to nonviolence in a talk at the St. James Baptist Church, and Birmingham detectives dutifully relayed the message to Connor.

"You must always refuse to use violence on your opponent," King told his St. James audience. "I know sometimes this is hard to do, but our cause is great and noble, no physical violence and no violence of spirit. Remember our white brothers are just misguided. We are not going to give up and we must let them know that, but we must not lower our love for our white brother."

King said blacks were "embarking on a mission to break down the barrier of segregation in Birmingham," which he described as "the last big city in the United States that is segregated" and the city with "the worst record for police brutality in the United States." The SCLC leader outlined several steps for nonviolent action: First, "collect the facts, be sure that there is some evil alive, and I tell you there is evil in Birmingham." Second, negotiate with an opponent by sitting down at a table and discussing problems. Third, use direct action such as sit-ins and ride-ins to create tension and attract attention to a cause, which "may mean going to jail, but we are ready." Fourth, always use nonviolence.

"We are not out to defeat the white man but to save him," said King. "We are struggling to set twenty million Negroes free, in so doing we will set eighty million whites free."[42]

Connor refused Shuttlesworth's request for a picketing permit at the outset of Project C, noting that such a permit "cannot be granted by me individually but is the responsibility of the entire Commission." He added, "I insist that you and your people do not start any picketing in the streets of Birmingham, Alabama,"[43] but the suggestion was ignored. The early demonstrations were peaceful and the police restrained in their handling of demonstrators. Police dogs and patrolmen armed with clubs appeared briefly during a demonstration on Palm Sunday, 7 April, but these symbols of force quickly disappeared. The arrests continued as the demonstrations grew stronger each day, but Connor and his policemen remained calm and businesslike. Then the reason for the restraint became apparent. Connor and his men were awaiting an injunction against marching without a permit, which they felt would halt the demonstrations.[44] On the night of 10 April, Circuit Judge William A. Jenkins issued the injunction; it was served against King, Shuttlesworth, Ralph Abernathy, and other campaign leaders on the morning of 11 April.[45]

Although the demonstrations had been mild, representatives of the business community were already attempting to negotiate a settlement. On 9 April a small group of whites led by Sidney Smyer met with Shuttlesworth and other ACMHR members. Shuttlesworth demanded that the whites go beyond their agreements of the previous fall and institute a school desegregation program, but little was accomplished. The groups met again on 11 April, agreed to enlarge their ranks, and scheduled a meeting for the following Tuesday, 16 April.[46]

The same day, Shuttlesworth received a telephone call from a white man who told the black leader, "You are doing more to create hate than any man has ever done before."

"Brother," Shuttlesworth answered, "we have got a movement going here in Birmingham that's not creating hate, but is going to set men free. Today is the first time that Bull has ever smiled at me. . . . As I walked out of the courtroom and saw Bull standing there, Bull looked at me and I looked at him and Bull smiled and said, 'Hi, Shuttlesworth,' and I said, 'Hi, Bull.' And then Bull made a remark about my overalls [the uniform of the day for the protesters]. He said, 'Shuttlesworth, if you wear those overalls to jail, they are going to work you real hard over there.' I said I was wearing them so that I might save the city a few pennies worth of work clothes."[47]

About this time, at the suggestion of Chief Jamie Moore, Connor invited Albany's police chief, Laurie Pritchett, to Birmingham for consultation. Moore had known Pritchett for many years and "wanted to follow the same procedures" in Birmingham that had been so effective in Albany the previous year. Pritchett traveled to Birmingham and went to Connor's office, where he "was expectin' some big robust man" with a nickname such as "Bull." "I never will forget," said Pritchett, "when we entered his office, his back was to us . . . some big executive chair, you know, and when he turned around, there was this little man—you know, in stature. But he had this boomin' voice, and he was tellin' me how they closed the golf course. . . . Said, 'They can play golf, but we put concrete in the holes. They can't get the ball in the holes.' And this give me some indication as to what type man he was.

You know, I think he was an opportunist that could see if he did this he could reach political power."[48]

Pritchett's advice to Connor was to afford King protection at all times because "if he were ever killed in any city that the fires would be there." Fearful of how the Klan might react to King's demonstrations and unsure that Connor would follow his suggestions, Pritchett left Birmingham quickly. "I didn't want to be associated with this in any way that it could cast a reflection back on me or the city which I represent," he said.[49]

Meanwhile, King and his colleagues were considering how to deal with the injunction. The tactic had not been unexpected, for it had successfully quelled earlier SCLC efforts. Mindful of these previous frustrations, the group decided it "had no choice but to violate such an injunction." King intended to set the example of civil disobedience to what he felt was an unjust law and prepared to lead a demonstration on the following day, 12 April, which would be Good Friday. At this point, the city notified the bondsman who had been furnishing bail for demonstrators that his assets were insufficient for further bonding. This was news of crisis proportion, for approximately three hundred demonstrators remained in jail of the more than four hundred arrested to that point.[50]

Discussing the problem in Room 30 of the Gaston Motel, SCLC leaders encouraged King to return to fund-raising and not to lead the 12 April march. One man told King, "You are the only one who has the contacts to get it [the money]. If you go to jail, we are lost. The battle of Birmingham is lost." King was in a quandary, "in the midst of the deepest quiet I have ever felt, with two dozen others in the room." In his 1964 book *Why We Can't Wait*, he recalled thinking of the twenty-four people with him, of the three hundred in jail, and of the Birmingham black community. "Then," he wrote, "my mind leaped beyond the Gaston Motel, past the city jail, past city lines and state lines, and I thought of twenty million black people who dreamed that someday they might be able to cross the Red Sea of injustice and find their way to the promised land of integration and freedom. There was no room for doubt.

"I don't know what will happen," he told his colleagues. "I don't

Martin Luther King, Jr., right, leads a protest march in Birmingham on Good Friday, 12 April 1963, accompanied by Fred L. Shuttlesworth, left, and Ralph Abernathy. Because an injunction had been issued prohibiting such marches, Birmingham police arrested the trio and others involved. Shuttlesworth made bail to continue leading the Birmingham protest, but King and Abernathy remained in jail eight days to dramatize the campaign. During this period, King wrote his famous "Letter from the Birmingham Jail." (Courtesy Birmingham Public Library)

know where the money will come from. But I have to make a faith act." King asked Abernathy to accompany him on the march. Then they all stood, linked arms, and chanted the battle hymn of the civil rights movement, "We Shall Overcome."[51]

Meanwhile, in city hall, another group met in Chief Jamie Moore's conference room. The topic of discussion: who would arrest King if he marched. A warrant was prepared; then came word that King and a group of demonstrators were on the street. Jack Warren, in charge of the Patrol Division, recalled that Moore's group "had run that around about who was going to get him."

Finally, Moore looked at Warren and said, "Well, you're going to get him."[52]

As the demonstrators led by King and Abernathy walked toward the downtown area, Warren and his officers arrived. Two muscular policemen grabbed the leaders by the backs of their shirts and herded them into a paddy wagon. "I took him to jail and arrested him," said Warren.[53] King and Abernathy were separated from the other demonstrators, and then from each other. King was held incommunicado for more than twenty-four hours in solitary confinement, "the longest, most frustrating and bewildering hours I have lived," he wrote later.[54] In Atlanta, Georgia, King's wife Coretta became so concerned for her husband's safety that she attempted to telephone Pres. John F. Kennedy to ask for help. A few minutes later, Robert Kennedy returned her call, promising to "look into the situation. . . . We have a difficult problem with local officials," Kennedy added. "Bull Connor is very hard to deal with."[55]

The next day, following an FBI check of the Birmingham situation, President Kennedy telephoned Mrs. King to say that her husband was well and would call her within a few minutes. Fifteen minutes later, King was on the telephone with his wife.[56] Police Chief Jamie Moore had his secretary monitor the conversation and take a shorthand transcript. King seemed surprised when Mrs. King told him that President Kennedy had telephoned.

King: "Who did you say called you?"
Mrs. King: "Kennedy, the President."
King: "Did he call you direct?"
Mrs. King: "Yes, and he told me you were going to call in a few minutes. It was about thirty minutes ago. He called from Palm Beach. I tried to 'phone him yesterday."
King: "Is that known?"
Mrs. King: "It's known here; I just got it."
King: "Let Wyatt know."
Mrs. King: "The Executive in Birmingham?"
King: "Yes, do that right now."

The Kings discussed the display that the Birmingham demonstrations were receiving in the Atlanta newspapers and various family matters. He said he had mailed their income tax report, that his morale was high, and that he was getting his vitamins.

Then he reminded his wife, "Be sure and get in touch with the Reverend [Wyatt Tee Walker]. I think this gives it a new dimension."[57]

After a wire service news report that King had been able to talk to his wife only after President Kennedy's intervention, the *Washington Star* editorialized that the episode smacked of politics. The *Star* quoted Chief Moore as saying that the Kings had conversed via telephone the day prior to the Kennedy-inspired call.[58] Moore told the *Birmingham News* that King's call "was not arranged by Kennedy or anyone connected with the President" and that the civil rights leader had been permitted to telephone Mrs. King "the first time he had requested a chance to call his wife."

"We knew she just recently had had a baby and was home from the hospital only a few days," Moore added. "That's the only reason we let him call."[59]

Moore repeated this assertion during a 1981 interview: "I asked Bull what to do and he said let them talk."[60]

At the time of the incident, Moore termed "ridiculous" the claim that King was being held incommunicado, saying, "Apparently some people think our jail is to be used as an office with frequent long distance calls and press conferences. We have rules and regulations. We have to follow them when we have 400 prisoners."[61]

While King remained in jail, Albert Boutwell and the nine new council members were inaugurated by Probate Judge J. Paul Meeks on 15 April.[62] Yet Boutwell, the clear choice of the electorate, was not clearly the mayor. The city commission refused to give up its quarters, contending that it was still in office until resolution of the court case. An agreement was worked out whereby both governmental bodies had office space; both met in city hall on Tuesday mornings, and official minutes were kept for each. "If you came into the Mayor's suite wanting to speak to the Mayor, the receptionist would ask, 'Which one?'" recalled attorney David Vann.[63] The two mayors agreed to have both their names appear on checks issued by the city until the court decided which was the legal government. Political pundits had a field day, *News* Managing Editor John Bloomer recalled, calling Birmingham "the only city in the world with two mayors and a King."[64]

Although Birmingham's two governments met in city hall on 16 April, the date may be more significant for a meeting that did not occur. The Smyer and Shuttlesworth groups were scheduled to convene again that day, but the whites grew fearful that if the court left the city commission in office, the commission would overturn any agreements reached by the businessmen, just as Connor had forced restoration of the Jim Crow signs the previous fall. For that reason, and not wishing to appear to have given in to black demands, the Smyer group suddenly decided against further negotiations for the moment.[65] The stage thus was set for confrontation in the streets.

Several of Birmingham's most liberal white ministers criticized King for the timing of the SCLC demonstrations, reasoning that the Boutwell government should be given a period of grace. The ministers urged Birmingham blacks "to withdraw support from these demonstrations" and to press their demands "in the courts and in negotiations among local leaders, and not in the streets."[66] The *Birmingham World* carried a similar theme in a 10 April editorial, noting that a new mayor and city administration had just been elected and saying, "It is in the best interest of all concerned for a certain degree of restraint to be shown on the part of all responsible citizens."[67]

King answered the criticism in a document that later became famous as his "Letter from the Birmingham Jail." He handwrote the lengthy epistle over several days, passing the sheets to attorneys Shores, Billingsley, or Clarence Jones during their visits. Walker's secretary, Willie Pearl Mackey, typed the sheets, which were then returned to King for editing.[68]

In the letter, King wrote that blacks had "waited for more than 340 years for our constitutional and God-given rights." He then explained his reasons for leading the civil rights movement and justified his techniques. "The nations of Asia and Africa are moving with jetline speed toward gaining political independence, but we still creep at horse-and-buggy pace toward gaining a cup of coffee at a lunch counter," he wrote. He discussed the seeming paradox of breaking some laws while obeying others, saying two types of laws existed—just and unjust.

"I would be the first to advocate obeying just laws," he wrote. "One has not only a legal but a moral responsibility to obey just laws. Conversely, one has a moral responsibility to disobey unjust laws. I would agree with St. Augustine that 'an unjust law is no law at all.'"

King described an unjust law as "a code that is out of harmony with the moral law." Segregation, he said, "is not only politically, economically and sociologically unsound, it is morally wrong and sinful."[69]

With King and Abernathy in jail, Shuttlesworth filled the pulpit at the St. James Baptist Church, using his considerable oratorical talents to entertain and fire the crowds. He had visited King and Abernathy, Shuttlesworth told his audience, and taken them their overcoats because the jail was cold and neither had mattresses, as did the other prisoners. With his usual flair, he told of approaching the white water fountain at city hall "to see what white water tasted like." Suddenly, a door opened and Connor appeared, saying, "Well, I caught you."

On the same visit, Shuttlesworth found the city hall restrooms locked and was forced to walk to the Greyhound Bus Station across the street to use the toilet.

"I found five policemen doing the same thing," he said. "They told me, 'Bull has got us in the same position you Negroes are in. We have to come over here to use the restroom. We are locked out.'"[70]

Shores could have posted the $300 bond for King's release at any point during his jail stay, "but the funds were coming in from all over the country by the thousands" in support of the civil rights effort, and the civil rights leader elected to remain in jail to dramatize the Birmingham campaign.[71] While King was in jail, one city official approached Connor about checking the SCLC head out to the Street and Sanitation Department to "put him to work out on the street and let him see how the other folks lived." Connor declined, not wishing to parade his noted prisoner through the streets with chains on his legs.[72]

But while the money flowed in and Shuttlesworth entertained

the crowds at the St. James Baptist Church, the force of the street demonstrations ebbed during King's absence.[73] The campaign leader and his colleague Abernathy thus decided to come out of jail on 20 April to renew the effort. During late April, King issued a call for black students to join the demonstrations in order to "fill up the jails."[74] Despite fear on the part of some parents for the safety of their children, students by the hundreds began taking part in the daily marches during early May. The Reverend Abraham Woods, who encouraged his three children to participate and recruited other students for the demonstrations, remembered that "the question did come up as to subjecting these young people to possible harm," but that King answered by saying "they had already been subjected to brutality by living in the Southern way of life."[75] The decision to use children marked a turning point in the effectiveness of the demonstrations, particularly after Connor intensified his response to the campaign.

The police grew less restrained in their handling of the demonstrators during the first week in May. Connor remained on the street with his policemen, recalled Jack Warren, and "you could see the tension . . . he was beginning to see that this was so damn big, he wasn't sure what the hell to do." On 2 May, following a meeting in Sixteenth Street Baptist Church, hundreds of blacks—many of them children—flooded across the adjacent Kelly Ingram Park and headed toward downtown. "You could see Bull," said Warren, "moving, looking, concerned, fidgety. He was just desperate. 'What the hell do I do?'"[76] Some demonstrators carried signs that read "No Eat. No Dollars," "Segregation is a Sin," and "Equal Rights." As the mass of people approached downtown, police began making arrests.[77] "Hell, we made arrests, and put them in jail, and didn't even know what they were over there for, by the fifties and hundreds," said Warren. "The jail was full."[78] Approximately one thousand people were arrested for parading without a permit and refusing to move along when requested to do so by police. The offenders, who included 319 school-age children, were hauled away in police vans, sheriff's cars, and finally, in school buses. At this point, Birmingham firemen laid hoses with which to repel the marchers, and the police department's K-9 corps trotted out its German shepherds.[79]

Connor had initiated the K-9 corps in February 1960 with six officers and six dogs, and the unit remained about the same size in 1963. The unit was led by Sgt. Marvin McBride, who had studied K-9 methods in Baltimore, Maryland, one of the first U.S. cities to use police dogs.[80] A K-9 patrolman trained his own dog under McBride's watchful eye; a man and his dog worked eight hours a day for sixteen weeks to gain mutual understanding and respect. An officer would walk a downtown beat or patrol in a car with his dog, and when the shift ended, the two would go home together. The dogs were used as psychological devices in crowd control situations, and at least one K-9 team was patrolling in the area of the Greyhound Bus Station on the day Freedom Riders were attacked at the Trailways station in 1961.

Chief Jamie Moore opposed the use of the K-9 corps during the early civil rights demonstrations, fearing lawsuits, and except for a brief appearance on 7 April, the German shepherds were not used during the first month of King's campaign. As the demonstrations grew, however, Connor decided to bring out the dogs. As Jabo Waggoner recalled, "They can handle a crowd, I promise you that. A snarling German police dog can handle a crowd."[81]

After the mass arrests of 2 May, the demonstrations grew more intense each day. "At the beginning, the orders were that they can't come past this point," said Warren. "But nobody had ever gotten down to the crucial point of having to make a decision. That is to say, to use the dogs, the hoses, shoot, or whatever. You can understand the reluctance of all these policemen. Nobody wanted to do the damn thing first." On 3 May masses of black demonstrators appeared again at Kelly Ingram Park. "Aw, hell, there must have been three thousand, four thousand out there," recalled Warren, in charge of the Patrol Division that day. "I mean, it was just solid. So they were coming up Fifth Avenue. And when they got to 17th Street . . . they were going to City Hall. And the orders were, they can't come. So at that time, when it was obvious they were going to keep coming, that's when the fire hoses and the dogs were turned loose." Connor had issued the order earlier in the day.[82]

Several blacks were bitten when they ventured too close to the dogs. They retaliated with a barrage of bricks and bottles, hit-

Birmingham firemen spray blacks with power water hoses in an attempt to quell civil rights demonstrations during the first week of May 1963. The use of the hoses continued for several days, unifying the black community in support of Martin Luther King, Jr.'s campaign to end segregation in the city. (Courtesy the Birmingham News*)*

ting one dog in the head.[83] The demonstrators taunted the dogs, threw rocks at them, spit on them. On 4 May hundreds of black children and adults flooded out of Sixteenth Street Baptist Church and headed toward downtown once again. Firemen immediately began hosing them with powerful streams of water, and a crowd of about four hundred white office workers viewing the scene from behind the water lines cheered. Two fire hoses were equipped with monitor guns capable of blasting bark off a tree at a distance of one hundred feet. At one point, two black girls ran through Kelly Ingram Park clad in their undergarments after the water streams ripped away their outer clothing.[84]

"We've just begun to fight," said Connor after several days of hosing down the demonstrators.[85] The violent scene was repeated

As civil rights demonstrations grew in intensity during the first week in May 1963, Connor ordered the use of police dogs to control crowds. Newspapers and television stations around the world carried pictures of the dogs in action, dramatizing the plight of blacks in segregated cities and mobilizing support for the civil rights movement. (Courtesy Birmingham Public Library [above] and the Birmingham News *[right])*

5 May, with one departure from the familiar script. Mayor Art Hanes held what he described as an "impromptu" meeting with SCLC leaders Charles Billups and Wyatt Tee Walker and reported, "I told them I would talk to anybody anytime, but that I would not talk or negotiate as long as the demonstrations were continuing."[86] Hanes's ultimatum had little effect, and the demonstrations reached a crescendo on 7 May, when some fifteen hundred blacks—mostly school-age children—flooded the downtown area, causing massive traffic jams, singing freedom songs, and chanting "We want Bull Connor."[87] The use of children in the demonstrations, while appalling to A. G. Gaston and other conservative black leaders, gave Project C a much-needed boost. The crowds at the nightly

mass meetings grew, and media coverage became more sympathetic to the SCLC cause.[88]

Injuries resulting from the use of police dogs and fire hoses were
minimal. A total of eighteen policemen and firemen, two newsmen, and five blacks suffered injuries requiring medical attention
during the period 5 April–9 May, according to a report released

by University Hospital, where those injured were taken for treatment. The majority of the policemen, firemen, and newsmen suffered bruises and lacerations from being hit by thrown objects; two blacks were treated for dog bites, one for facial injuries, one for a knee injury, and another (Fred L. Shuttlesworth) for chest pains after being hit by water streams.[89] Informed of Shuttlesworth's injury, Connor retorted, "I wish they'd taken him away in a hearse."[90]

If the injuries were minimal, the impact of Connor's decision to employ the dogs and hoses was far-reaching. On 4 May newspapers across the nation and around the world ran wirephotos of barefanged German shepherds confronting young black children in the streets of Birmingham. One news photo pictured an older demonstrator taunting one dog as another canine sank his teeth into the man's posterior. Other images were equally dramatic—five policemen holding down one woman demonstrator, and marchers of all ages swept along and staggering under the pressure of the water streams.

Until the dogs and hoses appeared, King's support in the Birmingham black community had been only lukewarm, according to Citizens for Progress organizer David Vann. But Connor's extreme tactics provided "instant unification."

"I was talking to a black businessman [A. G. Gaston]," Vann recalled, "and he was laughing about how the King people didn't have salaries, only expense accounts. He said, 'I'll swap my salary for their expense account any day. I was down at the motel last night watching them.' And then he said, 'But Attorney Vann, they've just turned fire hoses on little black girls. They're rolling them right down the middle of the street. I can't talk to you no more.'"[91]

The first week in May "was the time of our greatest stress," said King, "and the courage and conviction of those students and adults made it our finest hour." Because the demonstrators remained nonviolent yet did not turn back, "the moral conscience of the nation was deeply stirred and, all over the country, our fight became the fight of decent Americans of all races," said King.[92]

"If you'd ask half of them what freedom means, they couldn't tell you," challenged Connor.[93]

During the height of the demonstrations, Connor and Chief Jamie Moore joined their men at the scene of the action on the streets. Connor, in his trademark short-brimmed straw hat, was a much-photographed figure during the first week in May. At midday, the public safety commissioner and a retinue of police officers led by Moore would retire to a downtown restaurant such as LaParee, three blocks east of Kelly Ingram Park, for lunch. Connor made his customary "grand entrance," speaking to patrons left and right in his unmistakably loud voice. During the meal, Connor would "always have a drink or two" and continue to talk loudly, at times using language "that embarrassed the rest of us," Moore recalled.

"Of course, we were in uniform and couldn't have a drink," said the chief.[94]

By now, Connor was "in his glory," recalled television newsman Dan Rather in his autobiographical best-seller *The Camera Never Blinks*. "On television every night. Pushing around blacks and reporters and anyone who got in his way." Rather sought an interview with King for a Columbia Broadcasting System special on Birmingham, but to gain credentials from Connor, he posed as a reporter from a regional newspaper, the *Houston Chronicle*, using an outdated identification card from his days in Houston. Connor had surrounded King's motel with policemen, and no one was allowed in without credentials from the police commissioner.

"What the hell you ovah here for, wantin' to give all these niggers mo' publicity?" Rather remembered Connor asking.

"Well, you know, it has become a national story," Rather answered, "and the position of our paper is that we try to see for ourselves."

"Well, all you'll see heah is a bunch of smart-ass niggers," said Connor.[95]

Rather received his credentials and interviewed King. The reporter recalled that King characterized Connor as "just a big, ill-tempered pit bulldog, attacking whatever came into his pit." The civil rights leader added, "We knew what he was. We simply had to decide whether to stay out of his pit."[96]

While King was fulfilling his promise to fill the Birmingham jails, and Connor and his forces were confronting the marchers daily in the streets around Kelly Ingram Park, Birmingham merchants were feeling the economic sting produced by the disruption. Shoppers who customarily visited downtown department stores and specialty shops in this pre–suburban shopping mall era chose to avoid the city center. Retail sales fell off between 15 and 20 percent[97] and, as Smyer recalled, "We did have a depression back in those days."[98] On 4 May Robert Kennedy dispatched assistant attorney general Burke Marshall to Birmingham to try his hand at peace-making. Marshall, who was known and respected by leaders of both SCLC and the Senior Citizens Committee, encouraged both sides to reestablish negotiations. The Senior Citizens Committee appointed Sid Smyer and David Vann (who had been a leader in the change-of-government campaign) to meet with local SCLC representatives, and the two set up a 5 May meeting with the help of Arthur Shores.[99]

In its Birmingham campaign, SCLC sought to negotiate with white leaders on four major issues—desegregation of lunch counters, restrooms, fitting rooms, and drinking fountains in variety and department stores; upgrading and hiring of blacks on a nondiscriminatory basis; the dropping of all charges against jailed demonstrators; and the creation of a biracial committee to work out a timetable for desegregation in all areas of Birmingham life.[100] At the 5 May meeting, the merchants indicated a preference to wait until the Boutwell government was officially ensconced before incorporating any changes, and the blacks insisted that desegregation of lunch counters be gradually undertaken as soon as the mayor-council form became the official government. Smyer and Vann surveyed downtown merchants and identified "five or six" black employees who could be promoted after the demonstrations ended.

At that point, Smyer and Vann decided that they could go no further without the support of the entire Senior Citizens Committee. Marshall telephoned Robert Kennedy, giving him the names of key members of the committee. Kennedy enlisted the aid of cabinet officers as well as Pres. John Kennedy in making calls to committee members, urging them to support an agreement with SCLC. Secretary of the Treasury Douglas Dillon telephoned three former business acquaintances—Edward Norton, chairman of the board of Royal Crown Cola; Frank Plummer, president of Birmingham Trust National Bank; and William Hulsey, chairman of the board of Realty Mortgage Company.[101]

By 7 May, with the demonstrations at full pitch, Connor and his police had arrested more than two thousand persons. That afternoon, the full Senior Citizens Committee gathered for a meeting chaired by Smyer.[102] Outside, blacks sang freedom songs in the streets, "a veritable sea of black faces."[103] Marshall spoke briefly, telling the group it had an opportunity and a responsibility to help find a solution to Birmingham's problem by endorsing a negotiated settlement. Several of the businessmen who had been telephoned by Kennedy cabinet members spoke in favor of such an accord. With only scattered dissent, the committee agreed to endorse the downtown merchants' proposed timetable for desegregating store facilities and upgrading jobs. The group pledged to support a public biracial committee that would consider a broad range of black problems and appointed a subcommittee to complete the negotiations. That night, Smyer, Vann, and William C. Hamilton—Boutwell's executive secretary—met with black negotiators to work out details,[104] and SCLC agreed to end the marches.

"Initially, when King came, he was demanding things like employment of black police officers and desegregation of public schools and parks," David Vann remembered. "One of the first things we had to convince him of was that the business community couldn't do those things. We only could do things businessmen could do." After that, said Vann, King began talking at the mass meetings about the "signs on lunch counters" and saying that "where black people spend dollars, they ought to have jobs." "He shifted his demands so that what we could agree to do would match the demands he was making."[105]

The day after the agreement was reached, two episodes threatened to upset the delicate balance struck between SCLC and the Senior Citizens Committee. First, Connor—who with his fellow commissioners had been left out of the negotiations entirely—arrested King, Abernathy, and twenty-six other demonstrators found guilty of parading without a permit on Good Friday and sentenced to 180 days in jail and $100 fines.[106] Bail for King and Abernathy was set at the unusually high sum of $2,500 each, but

Gaston paid the $5,000 out of his own pocket and the two black leaders remained free to participate in discussions. (King and Abernathy were convicted of the charge in 1965, but the U.S. Supreme Court overturned the convictions in 1969.[107])

The second disturbing episode occurred when Shuttlesworth—incensed by SCLC's agreement to halt demonstrations before negotiations were final—threatened to resume the marches himself. Shuttlesworth had been ill and under sedation at Gaston Motel, but he erupted when told that King agreed to stop the marches. "Did I hear you right?" he asked King, and then demanded to know *who* made the decision. He accused King of coming to Birmingham, getting people excited about desegregation, and then leaving. "But I live here," he said, "the people trust me, and I have the responsibility after SCLC is gone, and I'm telling you it will not be called off."[108]

King's decision to hold a press conference angered Shuttlesworth even more. "Now, Martin, you're mister big," he told the SCLC leader, "but you're soon to be mister nothing. You're going to fall from up here to down here, and you're dead. . . ." He threatened to wait until after King announced the cessation of marches, then return to Sixteenth Street Baptist Church and lead the black children back to the streets. As he attempted to leave, a Burke Marshall subordinate, Joseph Dolan, blocked his way and persuaded him to speak to Robert Kennedy by phone. Kennedy convinced the pastor that returning to the streets would jeopardize any progress made in the discussions. Shuttlesworth relented somewhat, but pressured King into announcing that if an agreement were not reached by 11 A.M. the following day, demonstrations would resume.[109]

Following two days of talks, King and Shuttlesworth announced to reporters on 10 May that "the city of Birmingham has reached an accord with its conscience."[110] The agreement contained the following pledges—desegregation of lunch counters, restrooms, fitting rooms, and drinking fountains within ninety days; the upgrading and hiring of blacks on a nondiscriminatory basis, including employment as clerks and salesmen, within sixty days; official cooperation with SCLC legal representatives in releasing all jailed persons on bond or their personal recognizance; and the establishment of communication between blacks and whites through the Senior Citizens Committee within two weeks.[111]

Connor condemned the accord, labeling it "a face-saving announcement,"[112] while Mayor Hanes described the settlement as "capitulation by certain weak-kneed white people under threats of violence by the rabble rousing Negro, King." Hanes still was not certain who the white negotiators were, but he castigated them as "a bunch of quisling, gutless traitors."[113] Boutwell disclaimed any direct connection with the negotiations and denounced King's pressure methods, but said he would "soon have complete freedom" to seek a solution and would use the mayor's office to "promote peace and good will."[114]

The agreement between SCLC and the white business leaders ended the demonstrations in downtown Birmingham, but—as Laurie Pritchett had feared—not the violence. While some members of Birmingham's white community were willing to accept the agreement as a desirable compromise, the extremists were incensed. The Ku Klux Klan scheduled a meeting on a vacant lot between Birmingham and Bessemer for Saturday 11 May.[115] The Klan had been quiet for six weeks, and some investigators, "aware of Bull Connor's close personal ties with several Klan activists," believe word had gone out to Klansmen to stay clear of the Birmingham situation.[116] That changed abruptly, however, when the home of King's brother, the Reverend A. D. King, and the Gaston Motel were rocked by bomb blasts late Saturday night. The Gaston bomb was planted so that it would kill or injure the person in Room 30, Martin Luther King's room—but the civil rights leader had returned to his Atlanta home for the night.[117]

The blasts touched off rioting by blacks in the area near the motel, located less than a block west of Kelly Ingram Park. Rioters hurled stones at police cars, started fires, and overturned cars. Curiously, Alabama state troopers under command of Col. Al Lingo, a Connor ally, had patrolled the area heavily, but were pulled out a few hours before the bomb exploded. SCLC staffers suspected a setup. After the blast, troopers returned, along with Connor police, dogs, and an armored riot tank. Their appearance fueled the riot, and state troopers used their billy clubs on anyone within reach. King observed, "Whoever planted those bombs had wanted

Violence rocked Birmingham Saturday night, 11 May 1963, after an agreement to end some aspects of segregation was announced by King and the Senior Citizens Committee. Bystanders comfort a man hit by a rock near the Gaston Motel, which was bombed during the violence. The Birmingham Police Department riot tank stands in the background. (Courtesy the Birmingham News)

Blacks jeer "Mister Bull," their symbol of hard-line segregation, as he walks in front of the 17th Street A.O.H. Church in Birmingham. (Courtesy the Birmingham News*)*

the Negroes to riot. They wanted the pact upset."[118] The *Birmingham World* said, "The new terrorism on the Negro community reflects the cruel resistance to peaceful change and also the failure of law enforcement to solve the long chain of hate-bombings."[119]

Following the bombings, President Kennedy ordered 3,000 federal troops into position near Birmingham and made preparations to federalize the Alabama National Guard. The outburst of violence was brief, however, and peace returned the following day. On Monday 13 May the Young Men's Business Club voted overwhelmingly to denounce the violence and to endorse the agreement reached by the SCLC and the Senior Citizens Committee.[120]

The Birmingham Board of Education, whose superintendent was appointed by Connor under the commission form of government, had threatened to expel any school children taking part in the dem-

onstrations. On 20 May the threat became reality as the board
suspended or expelled 1,081 black students arrested for marching
during Project C.[121] Ironically, on the same day, the U.S. Supreme
Court voided convictions of blacks in four Southern states for dem-
onstrating against segregation, ruling they had been lawfully exercising constitutional rights. The Birmingham school board post-
poned appeals hearings for the suspended students until June, after
the close of the school year on 31 May, meaning that high school
seniors involved would miss graduation and others would miss
promotion unless they attended summer school. Attorneys Arthur
Shores and Orzell Billingsley, Jr., sought a temporary restraining
order, contending that the students had been suspended without
warning, notice of charges, or opportunity to appear at a hearing—
violating the Fourteenth Amendment.[122]

U.S. District Judge Clarence Allgood of Birmingham refused to
order Superintendent Theo R. Wright to readmit the suspended
students. Judge Allgood noted that the court had been "shocked
to see hundreds of school children ranging in age from six to 16
running loose and wild without direction over the streets of Birmingham and in business establishments," adding that he found
it inconceivable that a federal court would tell the school board
no punishment should be meted out.[123] SCLC officials called Chief
Judge Elbert P. Tuttle of the U.S. Fifth Circuit Court of Appeals
asking for an immediate appeals hearing. Judge Tuttle, in Atlanta,
set the hearing for the very same day and agreed to hear the case
alone rather than calling in fellow judges, a rarity but not unprece-
dented.[124]

Tuttle's facial expression during the hearing "reflected anger and
distress over the treatment of the students."[125] Afterward, he dic-
tated an order against the school board directing all students to
return to school the next morning, saying the students had been
"engaged in legally permissable activities" and that the "illegality
of the arrests was necessarily apparent to the officials." Since Allgood had included some of his personal opinions in his ruling,
Tuttle felt justified in making some of his own. He said he found
it "shocking that a board of education, interested in the education
of the children committed to its care, should thus in effect destroy
one term of school for many children at a time when all persons

Commissioners Connor and Jabo Waggoner manage smiles as they pre-pare to vacate their offices 11 May 1963, following the Alabama Supreme Court ruling in favor of a Mayor-Council form of government. After Bir-mingham voters chose the Mayor-Council format in November 1962, the Commission sued to have the election thrown out. The Supreme Court decision ended Connor's more than 22 years as Commissioner of Public Safety. (Courtesy the Birmingham News*)*

professionally interested in the educational process and the wel-fare of young people are bending their efforts toward minimizing school drop-outs and emphasizing the need for continuing educa-tion."[126] It was obvious that the school board action had been Con-nor's final ploy to undermine the Birmingham truce, Tuttle said in a later interview, but the expulsion of hundreds of seniors who would never have returned to school was the more important fac-tor.[127]

The day after Tuttle's decision, 23 May, the Alabama Supreme

Court handed down its long-awaited decision on Birmingham's form of government, saying in an opinion written by Associate Justice John Goodwyn that the mayor-council form was legal and that the commissioners must vacate their offices immediately.[128] Five minutes after hearing the announcement, Mayor Hanes packed his few personal belongings into a cardboard box and left the mayor's office.[129]

Commissioners Connor and Waggoner were not far behind. "All I can say," said Connor, "is that I have enjoyed my 22 and a half years as Public Safety Commissioner. I don't believe I owe the taxpayers anything. They are going to owe me almost two and a half years of pay whether I can get it or not.

"I am going to make application for my pennies," Connor added, "and I'm going to get in line for food stamps. I am going on relief."

Connor gave a formal word of appreciation to the Birmingham fire, police, and other departments for which he was responsible "for their cooperation and encouragement." He picked up his final city paycheck, which had been signed by the new mayor, Albert Boutwell, only moments before.[130] Tears filled his eyes as he told a small group, "This is the worst day of my life." Then he left city hall as an ordinary citizen.

Within a few days, the new city council authorized Mayor Boutwell to appoint a special Committee on Community Affairs to advise on "difficulties which confront us as a community," taking the first step toward meeting the accord reached by SCLC and the Senior Citizens Committee. Examples of a newly harmonious approach to racial matters continued during the summer months. In June the Jim Crow signs over water fountains came down for good. On 16 July Boutwell named a biracial group of city leaders to the Committee on Community Affairs. One week later, on 23 July, the city council repealed the segregation ordinances that Bull Connor had defended with such vehemence. Thus the racial separation that Birmingham had required by law in restaurants, recreational areas, public auditoriums, and public restrooms became a vestige of the past. Finally, on 30 July lunch counters were desegregated, and small groups of blacks celebrated by munching sandwiches and sipping coffee in Loveman's, Kress, Britts, Woolworth's and Pizitz stores.[131]

On the national scene, "The sound of the explosion of Birmingham reached all the way to Washington," said King, and "abruptly transformed the mood of the nation," according to historian Arthur Schlesinger, Jr. In June President Kennedy asked Congress to commit itself to the proposition "that race has no place in American life or law,"[132] and called for the most far-reaching civil rights bill in history. Noting that one hundred years had passed since Abraham Lincoln freed the slaves, Kennedy said:

> We preach freedom around the world, and we mean it, and we cherish our freedom here at home, but are we to say to the world . . . that this is a land of the free except for the Negroes . . . ? Now the time has come for this nation to fulfill its promise. The events in Birmingham and elsewhere have so increased the cries for equality that no city or state or legislative body can prudently choose to ignore them.[133]

Later that summer, King led some two hundred thousand civil rights demonstrators marching on Washington for jobs and freedom. Kennedy's civil rights bill faced a long legislative fight, and although it ultimately passed, Kennedy did not live to sign it into law. The bill finally passed the House of Representatives in February 1964 and the Senate in June 1964. Lyndon B. Johnson, who had become president following Kennedy's assassination in November 1963, signed the civil rights bill on 2 July 1964. The measure prohibited discrimination in public accommodations; authorized the attorney general to institute suits to desegregate schools or other public facilities; outlawed discrimination in employment on the basis of race, color, religion, sex, or national origin; and gave added protection for voting rights.

Birmingham, unlike Albany, was an overwhelming success for Martin Luther King, Jr., and the SCLC and paved the way for later civil rights gains. The conscience of the nation was stirred by the confrontation between grim-faced, helmeted policemen with their dogs and black children chanting freedom songs and hymns. King's techniques in Albany and Birmingham were similar; the methods of law enforcement were markedly dissimilar. Albany police chief Laurie Pritchett avoided conflict; Birmingham police commissioner Bull Connor met confrontation head on. The result in Birmingham was the dramatic encounter that King needed to give national impetus to the civil rights movement. Fred Shuttlesworth believes "the massive demonstrations in Birmingham moved the country forward to change" by proving that blacks wanted freedom from segregation so strongly that "people would go to jail for it." Without the demonstrations, said Shuttlesworth, "we would not have the civil rights bill."[134]

King called Birmingham "the most segregated city in America,"[135] and Shuttlesworth described it as almost "a police state" in which blacks and whites "were captives within their own system," unable to talk to each other "about what ought to be done."[136] During the spring of 1963, one individual, Bull Connor, came to epitomize Birmingham's racism, the city's intransigence, and even the city itself. While Mayor Art Hanes shouted "Never!" and businessman Sidney Smyer negotiated in a closed room, Connor and his forces dominated television and news reports from the demonstration-wracked city. The eyes of the nation saw Connor's police dogs lunging at blacks, his power hoses drenching little girls in their Sunday finery, and his riot tank rumbling into position in the path of marchers singing freedom songs. "They never marched more than one block," recalled attorney David Vann, "but that was all they needed to dominate the 15-minute national news."[137] Wyatt Walker agreed, saying, "There was never any more skillful manipulation of the news media than there was in Birmingham." Andrew Young, another King lieutenant, recalled, "The movement was really about getting publicity for injustice."[138] This the SCLC accomplished with the help of Bull Connor and the national television networks. President Kennedy saw the reports and remarked at a staff meeting, "The civil rights movement should thank God for Bull Connor. He's helped it as much as Abraham Lincoln."[139] Indeed, Connor's repressive tactics in the name of crowd control did thrust the civil rights movement forward. As he sought to defend Birmingham segregation and his Southern way of life, the little man with the booming voice became a catalyst for dismantling the dual society for which he stood.

9

The Long Last Hurrah

I f Bull Connor sensed that he had heard his last political hurrah in 1963, he failed to show it. He accepted the ruling of the Alabama Supreme Court in favor of a mayor-council form of government in typical Connor fashion—philosophically and with a quip about applying "for my pennies." Connor "had a great trait of coming back," recalled his former campaign manager J. Morgan Smith, "and he would not retain a depressed feeling at all. He always snapped back."[1] His former city commission colleague, Jabo Waggoner, said, "I think it fell off his back like water off a duck's back. I don't think it bothered him a nickel's worth."[2]

During the weeks and months following the Supreme Court ruling, Connor continued his role as an outspoken opponent of the civil rights movement. On 7 June 1963, four days before Alabama governor George C. Wallace's "stand in the schoolhouse door" to block integration of the University of Alabama, Connor addressed a meeting of the Tuscaloosa County Citizens Council in Holt, less than five miles from the university. He "pleaded with the group not to appear at the University 6/11/63 and to let Governor Wallace and law enforcement agencies handle the problem," saying the message was "a personal request from the Governor." The relaying of the message "appeared to be the purpose of the meeting," according to an FBI informant in attendance.[3]

Having delivered Wallace's request, Connor revealed that he had "been approached by many people to form a white citizens boycott organization which he would head." The organization would "fight integration by the same tactics used by Reverend Martin Luther King, Jr., that is, using the boycott as a weapon." He told the gathering he was "undecided" as to whether he would head such an organization.[4] Connor referred to an Alabama branch of the People's Association for Selective Shopping, an Atlanta-based confederation headed by segregationist Lester Maddox.

PASS, as the organization was called, had as its stated purpose "to fight for the restoration and preservation of Constitutional Government and to protect the jobs and security of White Americans." Members of PASS pledged to "Pass By" the services and products "of merchants, manufacturers and industries that place Negro employees on jobs formerly held by White Citizens." PASS claimed that "tens of thousands of White Americans" were "losing their jobs, homes, schools, churches—other properties and their rights and freedom because of attacks from Communist inspired, lawless racial agitators that foster racial integration and amalgamation."[5] Clearly, here was a creed that Connor could embrace.

PASS was organized to the extent that it prepared a statement for distribution to Birmingham business and civic leaders urging "no further surrender" to integration and promising "a massive and never ending campaign" to prevent PASS members from shopping in downtown Birmingham, should there be "a general break through [sic] in integration in the hotels, motels, restaurants and other business concerns in Birmingham."[6] In Atlanta, the Maddox organization circulated a list of "integrated hotels, motels, restaurants and cafeterias" with the suggestion that PASS members "stay away from these places" and "not eat or sleep integrated." Some names on the list included notations, such as Herren's Restaurant, which was described as "top of the list for integration and has been bragging about it."[7]

Several weeks after his Tuscaloosa announcement, Connor received a letter from his longtime adviser, attorney Jim Simpson, which counseled noninvolvement in PASS. Simpson told Connor "if I were you I would be afraid to take it over in this state because of the very unusual and stringent laws we have against boycotting, inciting to boycott, agreeing to boycott, etc., etc." The attorney felt "nearly sure that you would wind up" being prosecuted "and the penalties are pretty severe."[8] As he usually did, Connor heeded Simpson's advice.

Connor continued to relish his role as a spokesman against integration, however. He espoused a kind of "white solidarity" based on "selective buying" to indicate disapproval of integration, drives to register and organize white voters by wards and precincts, and the enlistment of a maximum number of persons in White Citizens Councils to raise funds to fight the civil rights movement.[9] Connor denounced the use of violence as a means of stopping integration, saying, "We can't win with dynamite or shotguns or stones and knives." Speaking at a Mobile County White Citizens Council rally in the fall of 1963, he condemned the 15 September bombing of Sixteenth Street Baptist Church in Birmingham—a tragedy in which four young black girls were killed—as "the worst thing that ever happened to Alabama." Connor typically justified his use of dogs and fire hoses to control the demonstrations of May 1963 by saying, "Which is better—to use fire hoses and dogs or bullets? Not a shot was fired in Birmingham." He promised to "stand up and fight for what I know is right—segregation, until I die," but admitted that segregationists were "on the one-yard line" with "our backs to the wall."[10]

The speaking engagements were an enjoyable diversion, but they afforded the former commissioner more than an opportunity to lash out at such favored targets as "Bobby Sox" Kennedy and "integrationists with Communist ties." Connor—that intrepid campaigner—had his mind set on another political race, and periodic appearances around the state of Alabama served to remind the voters that the old war horse was still in harness. At sixty-six, with more than a quarter century of tenure in public office, Connor decided to run for the presidency of the Alabama Public Service Commission (PSC) in the spring of 1964. *New York Times* reporter Howell Raines, in his oral history of the civil rights movement *My Soul Is Rested*, asserts that Sidney Smyer helped Connor make the decision, offering him support from the Birmingham business community in return for his pledge to stay out of local politics.[11]

Eugene "Bull" Connor, pictured here on 14 June 1963, continued to speak out against civil rights reforms after leaving office as police commissioner. Less than a year later, he won election as President of the Alabama Public Service Commission—his first successful statewide race. (Courtesy the Birmingham News*)*

In all likelihood, Smyer found it unnecessary to twist Connor's arm, for Bull was if anything a willing candidate. He probably would have made the race anyway.

Connor had run for governor twice, finishing sixth in a field of fifteen in 1950 and fifth among seven candidates in 1962. But his lack of success in statewide races failed to quash his enthusiasm for the Public Service Commission contest. Now, more than ever, his name was known throughout Alabama. He faced strong opposition for the PSC post in incumbent C. C. "Jack" Owen, who had served on the commission since 1946, and former governor James E. "Big Jim" Folsom. But campaign manager J. Morgan Smith recalled that Connor "was a great campaigner."

"Bull was anything but lazy," Smith said, "and he got in his car and he covered the state. On the stump."[12]

Owen, who had won five consecutive races for membership on the PSC, led the first primary on 5 May, collecting 198,787 votes to Connor's 163,804 and Folsom's 95,179.[13] Connor hit the stumps again, seeking to win enough of Folsom's first-round votes to capture the 2 June runoff with Owen.

At this point, Connor's "very strong" name identification, his image as a staunch segregationist, and his well-known friendship with Gov. George C. Wallace came into play. In the runoff election, he carried forty-eight of Alabama's sixty-seven counties, scoring heavily in the rural areas, and overcame Owen's 35,168-vote lead in the first primary to win the PSC presidency. In what the *Birmingham News* termed "a major political upset," Connor polled more than 209,000 votes to Owen's 201,000.

Connor won by siphoning off the majority of Folsom's first-round votes, effectively tying himself to Wallace in the public mind. Wallace endorsed no one publicly, but the "Wallace-Connor personal friendship was well known among many voters, and Connor's persistence in exploiting the relationship during the campaign paid off."[14] Smith believes the segregation issue—while it was "not openly" discussed during the campaign—was the deciding factor for many voters.[15] The president of the PSC made few if any decisions that might be affected by racial considerations, but for those Alabamians who felt threatened by the civil rights gains of the early 1960s, a proven segregationist was to be desired in any public office, however unrelated to matters of race. A jubilant Connor promised, "I will work most diligently to carry out my pledge to work for fair utility rates and to encourage local hearings in matters affecting individual communities."[16]

During the spring of 1960 Connor had sought election as a Democratic national committeeman from Alabama. With the support of the Ku Klux Klan, he defeated incumbent Charles W. McKay, Jr., of Sylacauga, 189,383 votes to 127,346. "I enter upon the discharge of these duties with earnest desire to serve this state and its people who are going through a crisis now second only to that of the Civil War time," he said after the victory.[17] His term would begin at the close of the 1960 Democratic convention in Los Angeles; thus his first national convention as committeeman would be in 1964.

By the spring of 1964 Alabama governor George C. Wallace had begun his national campaign as a third-party presidential candidate. As the Alabama Democratic primary approached, Wallace hand-picked a slate of unpledged electors to run against delegate candidates who would remain pledged to the national party's ticket. Wallace's unpledged electors won a landslide victory, taking all thirty-six places, and committed to support Wallace for president at the convention in Atlantic City, New Jersey.[18]

Pres. Lyndon B. Johnson's renomination was a foregone conclusion, so that the 1964 Democratic gathering was concerned primarily with choosing a vice presidential candidate and fashioning a platform. Minnesota senator Hubert H. Humphrey went to Atlantic City with wide support for the second spot on the ticket, but not among the Alabama delegation, which voted 33–3 against signing a loyalty pledge to support the party's ticket. In addition to their allegiance to Wallace, many Alabamians disliked Humphrey because of his support of civil rights programs. This was especially true of Connor, who recalled with distaste Humphrey's influence on the 1948 convention, which prompted the Dixiecrat revolt.

The Democratic National Committee ruled that only delegates signing the pledge would be issued convention credentials. But when Connor and Alabama committeewoman Ruth Johnson Owens presented themselves, a clerk mistakenly issued the two credentials for the entire Alabama delegation. Connor proceeded to hand out the credentials, even talking some reticent members into accepting their badges. "I hate to get mad at you but you better listen to me," he shouted.[19]

The national party officials, shaken by their mistake, then ruled that Alabama's delegation would be denied their seats by sergeants-at-arms unless they signed the pledge. Some members relented, but others—Connor included—were adamant. When Connor tried to take his seat on Wednesday night, 26 August, he was denied access. "I'm not walking out of this Convention," he said. "You are throwing me out." He was about to leave when suddenly his young grandson, who had accompanied him to the hall, began crying. Some reporters wrote that the party's decision to deny Connor his seat upset the boy, but actually, someone had stepped on the child's foot.[20]

At the close of the convention, with the Johnson-Humphrey ticket a fact, Connor attended the meeting of the Democratic National Committee. As President Johnson strode in to address the group, Connor stood and applauded with the entire committee and frequently applauded throughout the speech. Yet he continued to refuse to sign the loyalty pledge, the only member of the 108-person committee to decline support of the ticket. Later in the session, he was given thirty days to sign the pledge; failure to do so would forfeit his position as Democratic national committeeman for the 1968 convention. Finally, he signed, saying he had been willing to do so earlier until he was denied his seat for the Wednesday session. He blamed Attorney General Robert Kennedy for having "something to do with my not being seated," saying Kennedy acted through the Democratic national chairman John Bailey, who had been appointed by Kennedy's brother John.[21]

While Connor was concentrating on the Democratic National Convention and his upcoming inauguration as PSC president during the late summer and fall of 1964, opponents of the mayor-council form of government in Birmingham campaigned to bring back the city commission. Led by Raymond Rowell, who had been defeated as a city council candidate, the commission group obtained 21,000 signatures on a petition to call yet another election to determine Birmingham's form of government. As the 1 December election approached, former Mayor Art Hanes campaigned for the commission format, making a television appearance on 28 November in which he accused the Birmingham newspapers of trying to run the city. On election day, Birmingham voters underscored their satisfaction with the new mayor-council format, giving the Boutwell government 27,075 votes and the commission format 15,029. Ironically, the pro-commission vote fell some six thousand short of the number of signatures collected on the pro-commission petition. "The citizens of Birmingham have declared themselves for progress," said David Vann. Mayor-council boosters had stressed such achievements as putting Birmingham in the black fiscally, reopening the parks, enlarging Legion Field, and bringing harmony to city government and peace to the city.[22]

Connor took no public role in the 1964 change-of-government campaign, preparing instead to take his seat on the PSC. Facing no opposition in the general election of 1964, he joined Associate Comissioners Ed Pepper and Sybil Poole on the three-member body. To serve as his executive assistant, he called on his former colleague, James T. "Jabo" Waggoner, who was in Canada working as a staff member of Civitan International at the time of Connor's election. Waggoner believes attorney Jim Simpson suggested that Connor hire him because "he knew Bull would need somebody down there to sort of hold his hand." Simpson "knew I wouldn't tell him a lie" and "he knew I wouldn't doublecross Bull." Waggoner accepted the offer after Connor "promised me" that he would "just serve one term and he would support me for the next term."[23]

During this period, the bulk of Public Service Commission work was taken up with handling rate and route requests from motor carriers, railroads, and natural gas pipelines. Associate Commissioners Pepper and Poole tended to vote together on requests, thereby controlling the commission. Connor's predecessor as PSC president, Owen, had found himself on the losing side of numerous 2-to-1 votes, and Connor had the same experience during his early weeks on the commission. He and Waggoner began to suspect that Pepper used his position for personal gain.[24] Attorney Henry Simpson, who represented Connor at times for the law firm of his father Jim Simpson, recalled Connor saying, "I'm going to break this thing up."[25] An insignificant request from trucker Ross Neely for permission to transport material on a rural route in Tuscaloosa County provided Connor the opportunity.

Neely appeared before the PSC requesting additional authority in Tuscaloosa County during early 1965, and Waggoner recalled that "he didn't have a single witness against him." When the presentation ended, Connor moved to give Neely the authority, but Pepper and Poole requested additional time to consider the matter. While Neely's request gathered dust on Pepper's desk, Connor had Waggoner telephone Neely with the warning that someone "might try to shake you down."

"The sons of bitches, I hope they do!" Neely retorted.

"I hope they do, too, Ross," said Waggoner, "because we want you to go along with it," and then call the FBI.

Shortly thereafter, Neely received a telephone call from a man offering to help him get action on his PSC request in return for $5,000. He agreed to pay $3,500 (Waggoner had suggested that he negotiate the fee downward to avoid creating suspicion), and the two set up a meeting in an office. The caller appeared at the appointed time, and Neely "had one-way glass in there and he had FBI men sweeping the floor, and they had it bugged, and they took pictures of the guy, and they gave him money" that "had all this purple stuff on it that you can't get off your hands." Having been "caught as red-handed as he could be," the offender helped supply evidence that resulted in an indictment of Pepper on extortion charges.[26]

Following a federal grand jury investigation that included testimony from Commissioners Connor and Poole, Pepper and five others—including Demopolis cafe owner Thomas J. Dunnavant, the alleged recipient of the marked money—were indicted on five counts of extortion in connection with PSC applications on 17 November 1966.[27] By this time, Pepper was no longer a PSC member, having chosen to run for a U.S. congressional seat (a race he lost to Cong. Bill Nichols) during the spring of 1966. On the afternoon of 7 February 1967, a federal grand jury in Birmingham handed down two additional indictments against Pepper for extortion while on the PSC. He never went to trial, however, for that night he and his wife, along with twenty-four other persons, died in a spectacular restaurant fire at Dale's Penthouse in Montgomery.[28]

During the second year of his tenure on the commission, in December 1966, Connor was felled by a crippling stroke that left him confined to a wheelchair for the remainder of his life. Waggoner gradually assumed more and more of the duties of the PSC president, signing Connor's name to orders and voting for him on numerous occasions. "I signed his name 10,000 times," Waggoner recalled.[29]

Henry Simpson, who argued cases before Connor, said PSC records indicate that "Bull voted down the middle," adding, "His decisions were almost intuitive." Connor voted as Waggoner suggested at times, but not always, according to Simpson. "I believe he always wanted Jabo to know who was boss," he said.[30]

Despite his physical condition, Connor decided to run for reelection to the PSC presidency in 1968, and Waggoner supported the decision "because Bull had never made a whole lot of money . . . and I felt Bull, having had his stroke, that he ought to have another term down there." Waggoner threw himself into the campaign in behalf of Connor, performing fund-raising and speaking duties around the state.[31] Jack Owen, who had been reelected as an associate commissioner in 1966, ran for the PSC presidency against Connor, even though the two "frequently voted alike" in commission hearings.[32]

Connor and Owen far outdistanced three other candidates in the first primary, Connor collecting 198,345 votes and Owen 137,807 to set up a 2 June runoff.[33] But Owen, who had not been required to relinquish his associate commissioner post to run for PSC president, pulled out of the runoff, conceding the race to Connor. With two years remaining on his term as associate, Owen chose to avoid "a strenuous and expensive" runoff campaign, saying his withdrawal would "serve the interest of harmony on the Commission." He added, "Mr. Connor and I have in the past and will in the future work to maintain stability of this important body."[34]

Connor's confinement to a wheelchair failed to quash his enthusiasm for his quadrennial trip to the Democratic National Convention. Accordingly, he headed north in August 1968 to Mayor Richard Daley's Chicago. His physical condition already had prompted his decision to step down as Democratic national committeeman

Connor—recovering from a stroke suffered in December, 1966—presides over a session of the Alabama Public Service Commission in his hospital room 20 January 1967. Associate Commissioner C. C. "Jack" Owen sits in background. (Courtesy the Birmingham News)

following the 1968 gathering. As the convention opened, Connor spent some time scrutinizing the thirty-three-year-old executive director of Alabama's State Democratic Committee, Chriss H. Doss. Finally, he decided Doss could be trusted.

"You can do anything you want to with my vote," he told Doss, "but when it comes time to vote for the nominee, I'm going to vote for 'Bear' Bryant" (whose University of Alabama football teams had won three national titles since 1961).[35]

The Alabama delegation found itself situated on the floor just below the CBS News booth staffed by Walter Cronkite. This Alabama delegation was the first comprised of both black and white membership, and when CBS noticed Connor and civil rights attorney Arthur Shores in the same delegation, the network set up an interview with the two. Before the interview, Connor began fortifying himself with a liquid he drank from a coffee cup, but which fellow delegates suspected was stronger than Maxwell House. By the time CBS appeared, Connor was fast asleep in his wheelchair, impervious to the convention floor bedlam. A relative who had accompanied Connor to Chicago cut short the interview attempt.[36]

Connor was "pretty much on his good behavior throughout the convention," Doss recalled. He "even granted an apparent telephone interview to Ralph McGill, the liberal Atlanta newspaperman," although the actual caller was a north Alabama attorney, Bill Fite, who telephoned pretending to be McGill on a dare from Doss. Connor followed through on his plan to vote for "Bear" Bryant, after which the Birmingham News pontificated, "the seeming disregard for the seriousness of the moment probably embarrassed even Coach Bryant."[37] After introducing Earl Goodwin, his successor as committeeman, Connor told the Democratic National Committee, "I'm going on vacation."[38]

"He was fairly quiet until we got on the plane at O'Hare Field," said Doss. "As he rolled down the aisle, he let everyone know he had arrived by screaming, 'Vote for George Wallace.' Bull never could resist speaking to a crowd."[39]

Back home in Alabama, Connor chose not to campaign against two opponents in the fall general election for PSC president, saying his record "speaks for itself." He was an easy winner, polling 315,731 votes to 84,888 for Republican Fred Jones and 52,009 for

National Democratic Party of Alabama candidate John Henry Davis.[40]

Connor's health continued to deteriorate during his second PSC term. Frequently, he fell asleep during hearings "with a dozen lawyers out there for maybe the power company or Southern Bell or some railroad or somebody." On these occasions, Waggoner would go to the rostrum and awaken him "and it wouldn't be three minutes" before Connor "would go to snoring again." Finally, Waggoner would "take his wheelchair and roll him off and take him somewhere and just keep him out of the hearing" because "it was embarrassing to me and to everybody else." When the time came to vote, Connor would say, "Jabo, you do it."[41]

As the 1972 election approached, Waggoner hoped Connor would choose to retire. "He had deteriorated to the point that I felt like somebody ought to be there that had his own mind and could make his own judgments." Yet despite his infirmities, Connor made plans to run again. "Some people have been trying to put old Bull out to pasture for a long time," Connor said in a press release, and added, "My eight years of 'on-the-job training' are the best qualifications that a candidate could offer for this office."[42] Waggoner told Connor's supporters "it would be a mistake for Bull to run again" because "too many people had seen him go to sleep down there" while he was "supposed to be exercising some judgment" as president of the commission. He and Connor discussed the matter "until I was blue in the face," Waggoner recalled, and Connor was "adamant" that he would run again.[43]

Seven candidates qualified to run against Connor in the 1972 Democratic primary, a clear sign of his presumed vulnerability. The key issue became "the sharp increases in utility rates during the past four years" as the PSC aspirants charged Connor and the other commissioners with favoring the large utility companies. Connor ran well in the first primary, leading the field with 169,432 votes to 119,838 for Kenneth "Bozo" Hammond, a state senator from northeast Alabama. None of the remaining six candidates received as many as ten percent of the votes,[44] leaving Connor and Hammond to face each other in a 30 May runoff.

At this point, Alabama attorney general Bill Baxley injected himself into the PSC race, endorsing Hammond and assailing Con-

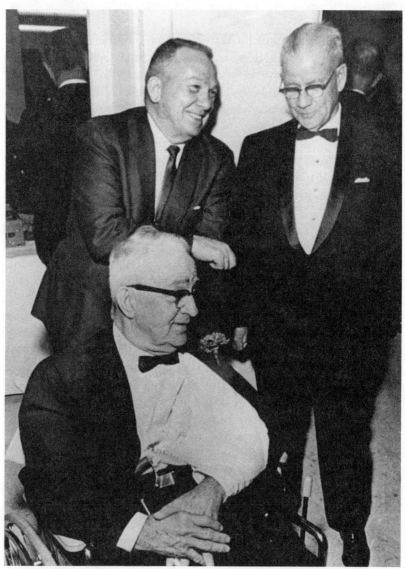

Connor named his former City Commission colleague, Jabo Waggoner, to serve as his administrative assistant on the Public Service Commission. After Connor's 1966 stroke left him confined to a wheelchair, Waggoner took the lead in Bull's successful 1968 campaign for re-election to the PSC. Here, Connor and Waggoner, standing left, chat with Southern Bell Telephone executive Frank Newton in February 1968. (Courtesy the Birmingham News)

nor as "the rubber stamp" of the utilities. Baxley urged Alabama voters to elect Hammond because Connor had made "a farce and mockery" of the PSC. The attempt to tie Connor to the large utilities was successful, and on election day, Hammond swamped his incumbent opponent, polling 270,301 votes to Connor's 149,341 ballots. The growing number of black voters was a factor also, for Connor was "trounced handily" in predominantly black polling places.[45]

Ironically, Connor "never gave Alabama Power Company what they deserved," according to Henry Simpson. "He gave them zero in 1968 and too little in later instances."[46] Nonetheless, Connor—as a lame duck commission president in late 1972—voted with Owen to give Alabama Power Company $26 million of its annual rate increase shortly before leaving office, prompting Baxley to say, "I told the people last May that is exactly what would happen if Bull Connor and Jack Owen were the majority of the commission."[47] Waggoner defended the rate increases that were approved during Connor's second term as "the only thing you could do, if you were honest," because of rapidly escalating inflation. The commission approved the increases the utilities "needed to stay in business and provide service, and that's what the law says you have to do." Despite his justification of Connor's PSC performance (and his own), Waggoner called his colleague's decision to run in 1972 "a doggoned shame" because he had been "a good PSC president" yet was "defeated by a man that he shouldn't have been defeated by" in Hammond,[48] who was later convicted of improprieties in office.

Connor's most significant PSC legacy probably stemmed from his stance in the case of *Alabama Public Service Commission* v. *Redwing Carriers, Inc.* during the early part of his first term. At issue was whether the PSC could render decisions while not formally in session. During the spring of 1965, Schwerman Trucking Company asked for authority to haul dry commodities over Alabama roads. Ten Alabama trucking companies protested, and a PSC hearing was held on 18 May. On 29 July Associate Commissioners Pepper and Poole granted Schwerman a certificate of authority to operate in Alabama. Later, several of the protesting truckers filed suit, claiming the PSC had considered the case without giving public notice. Connor testified that he had received no notice of the meeting at which Pepper and Poole had considered the request, thus invalidating the authority. The case went to the Alabama Supreme Court, which rendered a verdict on 1 June 1967, requiring that "members of the Commission must act as a body when a quorum is present, and each Commissioner must be given a reasonable notice of meetings of the Commission and accorded an opportunity to be present if feasible."[49] Thus Connor—who had made headlines early in his career by removing the door from his city hall office—struck a blow for open hearings and against informal decision making during the twilight of his lengthy tenure as a public servant.

With the loss to Hammond during the spring of 1972, Bull Connor at long last had heard his final hurrah. After more than three decades in public office, he retired to the solitude of his Crestwood home. The *Birmingham News*, which over the years had alternately fought and supported Connor while chronicling his colorful career, took note of the moment. In an editorial following his 30 May loss, the *News* said, "Connor has given a great deal of himself to his constituency in all his several offices. We wish him well."[50] Less than a year later, on 26 February 1973, Connor suffered another stroke. He lingered for twelve days in intensive care at Birmingham Medicenter before dying at age seventy-five on 10 March.[51] The voice that had earned him a lifelong nickname during the golden days of the twenties was silenced forever.

10

The Perfect Adversary

Bull Connor fit the mold of the stereotypical Southern politician of the first half of the twentieth century. He was loud, quick with the quip, racist, and theatrical, a compulsive campaigner who discovered early that entertaining his constituents was more effective than delivering stodgy preachments on dry political issues. He enjoyed a three-decade love affair with the white voters of Birmingham, who viewed him as a colorful, protective, "dollars-and-cents" honest man of the people. He graduated from the school of hard knocks to become a success, first in local radio and then in local politics; blue-collar Birmingham, attracted by his rough-hewn charisma, applauded each step along the way.

Connor's success in winning six city commission races could be attributed partially to his popularity with the rank-and-file elements of "the great workshop town" of Birmingham. Throughout the Connor era, Birmingham was one of the most unionized cities in the South. Connor usually carried a strong labor vote, stemming from his early days in the Alabama legislature and his longtime membership in the telegrapher's union. While some union leaders viewed Bull as a pawn of the corporate fathers, white union members applauded his willingness to keep blacks "in their place," and registered their support at the polls. They liked the commissioner's brash, down-home manner and his affinity for mixing with the working men and excused such antiunion measures as his 1958 opposition to a Police Department labor union.[1]

Connor epitomized the self-made man, coming from a poor background with little education to make a name for himself. His route into politics was almost intuitive, but his assertion that he was free of any entangling alliances ignored the influence of Jim Simpson. Birmingham was no "machine" town politically, but a consensus of industrial, banking, real estate, and other interests exercised wide influence over city affairs through a system of informal accord. In his 1964 book *A Time To Speak*, attorney Charles Morgan, Jr., described how these leaders would agree over lunch, at the country club, or on the telephone that a certain candidate or course of action was best for Birmingham. These men controlled the purse strings of the community; the knowledge that they were for or against this candidate or that activity carried great weight.[2] Simpson—whose law firm represented the city's largest employer, U.S. Steel—was a member of this influential group and provided Connor's route of access to the "big mules."

The struggle between union and antiunion elements often influenced politics in the industrial city, with corporate leaders tending to support politicians who would hold unions in check. While Connor enjoyed his image of independence and remained on good terms with union members, he encouraged support from the economic leaders by keeping taxes low and working to maintain the status quo. One study noted that Connor helped the industrial elite by "controlling strikes . . . and silencing radicals" while industry supported Connor by "private political contributions and discreet . . . reinforcement of his authority."[3] Connor was exactly what the companies that controlled Birmingham were looking for, according to *New York Times* reporter Harrison Salisbury. "He was sort of counted on to keep the status quo," said Salisbury.[4] As business editor Irving Beiman noted, Connor "stayed on the good side of the business leaders . . . [and] was always receptive to corporate suggestions."[5] His preaching about economy in government and no new taxes reflected the influence of Birmingham's industrial and financial interests, who, according to Beiman, "always insisted on cheap government" with "only bare essential services."[6]

One secret of Connor's political success, according to Jabo Waggoner, was his "innate ability of finding out beforehand" what people wanted to hear, and his willingness to tell them just that as election time drew near. "Of course, he had a pretty good network of four hundred policemen out there that could find out might' near anything he wanted to know," said Waggoner.[7] Over the years, Connor molded the police force into his own instrument of power. His control grew with each election success, becoming all the more pervasive after his return to power in 1957. Connor could afford to be honest in money matters, James Parsons felt, because "the power is what turned him on." Connor "loved people that hovered around his feet," said Parsons, "and he always had a bunch of cronies around him . . . always sycophants."[8]

Connor campaign manager J. Morgan Smith recalled that "Bull had a quick mind" and the ability to "size up a situation very clearly." Actually, "he could size up people, and he had a sixth sense of knowing people's tendencies," said Smith.[9] Although he was direct to the point of abrasiveness at times, Connor also practiced the art of flattery. Waggoner recalled with a laugh, "Every woman that would walk into his office, he'd say, 'Come in, Miss America. I'm so happy to see you.' "[10]

Yet Bull Connor was cut from a rough mold. He was more at home in the bleachers than in the box seats and preferred the rough-and-tumble talk of the detectives' room or convention floor to "old boy" boardroom banter. Birmingham business leaders were somewhat ashamed of Bull and snubbed him socially.[11] "Connor was a dirty name to anyone with a college degree," attorney Henry Simpson told a 1973 interviewer. "They felt only thieves and low-lifers talked to him."[12] Attorney Lee Bradley, Jr., a Jim Simpson contemporary who headed one of Birmingham's leading law firms, recalled, "Of course, I had no social contact with Connor. None of the politicians of that time had any social contacts with people in my group."[13] As long as Connor and his fellow commissioners posed no threat to economic interests, the business leaders "did not give a damn whether Tweedledee or Tweedledum occupied office space in City Hall."[14] But as the race issue grew in intensity during the 1950s and early '60s, the economic fathers were pleased to have Connor "guard the ramparts against the agents of change."[15]

Connor guarded the ramparts well, prompting Martin Luther King, Jr., to describe Birmingham as "the most segregated city in America." The police commissioner accepted the epithet as a compliment to his own effectiveness. Connor's tactics were as rough as his manner. He had returned to a Birmingham run by the Ku Klux Klan in the 1920s, and although he disclaimed ever having held membership in the hooded society, his extreme policies during 1958–63 offered encouragement to Klansmen[16] and others threatened socially and economically by the prospect of integration. Long years at the head of the police force bred a spirit of defiance in Connor, a sense that sheer obstinance would forestall the day when Birmingham society would be integrated. Jim Simpson, Connor's most trusted political ally, was an avowed segregationist who shared the police commissioner's unwillingness to bend in the direction of racial accommodation. Birmingham voters encouraged that defiance by their continued support at the polls, but never more strongly than in 1961, when Connor was rewarded for four years of stubborn resistance to integration by his most sweeping victory in nine political campaigns. Richard Arrington, Birmingham's first black mayor who was a young teacher at Miles College during the turbulent early 1960s, noted, "There is no way for us to heap upon the shoulders of 'Bull' Connor the full blame for what happened. Connor did not hold office by coup. He was elected." Arrington believes, as did King, that Birmingham's white moderates "just abdicated their responsibility" in the face of Connor's wide support and heavy-handed tactics.[17] In all likelihood, many remained silent because they shared Connor's basic belief in the dual society that had evolved over three centuries of Southern history. "Bull was doing what 90 percent of the (white) people in Birmingham wanted him to do," said Russell Yarbrough, a longtime Birmingham city councilman who served a few months as Connor's administrative assistant in 1962.[18] As the News noted following the Harrison Salisbury articles, Birmingham remained a city in which the vast majority of whites—moderates and otherwise—were "fiercely opposed to any integration."[19]

In the wake of the Brown decision, Connor sized up the Birmingham electorate correctly in 1957, using the race issue to reclaim his seat at city hall. The police commissioner rode a cresting wave of popularity into the early 1960s. But a series of events—the Freedom Riders episode, the parks closing, and the boycott of downtown stores—prompted economic leaders to reassess their support of Bull. Coupled with a lagging economy in which the city lost 10 percent of its jobs during 1958–61,[20] Connor's intransigence—once viewed as an asset for business—became a liability. The corporate fathers supported Connor as long as he "served their purpose, then they dumped him," said one longtime union official. Even before 1963, economic considerations had motivated many Southern communities to accept integration measures; Project C forced Birmingham to move with the times, albeit grudgingly.

After Connor's death, the *Birmingham News* commented editorially, "If his positions on racial questions prevented his city from going with the tide of social change . . . , Connor, in many respects, served his city well."[21] Yet despite the positive contributions he made in the area of public safety during his early tenure, his legacy grew out of a seven-day period of confrontation in May 1963, and he is remembered primarily for his use of fire hoses and police dogs against demonstrators. Connor learned the art of politics well, so well that he stayed too long in office. Thus during an era that increasingly called for compromise in race relations, he stubbornly played the hard line, resisting integration until the bitter end.

A memorabilia case in the home of a Connor relative keeps alive the memory of the flamboyant commissioner of public safety. Alabama's standard from the 1948 Democratic National Convention is there. Connor grabbed it as he and other delegates stormed out of the Philadelphia convention, irate that the Democrats would adopt a civil rights plank. "No use to leave this, they don't know we are here anyway," he had bellowed.[22] Other mementoes surround the banner—various community service awards, a scrapbook from Connor's early days as a sportscaster, photographs, news clippings, and a baseball autographed by Babe Ruth.

But more than these fragments of a man's life, and more than the banner snatched down in disgust in Philadelphia, one artifact epitomizes Bull Connor—a shiny white hard hat emblazoned with the words "Veteran of the Battle of Kelly Ingram Park." For it was Connor's direction of Birmingham police against black demonstrators in and around the park during the spring of 1963 that fired the civil rights movement and gave it national impetus. Perhaps John Kennedy was correct when he said Bull Connor helped civil rights as much as Abraham Lincoln did. As Birmingham newspaper editor John Bloomer observed, "King tried to get a confrontation in Albany, Georgia, but they were too nice to him. Then he came to Birmingham, and Bull accommodated him."[23] After the Birmingham elections under the mayor-council government in April 1963, SCLC was asked to delay its demonstrations "to give the new government a chance." But "we realized that this was our last chance to demonstrate against Bull Connor," recalled King aide Wyatt Tee Walker, "and we were confident that if we did it long enough, he would do something to help us."[24]

Help it he did. For the civil rights movement in America, Bull Connor was indeed the perfect adversary.

Notes

Chapter 1

1. David L. Lewis, *King: A Biography*, 2d ed. (Urbana, Ill.: Univ. of Illinois Press, 1970), p. 169.
2. Quoted in ibid., p. 169.
3. Ibid., p. 170.
4. Ibid.
5. Leah R. Atkins, *The Valley and the Hills: An Illustrated History of Birmingham and Jefferson County* (Woodland Hills, Calif.: Windsor Publications, 1981), p. 109.
6. Virginia V. Hamilton, *Alabama: A History* (New York: W. W. Norton, 1977), p. 137.
7. *Birmingham News* Centennial Edition, 13 March 1988.
8. Irving Beiman, "Birmingham: Steel Giant with a Glass Jaw," in *Our Fair City*, ed. Robert S. Allen (New York: Vanguard Press, 1947), p. 99.
9. Blaine A. Brownell, "The Urban South Comes of Age, 1900–1940," in *The City in Southern History: The Growth of Urban Civilization in the South*, ed. Blaine A. Brownell and David R. Goldfield (Port Washington, N.Y.: Kennikat Press, 1977), p. 132.
10. Interview with Lee C. Bradley, Jr., attorney, Birmingham, Alabama, 13 May 1988.
11. Beiman, "Birmingham: Steel Giant with a Glass Jaw," p. 100.
12. William Robert Snell, "The Ku Klux Klan in Jefferson County, Alabama 1916–1930" (M.A. thesis, Samford University, 1967), p 137.
13. Reference 44-2004-52, pp. 1, 2, U.S. Department of Justice, Federal Bureau of Investigation, Eugene ("Bull") Connor File.
14. "Integration's Hottest Crucible," *Time*, 15 December 1958.
15. Quoted in *Birmingham News*, 4 November 1957.
16. Edward S. LaMonte, "Politics and Welfare in Birmingham, Alabama 1900–1975" (Ph.D. dissertation, University of Chicago, 1976), p. 273.
17. Interview with Jack A. Warren, retired Birmingham city detective

and acting chief of police, Birmingham, Alabama, 16 February 1988.

18. Interview with James C. Parsons, former Birmingham police chief, Birmingham, Alabama, 10 July 1986.

19. "Wallace's Man Taylor Tilts at Birmingham's Race Laws," *Alabama*, 7 May 1948.

20. Geraldine H. Moore, *The Black Side of Birmingham's Story 25 Years Later* (Birmingham: Help One Another Club, 1985), p. 17.

21. Harrison Salisbury, "Fear and Hatred Grip Birmingham," *New York Times*, 8 April 1960.

22. *Birmingham News*, 15 April 1960.

23. Ibid.

24. Ibid., 15 May 1961.

25. *Atlanta Constitution*, 1 March 1961.

26. Wyatt Tee Walker speech, "Birmingham 1963: Strategy for Bringing Change," The Media and the Movement: The Role of the Press in a Changing Society, Symposium, Birmingham, Alabama, 15 April 1981.

27. David J. Garrow, *Bearing the Cross: Martin Luther King, Jr., and the Southern Christian Leadership Conference* (New York: William Morrow and Company, 1986), p. 228

28. Warren interview.

29. Garrow, *Bearing the Cross*, p. 248.

30. Michael Cooper Nichols, "Cities Are What Men Make Them: Birmingham, Alabama Faces the Civil Rights Movement 1963" (Senior honors thesis, Brown University, 1974), p. 286.

Chapter 2

1. *Birmingham News*, 18 October 1931.

2. *Birmingham News*, undated article from 1931, scrapbook of Eugene "Bull" Connor in possession of the Connor family, Birmingham, Alabama.

3. Ibid.; *The Sporting News* (St. Louis), 25 February 1932.

4. *Birmingham News*, undated 1931 article, Connor scrapbook.

5. Ibid.

6. Beiman, "Birmingham: Steel Giant with a Glass Jaw," p. 117.

7. Connor scrapbook.

8. *The Sporting News*, 25 February 1932.

9. *Birmingham News*, 31 October 1937.

10. Ibid., undated article in Connor scrapbook.

11. *Birmingham News*, 31 October 1937.

12. Certificate of Election signed by Pete B. Jarman, Jr., Secretary of State for Alabama, 6 November 1934, Connor scrapbook.

13. *Birmingham News*, undated article in Connor scrapbook.

14. Ibid.

15. Leah Rawls Atkins, "Senator James A. Simpson and Birmingham Politics of the 1930s: His Fight Against the Spoilsmen and the Pie-Men," *The Alabama Review* 41 (January 1988): 16–17.

16. Ibid., p. 18.

17. *Journal of the House of Representatives, State of Alabama, Session of 1935, Volume 1* (Birmingham, Ala.: Birmingham Printing Company, 1935), p. 1397.

18. *Journal of the House of Representatives, State of Alabama, Session of 1935, Volume 2* (Birmingham, Ala.: Birmingham Printing Company, 1935), pp. 1937–39, 2419, 2550.

19. Atkins, "Senator James A. Simpson and Birmingham Politics of the 1930s," pp. 21, 21n.56.

20. Ibid., p. 18n.48.

21. Interview with James T. "Jabo" Waggoner, former associate commissioner, Birmingham, Alabama, 25 April 1982.

22. *Birmingham News*, 9 and 19 May 1937.

23. Ibid., 3 and 4 May 1937.

24. Ibid., 5 May 1937.

25. Ibid., 6 May 1937.

26. Ibid., 10 May 1937.

27. Ibid., 11 May 1937.

28. Ibid., 13 and 16 May 1937.

29. Ibid., 19 May 1937.

30. Ibid.

31. Ibid., 5 May 1937.

32. Ibid., 31 October 1937.

33. *Summary of the Proceedings of the City Commission of Birmingham, Alabama 1937–38*, 1 November 1937.

34. *Birmingham News*, 1 November 1937.

35. Ibid.

36. *Birmingham Age-Herald*, 1 November 1937.

37. *Birmingham Post*, 2 November 1937.

38. Ibid.; *Birmingham News*, 4 November 1937.

39. Ibid., 11 November 1937 and 9 November 1937; *Birmingham Post*, 2 November 1937.

40. *Birmingham Age-Herald*, 24 and 25 November 1937.

41. *Birmingham Post*, 2 November 1937.

42. *Birmingham News*, 23 November 1937.

43. *Birmingham Post*, 30 November 1937.

44. Ibid., 14 December 1937.

45. Ibid., 1 December 1937.

46. *Birmingham News*, 26 November 1937, and 7 January 1938.

47. *Montgomery Advertiser*, 22 January 1938.

48. Interview with Tommy Hill, Birmingham, Alabama, 24 October 1978.

49. *Birmingham News*, 5 May 1941.

50. Atkins, "Senator James A. Simpson and Birmingham Politics of the 1930s," p. 26.

51. Beiman, "Birmingham: Steel Giant with a Glass Jaw," p. 117.

52. Carl V. Harris, *Political Power in Birmingham 1871–1921*, Twentieth Century America Series (Knoxville, Tenn.: Univ. of Tennessee Press, 1977), pp. 88–89.

Chapter 3

1. *Birmingham News*, 4 May 1941.
2. Ibid., 7 May 1941, 2 May 1945, 1 May 1949.
3. Interview with George A. Palmer, Sr., retired Birmingham city detective, Birmingham, Alabama, 17 April 1986.
4. Reference 80-606-54-5, pp. 1, 2, 3 (11, 28), Connor file, FBI.
5. *Birmingham News*, 4 May 1941.
6. Ibid., 7 May 1941.
7. Palmer interview.
8. Ibid.
9. Interview with Jamie Moore, former police chief, Birmingham, Alabama, 15 May 1981.
10. Parsons interview.
11. Eugene "Bull" Connor to Mr. and Mrs. Frank A. Beavers, Sr., 16 June 1944, in possession of Leah R. Atkins, Birmingham, Alabama.
12. *Birmingham News*, 29 April 1945.
13. Reference 66-8054-4-46, p. 1 (11, 28), Connor file, FBI.
14. *Birmingham News*, 29 April 1945.
15. Ibid., 22 April 1945.
16. Ibid., 29 April 1945.
17. Ibid., 2 May 1945.
18. Palmer interview.
19. Ibid.; Parsons interview.
20. Parsons interview.
21. *Birmingham Post*, 9 May 1941.
22. Parsons interview.
23. Ibid.
24. Moore interview.
25. Warren interview.
26. Moore interview.
27. Waggoner interview.
28. Interview with Irving Beiman, Birmingham, Alabama, 15 February 1988.
29. William D. Barnard, *Dixiecrats and Democrats: Alabama Politics 1942–50* (University, Ala.: Univ. of Alabama Press, 1974), pp. 56–57, 3.
30. Notebook on 1944 Senate race, James Alexander Simpson Papers, Alabama State Department of Archives and History, Montgomery, Alabama.
31. Barnard, *Dixiecrats and Democrats*, p. 57.
32. George B. Tindall, *The Emergence of the New South 1913–1945*, A History of the South Series, no. 10 (Baton Rouge, La.: Louisiana State Univ. Press, 1967), pp. 636–37.
33. Beiman, "Birmingham: Steel Giant with a Glass Jaw," p. 118.
34. Tindall, *The Emergence of the New South 1913–1945*, pp. 636–37.
35. Beiman interview.
36. *Smith v. Allwright*, 321 U.S. 649 (1944).
37. Valdimer O. Key, *Southern Politics in State and Nation* (New York: A. A. Knopf, 1949), p. 330.

38. *Birmingham News,* 8 February 1948.
39. Key, *Southern Politics,* p. 331; *Birmingham News,* 8 February 1948.
40. Key, *Southern Politics,* p. 329.
41. *Birmingham News,* 20 February 1948.
42. Eugene "Bull" Connor campaign letter, 8 March 1948, James A. Simpson Papers, Birmingham, Alabama.
43. Key, *Southern Politics,* p. 332.
44. *New York Times,* 2 May 1948.
45. *Birmingham News,* 2 May 1948.
46. *New York Times,* 2 May 1948.
47. Ibid., 3 May 1948.
48. *Birmingham News,* 4 May 1948.
49. Ibid., 2 May 1948.
50. Ibid.
51. Barnard, *Dixiecrats and Democrats,* pp. 110–11.
52. Delores Ann Hobbs, "States' Rights Movement of 1948" (M.A. thesis, Samford University, 1968) pp. 31–32.
53. *Birmingham News,* 17 July 1948.
54. J. Barton Starr, "Birmingham and the Dixiecrat Convention of 1948," *Alabama Historical Quarterly* 32 (Spring and Summer 1970): 44.
55. *Birmingham News,* 1 August 1947.
56. Ibid., 19 August 1947.
57. Interview with Arthur D. Shores, civil rights attorney, Birmingham, Alabama, 6 May 1982.
58. LaMonte, "Politics and Welfare in Birmingham," p. 263.
59. Shores interview.
60. *Birmingham News,* 25 March 1949.
61. Shores interview.
62. Warren interview.
63. Shores interview.
64. Reference 44-2004-52 pp. 1, 2, Connor file, FBI.
65. Shores interview. Jack Warren recalled an incident at about the same time in which policemen investigating one bombing episode suddenly heard "12 or 15 gunfire shots" nearby. "We didn't know where it was coming from or who was doing it, and as I recall, we never did catch nobody," he said. Neither Warren nor other policemen interviewed could confirm the incident related by Shores, although George Palmer had "a faint recollection of something like that." Warren said it was a plausible explanation of the cessation of bombings for several years.
66. *Birmingham News,* 4 May 1949.
67. Barnard, *Dixiecrats and Democrats,* p. 141.
68. *Alabama Official and Statistical Register 1951* (Montgomery, Ala.: Alabama State Department of Archives and History, 1951), pp. 527–29.
69. Palmer interview.
70. *Birmingham News,* 22 August 1950.
71. Hamilton, *Alabama: A History,* p. 137.
72. Nell Irvin Painter, *The Narrative of Hosea Hudson: His Life as a Negro Communist in the South* (Cambridge, Mass.: Harvard Univ. Press, 1979), pp. 308–9.

73. Warren interview; Palmer interview.
74. *Birmingham News*, 21 October 1950.
75. Ibid., 4 June 1989.
76. Ibid., 21 December 1950.
77. Ibid., 5 January 1952.
78. Ibid., 6 January 1952.
79. Ibid., 5 January 1952.
80. Ibid., 7 January 1952, 15 July 1952, 28 August 1952.
81. Ibid., 20 February 1952.
82. Ibid., 21 February 1952.
83. Ibid., 27, 29, and 31 March 1952.
84. Ibid., 18 October 1952.
85. Reference 62-75147-4-56, p. 1, Connor file, FBI.
86. *Birmingham News*, 1 March 1953.
87. Ibid.
88. Clark Hungerford to Eugene Connor, 2 March 1953, James A. Simpson Papers, Birmingham, Alabama.
89. Gerald E. Caiden, *Police Revitalization* (Lexington, Mass.: D. C. Heath and Company, 1977), pp. 304, 310.
90. *Birmingham News*, 2 November 1953.
91. Ibid., 22 October 1954.
92. Parsons interview.
93. *Birmingham News*, 1 March 1953.

Chapter 4

1. *Birmingham News*, 2 November 1953.
2. Parsons interview.
3. Ibid.
4. *Birmingham Post-Herald*, 12 August 1954.
5. Parsons interview.
6. *Birmingham News*, 22 October 1954.
7. Waggoner interview.
8. Ibid.
9. *Birmingham News*, 5 May 1954.
10. James A. Simpson to Eugene "Bull" Connor, 5 May 1954, James A. Simpson Papers, Birmingham, Alabama.
11. *Birmingham Post-Herald*, 3 and 5 June 1953.
12. Waggoner interview.
13. *Birmingham News*, 30 May 1956.
14. Waggoner interview.
15. Ibid.
16. Interview with J. Morgan Smith, retired advertising and public relations executive, Birmingham, Alabama, 5 May 1982.
17. *Birmingham News*, 30 May 1956.
18. Connor file, FBI, pp. 33–34.
19. *Birmingham News*, 11 April 1956.
20. Nichols, "Cities Are What Men Make Them," p. 109.

21. *Birmingham News*, 12 April 1956.
22. Ibid., 2 May 1956.
23. Ibid., 27 May 1956.
24. Ibid.
25. Ibid., 30 May 1956.
26. Waggoner interview.
27. Smith interview.
28. *Birmingham News*, 30 May 1956.
29. Ibid., 12 August 1956.
30. Ibid., 13 August 1956.
31. Ibid., 15 August 1956.
32. Ibid.
33. Ibid., 19 August 1956.
34. Ibid., 17 April 1957.
35. Ibid., 21 April 1957.
36. Ibid., 22 April 1957.
37. Ibid., 24 April 1957.
38. Ibid., 26 April 1957.
39. Ibid., 1 May 1957.
40. Ibid., 5 May 1957.
41. Ibid., 8 May 1957.
42. Ibid., 1 May 1957.
43. J. Mills Thornton III, "Challenge and Response in the Montgomery Bus Boycott of 1955–1956," *The Alabama Review* 33 (July 1980): 234–35.
44. Numan V. Bartley, *The Rise of Massive Resistance: Race and Politics in the South during the 1950's* (Baton Rouge, La.: Louisiana State Univ. Press, 1969), p. 146.
45. *Birmingham News*, 22 April 1957.
46. Ibid., 27 May 1957.
47. Ibid., 31 May 1957, 2 June 1957.
48. Ibid., 27 May through 2 June 1957.
49. Waggoner interview.
50. Ibid.
51. Smith interview.
52. *Birmingham News*, 3 June 1957.
53. Waggoner interview.
54. Moore interview.
55. Smith interview.
56. *Birmingham News*, 3 June 1957.
57. Ibid., 5 June 1957.
58. Henry J. Abraham, *Freedom and the Court: Civil Rights and Liberties in the United States*, 2d ed. (New York: Oxford Univ. Press, 1972), p. 321.
59. Bartley, *The Rise of Massive Resistance*, pp. 263–68.
60. *Birmingham News*, 4 November 1957.
61. Ibid.
62. Ibid.
63. James A. Simpson to Commissioner Eugene ("Bull") Connor, James A. Simpson Papers, Birmingham, Alabama, 12 November 1957.

64. *Birmingham News*, 10 November 1957.
65. Moore interview.
66. Waggoner interview.
67. Moore interview.
68. *Birmingham News*, 10 November 1957.
69. Ibid., 13 November 1957.
70. Ibid., 15 November 1957.
71. Moore interview.
72. *Birmingham News*, 18 January 1958.
73. Moore interview.
74. *Birmingham News*, 18 January 1958.
75. Ibid., 17 January 1958.
76. Ibid., 17 and 19 January 1958.
77. Ibid., 17 January 1958.
78. Ibid., 19 January 1958.
79. Ibid., 22 January 1958.
80. Moore interview.
81. Parsons interview.
82. *Birmingham News*, 2 November 1961.
83. Parsons interview.
84. Ibid.
85. Smith interview.
86. Robert Corley, "In Search of Racial Harmony: Birmingham Business Leaders and Desegregation, 1950–53," in *Southern Businessmen and Desegregation*, ed. Elizabeth Jacoway and David R. Colburn (Baton Rouge, La.: Louisiana State Univ. Press, 1982), pp. 173–74.
87. Eugene ("Bull") Connor to James A. Simpson, 9 October 1952, James A. Simpson Papers, Birmingham, Alabama.
88. Corley, "In Search of Racial Harmony," pp. 175–79.

Chapter 5

1. *Birmingham News*, 26 December 1956.
2. Glenn T. Eskew, "The Alabama Christian Movement and the Birmingham Struggle for Civil Rights, 1956–1963" (M.A. thesis, University of Georgia, 1987), p. 4.
3. Interview with Fred L. Shuttlesworth, civil rights leader, Birmingham, Alabama, 23 October 1981.
4. Eskew, "The Alabama Christian Movement and the Birmingham Struggle for Civil Rights," p. 5.
5. *Birmingham News*, 2 June 1956. Also see *NAACP v. Alabama ex rel. Patterson*, 357 U.S. 449 (1956).
6. Eskew, "The Alabama Christian Movement and the Birmingham Struggle for Civil Rights," p. 6.
7. Ibid., p. 7.
8. *Birmingham World*, 8 June 1956.
9. *Birmingham News*, 6 June 1956.
10. Garrow, *Bearing the Cross*, p. 90.

11. Shores interview.

12. Eskew, "The Alabama Christian Movement and the Birmingham Struggle for Civil Rights," pp. 9–10.

13. Garrow, *Bearing the Cross*, p. 199.

14. Lee Edmundson Bains, Jr., "Birmingham 1963: Confrontation over Civil Rights" (Senior honors thesis, Harvard College, 1977), p. 126.

15. *Gayle v. Browder*, 352 U.S. 903 (1956).

16. Shuttlesworth interview.

17. *Birmingham News*, 26 December 1956.

18. Ibid.

19. Shuttlesworth interview.

20. Ibid.

21. Ibid.

22. *Birmingham News*, 27 December 1956.

23. Ibid., 28 December 1956.

24. Eskew, "The Alabama Christian Movement and the Birmingham Struggle for Civil Rights," p. 45.

25. Abraham, *Freedom and the Court*, p. 345.

26. *Birmingham News*, 3 September 1957.

27. Robert G. Corley, "The Quest for Racial Harmony: Race Relations in Birmingham, Alabama, 1947–63" (Ph.D. dissertation, University of Virginia, 1979), p. 136; *Birmingham Post-Herald*, 10 September 1957.

28. *Birmingham News*, 3 September 1957.

29. Ibid., 9 September 1957.

30. Ibid., 10 September 1957.

31. Eskew, "The Alabama Christian Movement and the Birmingham Struggle for Civil Rights," p. 34; Corley, "The Quest for Racial Harmony," pp. 138–39.

32. Reference 100-135-61-523 enclosure, p. 4, Connor file, FBI.

33. *Birmingham News*, 25 October 1961.

34. Ibid., 7 December 1957.

35. Ibid., 8 December 1957.

36. Reference 105-61538-14 enclosure, p. 2, Connor file, FBI.

37. LaMonte, "Politics and Welfare in Birmingham," p. 273.

38. Shuttlesworth interview.

39. Ibid.

40. *Birmingham News*, 4 June 1958.

41. Shuttlesworth interview.

42. *Birmingham News*, 8 December 1958.

43. Shores interview.

44. Warren interview.

45. Fred L. Shuttlesworth to Federal Bureau of Investigation, 9 August 1958, Connor file, FBI.

46. *Birmingham News*, 30 June 1958.

47. Fred L. Shuttlesworth to Eugene ("Bull") Connor, 9 August 1958, Connor file, FBI.

48. Ibid.

49. Ibid.

50. Report of 12 August 1958, Birmingham Office of Federal Bureau

of Investigation, Connor file, FBI. Both Shuttlesworth's letter and his comment about having Connor "where we want him" are included in this report.

51. Reference 100-135-4-365, pp. 1–3, Connor file, FBI.
52. *Birmingham News*, 29 April 1958.
53. Ibid., 1 May 1958.
54. Ibid., 4 May 1958.
55. Reference 94-8-173-A, Connor file, FBI.
56. Reference 100-135-4-365, pp. 1–3, Connor file, FBI.
57. Reference 62-105210-A (10), Connor file, FBI; *Birmingham News*, 12 September 1958.
58. Eskew, "The Alabama Christian Movement and the Birmingham Struggle for Civil Rights," p. 37; *Birmingham News*, 1 September 1958.
59. *Birmingham News*, 14 October 1958.
60. Shuttlesworth interview.
61. *Birmingham News*, 21 October 1958.
62. Ibid., 24 October 1958.
63. Ibid., 26 October 1958.
64. Reference 100-135-61-521, p.1, Connor file, FBI.
65. *Birmingham News*, 28 October 1958.
66. Ibid., 21 October 1958.
67. Shuttlesworth interview.
68. *Birmingham News*, 29 October 1958.
69. Reference 44-13806-A, Connor file, FBI; *Birmingham News*, 16 January 1959.
70. *Time*, 15 December 1958.
71. *Birmingham News*, 16 January 1958.
72. Reference 62-105051-387, p. 2, Connor file, FBI.
73. *Birmingham News*, 12 February 1960.
74. Ibid., 27 February 1960.
75. Ibid., 8, 12, and 14 February 1960.
76. Ibid., 26 February 1960.
77. Shuttlesworth interview.
78. *Birmingham News*, 31 March 1960.
79. Shuttlesworth interview.
80. Ibid.
81. Garrow, *Bearing the Cross*, p. 237.
82. Ibid., p. 238.
83. Shuttlesworth interview.

Chapter 6

1. Earl Black, *Southern Governors and Civil Rights: Racial Segregation as a Campaign Issue in the Second Reconstruction* (Cambridge, Mass.: Harvard Univ. Press, 1976), p. 55.
2. Ibid. Black contends that Alabama selected the most militant of the available segregationists through the 1970 gubernatorial election (see p. 52).

3. 1956 Alabama Acts No. 67, H. 106 and 1956 Alabama Acts No. 103, H. 107; 1956 Alabama Acts No. 42, H.J.R. 18 and 1956 Alabama Acts No. 58, H.J.R. 10.

4. *Orleans Parish School Board v. Bush*, 268 F.2d 78 (1959); *United States v. Association of Citizens Councils of Louisiana*, 196 F. Supp. 908 (1961).

5. Bartley, *The Rise of Massive Resistance*, p. 339.

6. Salisbury, "Fear and Hatred Grip Birmingham," *New York Times*, 8 April 1960.

7. *Birmingham News*, 15 April 1960.

8. Ibid., 18 April 1960.

9. Ibid., 15 April 1960.

10. Ibid., 21 April 1960.

11. Ibid., 18 April 1960.

12. Ibid., 20 April 1960.

13. Ibid., 26 April 1960.

14. Ibid., 20 April 1960.

15. Ibid., 15 April 1960.

16. Ibid.

17. Warren interview.

18. Shuttlesworth interview.

19. *Birmingham News*, 14–15 April 1960. Salisbury's articles on Birmingham appeared in the *New York Times* on 8–9 April 1960 and were reprinted by the *News* the following week.

20. Ibid., 27 April 1960.

21. *New York Times v. Connor*, 365 F. 2d 567 (1966).

22. Eugene ("Bull") Connor Papers, Birmingham Public Library Archives, Birmingham, Alabama.

23. Waggoner interview.

24. Smith interview.

25. Warren interview.

26. *Birmingham World*, 3 May 1961.

27. Shores interview; Shuttlesworth interview.

28. *Birmingham News*, 19 April 1961.

29. Ibid., 20 April 1961.

30. Ibid., 18 April 1961.

31. Ibid., 3 May 1961.

32. Ibid., 19 April 1961.

33. Ibid., 1 May 1961.

34. Ibid., 3 May 1961.

35. Ibid.

36. Ibid.

37. Interview with J. Thomas King, attorney, Birmingham, Alabama, 1 February 1989.

38. Ibid.

39. Arthur M. Schlesinger, Jr., *Robert Kennedy and His Times* (Boston: Houghton Mifflin, 1978), 1:307.

40. King interview; *Birmingham News*, 22 December 1975.

41. King interview.

42. *Birmingham News*, 14 May 1961.

43. Ibid., 15 May 1961.

44. Deposition of David Lowe, *United States v. United States Klans, Knights of the Ku Klux Klan, Inc., et al.*, Civil Action No. 1718-N, 26 May 1961, James A. Simpson Papers, Birmingham, Alabama.

45. Interview with Tom E. Langston, *Birmingham Post-Herald* photographer, 23 April 1986. A personal note: I was a fledgling reporter with the *Post-Herald* the day the Freedom Riders were attacked, working my first Sunday afternoon shift. I remember looking up and seeing Langston walk in to confer with the city editor following the incident. It was with some trepidation that I wondered whether journalism would be my appropriate calling.

46. *Birmingham News*, 15 May 1961.

47. Langston interview.

48. Ibid. Langston's photograph was nominated for a Pulitzer Prize, but was beaten out by a picture of a Japanese politician being run through with a sword while making a speech.

49. Schlesinger, *Robert Kennedy and His Times*, p. 307; Howell Raines, *My Soul Is Rested: Movement Days in the Deep South Remembered* (New York: G. P. Putnam's Sons, 1977), p. 114.

50. Report on Miscellaneous Activities of Eugene ("Bull") Connor, Connor file, FBI.

51. *Birmingham Post-Herald*, 27 January 1983.

52. Moore interview.

53. Gary Thomas Rowe, Jr., *My Undercover Years with the Ku Klux Klan* (New York: Bantam Books, 1976), pp. 41–42.

54. Ibid., pp. 42–43.

55. *Birmingham News*, 15 May 1961.

56. Fred L. Shuttlesworth to Eugene ("Bull") Connor, 14 May 1961, Connor Papers; Connor file, FBI.

57. Interview with John E. Bloomer, former editor, *Birmingham News*, Birmingham, Alabama, 26 August 1980.

58. Affidavit of Sgt. Thomas H. Cook, *United States v. United States Klans, Knights of Ku Klux Klan, Inc., et al.*, Civil Action No. 1718-N, 26 May 1961.

59. *Birmingham News*, 15 May 1961.

60. *Birmingham World*, 20 May 1961.

61. *Birmingham News*, 15 May 1961.

62. Deposition of James William Zwerg, *United States v. United States Klans, Knights of Ku Klux Klan, Inc., et al.*, Civil Action No. 1718-N, 25 May 1961, James A. Simpson Papers, Birmingham, Alabama.

63. Cook Affidavit, *U.S. v. U.S. Klans, et al.*

64. Raines, *My Soul Is Rested*, p. 118.

65. Ibid.

66. Affidavit of Lt. J. T. Holtam, *United States v. United States Klans, Knights of Ku Klux Klan, Inc., et al.*, Civil Action No. 1718-N, 26 May 1961, James A. Simpson Papers, Birmingham, Alabama.

67. Raines, *My Soul Is Rested*, p. 119.

68. Affidavit of Lt. Jack A. Warren, *United States v. United States*

Klans, Knights of Ku Klux Klan, Inc., et al., Civil Action No. 1718-N, 26 May 1961, James A. Simpson Papers, Birmingham, Alabama.

69. Schlesinger, *Robert Kennedy and His Times*, pp. 308–9.

70. Edwin Guthman, *We Band of Brothers*, p. 171, quoted in Schlesinger, *Robert Kennedy and His Times*, p. 309.

71. Zwerg Deposition, *U.S. v. U.S. Klans, et al.*

72. Schlesinger, *Robert Kennedy and His Times*, p. 309.

73. Affidavits of F. C. Garrett and A. Y. Parker, *United States v. United States Klans, Knights of Ku Klux Klan, Inc., et al.*, Civil Action No. 1718-N, 27 May 1961, James A. Simpson Papers, Birmingham, Alabama.

74. Affidavit of Sgt. T. E. Sellers, *United States v. United States Klans, Knights of Ku Klux Klan, Inc., et al.*, Civil Action No. 1718-N, 26 May 1961, James A. Simpson Papers, Birmingham, Alabama.

75. *Birmingham News*, 30 May 1961; affidavit of Thomas E. Lankford, *United States v. United States Klans, Knights of the Ku Klux Klan, Inc., et al.*, Civil Action No. 1718-N, no date, James A. Simpson Papers, Birmingham, Alabama.

76. *Birmingham News*, 15 May 1961.

77. Affidavit of Paul G. Sutter, *United States v. United States Klans, Knights of Ku Klux Klan, Inc., et al.*, Civil Action No. 1718-N, 27 May 1961, James A. Simpson Papers, Birmingham, Alabama.

78. *Birmingham News*, 31 May 1961. See also *United States v. United States Klans, Knights of Ku Klux Klan, et al.*, 194 F. Supp. 897 (1961).

79. *Birmingham News*, 2 June 1961. See also *United States v. United States Klans, Knights of Ku Klux Klan, et al.*, 194 F. Supp. 897 (1961).

80. Moore interview.

81. *Bergman v. United States*, 565 S. Supp. 1353 (W. D. Mich. 1983).

82. Parsons interview.

83. Cook Affidavit, *U.S. v. U.S. Klans, et al.*

84. *Birmingham Post-Herald*, 27 January 1983.

85. *Birmingham News*, 24 March 1983.

86. Ibid.

87. Ibid.

88. *Birmingham Post-Herald*, 29 March 1983.

89. Ibid., 3 December 1975.

90. Affidavit of Detective L. J. Wilson, *United States v. United States Klans, Knights of Ku Klux Klan, Inc., et al.*, Civil Action No. 1718-N, 26 May 1961, James A. Simpson Papers, Birmingham, Alabama.

91. Affidavit of Detective J. E. Allbritton, *United States v. United States Klans, Knights of Ku Klux Klan, Inc., et al.*, Civil Action No. 1718-N, 26 May 1961, James A. Simpson Papers, Birmingham, Alabama.

92. Affidavit of Lt. George Wall, *United States v. United States Klans, Knights of Ku Klux Klan, Inc., et al.*, Civil Action No. 1718-N, 27 May 1961, James A. Simpson Papers, Birmingham, Alabama.

93. *Birmingham News*, 30 May 1961.

94. Interview with David J. Vann, attorney, Birmingham, Alabama, 31 July 1986.

95. Langston interview.
96. Charles Morgan, Jr., *A Time to Speak* (New York: Harper and Row, 1964), p. 93.
97. *Birmingham News*, 31 May 1961.
98. Ibid., 29 May 1961.
99. Ibid., 31 May 1961.
100. Ibid.
101. Morgan, *A Time To Speak*, pp. 94–95.
102. King interview; *Birmingham News*, 22 December 1975.
103. *New York Times*, 9 April 1960.

Chapter 7

1. *Birmingham News*, 25 October 1961. Case not reported in federal citations. See also *F. L. Shuttlesworth v. Gaylord*, 202 F. Supp. 59 (N. D. Ala. 1961).
2. *Birmingham News*, 25 October 1961.
3. Ibid.
4. Ibid., 6 November 1961.
5. Ibid., 1 November 1937.
6. Ibid., 6 November 1961.
7. *Proceedings of Birmingham City Commission*, 14 November 1961.
8. *F. L. Shuttlesworth v. Gaylord*, 202 F. Supp. 59 (N. D. Ala. 1961).
9. *Birmingham News*, 9 November 1961.
10. Ibid., 9 December 1961.
11. Ibid., 29 November 1961.
12. Ibid., 9 December 1961.
13. Ibid., 12 December 1961.
14. Ibid., 13 December 1961.
15. Ibid., 10 December 1961.
16. Ibid., 9 December 1961.
17. Ibid., 11 December 1961.
18. Ibid., 12 December 1961.
19. Waggoner interview.
20. Ibid.
21. *Birmingham News*, 13 December 1961.
22. *Birmingham World*, 6 January 1962.
23. Schlesinger, *Robert Kennedy and His Times*, pp. 298, 299–300.
24. Ibid., p. 313.
25. *Birmingham News*, 3 November 1961.
26. Ibid.
27. Ibid., 6 November 1961.
28. Ibid., 8 November 1961.
29. Ibid., 4 December 1961.
30. *Proceedings of Birmingham City Commission*, 19 December 1961.
31. *Birmingham News*, 14 December 1961.
32. Bartley, *The Rise of Massive Resistance*, pp. 338–39, 342.
33. Anthony Paul Underwood, "A Progressive History of the Young

Men's Business Club of Birmingham, Alabama 1946–70" (M.A. thesis, Samford University, 1980), pp. 101, 105–6.

34. Eskew, "The Alabama Christian Movement and the Birmingham Struggle for Civil Rights," p. 88.

35. Boycott handout, files of Fred L. Shuttlesworth, Martin Luther King Center for Social Change, Atlanta, Ga.

36. Eskew, "The Alabama Christian Movement and the Birmingham Struggle for Civil Rights," p. 89; Garrow, *Bearing the Cross*, p. 199.

37. Eskew, "The Alabama Christian Movement and the Birmingham Struggle for Civil Rights," p. 89.

38. Ibid., pp. 90, 91.

39. James A. Simpson to Eugene ("Bull") Connor, 7 September 1961, James A. Simpson Papers, Birmingham, Alabama.

40. Statement from Eugene ("Bull") Connor Speech, 1962 governor's race, James A. Simpson Papers, Birmingham, Alabama.

41. Speech draft of Eugene ("Bull") Connor, 1962 governor's race, James A. Simpson Papers, Birmingham, Alabama.

42. Eugene ("Bull") Connor to Andy (no last name), Connor for Governor file, James A. Simpson Papers, Birmingham, Alabama.

43. Marshall Frady, *Wallace* (New York: World Publishing, 1968), p. 133.

44. *Alabama Official and Statistical Register 1963* (Montgomery, Ala.: Alabama State Department of Archives and History, 1963), pp. 736–37.

45. George E. Sims, *The Little Man's Big Friend: James E. Folsom in Alabama Politics 1946–58* (University, Ala.: Univ. of Alabama Press, 1985), p. 221.

46. *Alabama Official and Statistical Register 1963*, pp. 736–37.

47. Eugene ("Bull") Connor press release, 17 May 1962, James A. Simpson Papers, Birmingham, Alabama.

48. *Alabama Official and Statistical Register 1963*, pp. 763–64.

49. Underwood, "A Progressive History of the Young Men's Business Club of Birmingham," p. 101.

50. Morgan, *A Time To Speak*, p. 9.

51. Vann interview.

52. Ibid.

53. *Birmingham News*, 29 August 1962.

54. Ibid., 20 September 1962.

55. Moore interview.

56. *Birmingham News*, 28 September 1962.

57. Ibid., 29 September 1962.

58. Moore interview.

59. Vann interview.

60. *Birmingham News*, 16 October 1962.

61. Vann interview.

62. Ibid.

63. In addition to these totals, the council-manager form of government received 999 votes (*Birmingham News*, 7 November 1962).

Chapter 8

1. Raines, *My Soul Is Rested*, pp. 361–62.
2. Martin Luther King, Jr., *Why We Can't Wait* (New York: Harper and Row, 1963), p. 45.
3. Eskew, "The Alabama Christian Movement and the Birmingham Struggle for Civil Rights," pp. 92–93; Garrow, *Bearing the Cross*, p. 220.
4. Shuttlesworth interview.
5. Corley, "The Quest for Racial Harmony," pp. 130–31.
6. Shuttlesworth interview.
7. Ibid.
8. Ibid.
9. Garrow, *Bearing the Cross*, p. 220.
10. *Birmingham World*, 19 September 1962.
11. Garrow, *Bearing the Cross*, p. 221.
12. Reference 157-6-4-440 Enclosure, p. (17), Connor file, FBI.
13. Vann interview.
14. Corley, "The Quest for Racial Harmony," p. 240.
15. Ibid.
16. King, *Why We Can't Wait*, p. 47.
17. *Birmingham Post-Herald*, 19 January 1963.
18. Ibid.
19. Ibid., 10 January 1963.
20. *Birmingham News*, 22 January 1963.
21. Ibid., 1 February 1963.
22. Connor Papers, 12 March 1963.
23. *Birmingham News*, 4 June 1958.
24. Ibid., 21 January, 1963.
25. Ibid., 6 March 1963.
26. King, *Why We Can't Wait*, pp. 48–50.
27. Corley, "The Quest for Racial Harmony," p. 249.
28. King, *Why We Can't Wait*, pp. 50, 51–52.
29. Corley, "The Quest for Racial Harmony," pp. 245–47.
30. *Birmingham News*, 28 March 1963.
31. Ibid., 30 March 1963.
32. Ibid.
33. Waggoner interview.
34. *Birmingham News*, 31 March 1963.
35. *Birmingham World*, 27 March 1963.
36. Reference 157-6-4-504 Enclosure, p. 1 (17, 32), Connor file, FBI.
37. *Birmingham Post-Herald*, 3 June 1983.
38. Corley, "The Quest for Racial Harmony," p. 248; *Birmingham News*, 3 April 1963.
39. *Birmingham News*, 4 April 1963. See also *Connor v. State ex rel. Boutwell*, 275 Ala. 230, 153 So. 2d 787 (1963).
40. King, *Why We Can't Wait*, p. 56.
41. Lewis, *King: A Biography*, pp. 171–72.
42. Connor Papers, 5 April 1963.
43. Ibid.

44. King, *Why We Can't Wait*, p. 68.
45. Lewis, *King: A Biography*, p. 182.
46. Corley, "The Quest for Racial Harmony," p. 254.
47. Connor Papers, 12 April 1963.
48. Raines, *My Soul Is Rested*, p. 365.
49. Ibid.
50. King, *Why We Can't Wait*, p. 69.
51. Ibid., pp. 70, 71, 72.
52. Warren interview.
53. Ibid.
54. King, *Why We Can't Wait*, p. 73.
55. Schlesinger, *Robert Kennedy and His Times*, p. 342.
56. Ibid.
57. Connor Papers, undated transcript; Moore interview.
58. *Birmingham News*, 18 April 1963.
59. Ibid., 16 April 1963.
60. Moore interview.
61. *Birmingham News*, 16 April 1963.
62. The newly elected city council members were Dr. John E. Bryan, Alan T. Drennen, Jr., John Golden, Don A. Hawkins, Nina Miglionico, Dr. E. C. Overton, George Seibels, Jr., M. E. Wiggins, and Tom Woods (ibid., 15 April 1963).
63. Speech delivered by Mayor David J. Vann, Duard LeGrand Conference, Birmingham, Alabama, 15 November 1978.
64. Bloomer interview.
65. Corley, "The Quest for Racial Harmony," p. 254.
66. *Birmingham News*, 12 April 1963.
67. *Birmingham World*, 10 April 1963.
68. Garrow, *Bearing the Cross*, p. 246.
69. King, *Why We Can't Wait*, pp. 83, 84, 85.
70. Connor Papers, 17 April 1963.
71. Shores interview.
72. Confidential interview with an eyewitness.
73. Lewis, *King: A Biography*, pp. 185–86.
74. King, *Why We Can't Wait*, p. 104.
75. Raines, *My Soul Is Rested*, p. 151.
76. Warren interview.
77. *Birmingham News*, 2 May 1963.
78. Warren interview.
79. *Birmingham News*, 3 May 1963.
80. Ibid., 23 November 1959.
81. Waggoner interview.
82. Warren interview.
83. *Birmingham News*, 3 May 1963.
84. Ibid., 4 May 1963.
85. *New York Times*, 8 May 1963.
86. *Birmingham News*, 5 May 1963.
87. Ibid., 7 May 1963.
88. Corley, "The Quest for Racial Harmony," pp. 258–60.

89. *Birmingham News*, 9 May 1963.
90. *New York Times*, 8 May 1963.
91. Vann interview.
92. King, *Why We Can't Wait*, p. 106.
93. Lewis, *King: A Biography*, p. 193.
94. Moore interview.
95. Dan Rather with Mickey Herskowitz, *The Camera Never Blinks: Adventures of a TV Journalist* (New York: Ballantine Books, 1977), p. 96.
96. Ibid., p. 102.
97. Corley, "The Quest for Racial Harmony," p. 262.
98. Raines, *My Soul Is Rested*, p. 166.
99. Corley, "The Quest for Racial Harmony," p. 263.
100. King, *Why We Can't Wait*, p. 109.
101. Corley, "The Quest for Racial Harmony," pp. 265–68.
102. Ibid., p. 260.
103. King, *Why We Can't Wait*, p. 109.
104. Corley, "The Quest for Racial Harmony," p. 269.
105. *Birmingham News*, 16 January 1986.
106. Ibid., 9 May 1963.
107. *Shuttlesworth v. Birmingham* 394 U.S. 147 (1969).
108. Garrow, *Bearing the Cross*, pp. 256–57.
109. Ibid., pp. 257–58.
110. *Birmingham News*, 10 May 1963.
111. King, *Why We Can't Wait*, pp. 112–13; *Birmingham News*, 10 May 1963.
112. *Birmingham News*, 16 May 1963.
113. Corley, "The Quest for Racial Harmony," p. 273.
114. *Birmingham News*, 10 May 1963.
115. Ibid.
116. Garrow, *Bearing the Cross*, p. 260.
117. King, *Why We Can't Wait*, p. 113.
118. Garrow, *Bearing the Cross*, pp. 114, 260.
119. *Birmingham World*, 20 May 1963.
120. Corley, "The Quest for Racial Harmony," p. 275.
121. *Birmingham News*, 20 May 1963.
122. Jack Bass, *Unlikely Heroes: The Dramatic Story of the Southern Judges of the Fifth Circuit Who Translated the Supreme Court's Brown Decision into a Revolution for Equality* (New York: Simon and Schuster, 1981), p. 206.
123. *Birmingham News*, 22 May 1963.
124. Bass, *Unlikely Heroes*, p. 207.
125. *New York Times*, 23 May 1963.
126. Bass, *Unlikely Heroes*, p. 208; Abraham, *Freedom and the Court*, p. 357. Case not reported in federal citations.
127. Bass, *Unlikely Heroes*, p. 209.
128. *Connor v. State ex rel. Boutwell*, 275 Ala. 230, 153 So. 2d 787 (1963).
129. *Birmingham News*, 23 May 1963.
130. Ibid.

131. Corley, "The Quest for Racial Harmony," pp. 276, 277.

132. Lewis, *King: A Biography*, p. 208; Arthur M. Schlesinger, Jr., *A Thousand Days: John F. Kennedy in the White House* (Boston: Houghton Mifflin Company, 1965), pp. 959, 965.

133. *Public Papers of the Presidents of the United States, John F. Kennedy, Containing the Public Messages, Speeches, and Statements of the President 1963* (Washington: Office of the Federal Register, National Archives and Records Service, General Services Administration, 1964), p. 469.

134. Shuttlesworth interview.

135. King, *Why We Can't Wait*, p. 43.

136. Shuttlesworth interview.

137. Vann interview.

138. Garrow, *Bearing the Cross*, p. 264.

139. Theodore C. Sorensen, *Kennedy* (New York: Harper and Row, 1965), p. 489.

Chapter 9

1. Smith interview.

2. Waggoner interview.

3. FBI memorandum of 8 June 1963, Connor file, FBI.

4. Ibid.

5. PASS statement dated June 1963, Connor file, James A. Simpson Papers.

6. Ibid.

7. List of integrated hotels, motels, restaurants and cafeterias, Connor file, James A. Simpson Papers.

8. James Simpson to Eugene ("Bull") Connor, 23 July 1963, Connor file, James A. Simpson Papers.

9. FBI report of 19 September 1963, Connor file, FBI.

10. *Mobile Press-Register*, 18 September 1963.

11. Raines, *My Soul Is Rested*, p. 166.

12. Smith interview.

13. *Birmingham News*, 6 May 1964.

14. Ibid., 3 June 1964.

15. Smith interview.

16. *Birmingham News*, 3 June 1964.

17. Ibid., 2 and 6 May 1960.

18. Ibid., 6 May 1964.

19. Ibid., 24 August 1964.

20. Ibid., 27 August 1964.

21. Ibid.

22. Ibid., 2 December 1964.

23. Waggoner interview.

24. Ibid.

25. Interview with Henry Simpson, attorney, Birmingham, Alabama, 9 September 1981.

26. Waggoner interview.
27. *Birmingham News*, 18 November 1966.
28. Ibid., 8 February 1967.
29. Waggoner interview.
30. H. Simpson interview.
31. Waggoner interview.
32. *Birmingham News*, 8 May 1966.
33. Ibid., 14 May 1968.
34. Ibid., 15 May 1968.
35. Interview with Chriss H. Doss, former executive director, Alabama State Democratic Committee, Birmingham, Alabama, 17 April 1987.
36. Ibid.
37. *Birmingham News*, 30 August 1968.
38. Ibid., 31 August 1968.
39. Doss interview.
40. *Birmingham News*, 6 November 1968.
41. Waggoner interview.
42. Draft of press release included with Henry E. Simpson to Eugene ("Bull") Connor, 6 October 1971, Connor file, James A. Simpson Papers.
43. Waggoner interview.
44. *Birmingham News*, 3 May 1972.
45. Ibid., 31 May 1972.
46. Simpson interview.
47. *Birmingham Post-Herald*, 14 December 1972.
48. Waggoner interview.
49. *Alabama Public Service Commission v. Redwing Carriers, Inc.*, 199 *Southern Reporter*, 2d ser., pp. 653–59.
50. *Birmingham News*, 31 May 1972.
51. Ibid., 11 March 1973.

Chapter 10

1. *Birmingham News*, 6 May 1958. When a Police Department labor union was proposed, the City Commission passed an ordinance sponsored by Connor that called for the dismissal of any policeman involved in union activity. "Policemen can't serve two masters," said Connor. "They've got to enforce the law equally against labor and management."
2. Morgan, *A Time To Speak*, p. 88.
3. Nichols, "Cities Are What Men Make Them," p. 62.
4. *Birmingham News*, 3 April 1988.
5. Beiman interview.
6. Beiman, "Birmingham: Steel Giant with a Glass Jaw," p. 118.
7. Waggoner interview.
8. Parsons interview.
9. Smith interview.
10. Waggoner interview.
11. Hamilton, *Alabama: A History*, p. 146.
12. Nichols, "Cities Are What Men Make Them," p. 73.

13. Bradley interview.

14. Morgan, *A Time To Speak*, p. 89.

15. Hamilton, *Alabama: A History*, p. 146.

16. David M. Chalmers, *Hooded Americanism: The First Century of the Ku Klux Klan 1865–1965* (Garden City, N.Y.: Doubleday, 1965), p. 372.

17. *Birmingham News*, 28 February 1988.

18. Ibid., 25 September 1988.

19. Ibid., 20 April 1960.

20. Joe David Brown, "Birmingham—A City in Fear," *Saturday Evening Post*, 2 March 1963, p. 17.

21. *Birmingham News*, 12 March 1973.

22. Ibid., 3 May 1961.

23. Bloomer interview.

24. Vann interview.

Bibliography

Unpublished Materials and Manuscripts

Connor, Eugene ("Bull"). Letter. In possession of Leah R. Atkins, Birmingham, Alabama.

Connor, Eugene ("Bull"). Papers. Birmingham Public Library, Birmingham, Alabama.

Connor, Eugene ("Bull"). Scrapbook. In possession of the Connor family, Birmingham, Alabama.

Shuttlesworth, Fred L. Files. Martin Luther King, Jr., Center for Social Change, Atlanta, Georgia.

Simpson, James Alexander. Papers. Alabama State Department of Archives and History, Montgomery, Alabama.

Simpson, James A. Papers. In possession of his son, Henry Simpson, Birmingham, Alabama.

Walker, Wyatt Tee. "Birmingham 1963: Strategy for Bringing Change" (speech). Symposium on The Media and the Movement: The Role of the Press in a Changing Society, 15 April 1981, Birmingham, Alabama.

Vann, David J. Speech. Duard LeGrand Conference, 15 November 1978, Birmingham, Alabama.

Government Documents

Alabama Acts (1956).

Alabama State Department of Archives and History, Montgomery, Alabama. *Journal of the House of Representatives, State of Alabama, Session of 1935*, vols. 1 and 2.

Birmingham Public Library, Birmingham, Alabama. *Alabama Official and Statistical Register* 1951, 1963.

Birmingham Public Library, Birmingham, Alabama. *Proceedings of the City Commission of Birmingham, Alabama 1937–63*.

Federal Bureau of Investigation, U.S. Department of Justice, Washington, D.C. Miscellaneous Files. Reports on Eugene ("Bull") Connor.

Samford University Library, Birmingham, Alabama. *Public Papers of the President of the United States, Harry S. Truman, Containing the Public Messages, Speeches, and Statements of the President 1948.*
Samford University Library, Birmingham, Alabama. *Public Papers of the President of the United States, John F. Kennedy, Containing the Public Messages, Speeches, and Statements of the President 1963.*

Newspapers

Atlanta Constitution, 1961.
Birmingham Age-Herald, 1937.
Birmingham News, 1931-89.
Birmingham Post, 1937, 1941.
Birmingham Post-Herald, 1953-83.
Birmingham World, 1956-63.
Mobile Press-Register, 1963.
Montgomery Advertiser, 1938.
New York Times, 1948-73.
The Sporting News (St. Louis, Mo.), 1932.

Interviews

Beiman, Irving. Birmingham, Alabama. 15 February 1988.
Bloomer, John E. Birmingham, Alabama. 26 August 1980.
Bradley, Lee C., Jr. Birmingham, Alabama. 13 May 1988.
Confidential interview.
Doss, Chriss H. Birmingham, Alabama. 17 April 1987.
Hill, Tommy. Birmingham, Alabama. 24 October 1978.
King, J. Thomas. Birmingham, Alabama. 1 February 1989.
Langston, Thomas E. Birmingham, Alabama. 23 April 1986.
Moore, Jamie. Birmingham, Alabama. 15 May 1981.
Palmer, George A. Birmingham, Alabama. 17 April 1986.
Parsons, James C. Birmingham, Alabama. 10 July 1986.
Shores, Arthur D. Birmingham, Alabama. 6 May 1982.
Shuttlesworth, Fred L. Birmingham, Alabama. 23 October 1981.
Simpson, Henry. Birmingham, Alabama. 9 September 1981.
Smith, J. Morgan. Birmingham, Alabama. 5 May 1982.
Vann, David J. Birmingham, Alabama. 31 July 1986.
Waggoner, James T. ("Jabo"). Birmingham, Alabama. 25 April 1982.
Warren, Jack A. Birmingham, Alabama. 16 February 1988.

Journal and Popular Magazine Articles

Atkins, Leah R. "Senator James A. Simpson and Birmingham Politics of the 1930s: His Fight Against the Spoilsmen and the Pie-men." *The Alabama Review* 41 (January 1988): 3–29.

Brown, Joe David. "Birmingham—A City in Fear." *Saturday Evening Post* (2 March 1963): 11–19.
"Integration's Hottest Crucible." *Time*, 15 December 1958.
Starr, J. Barton. "Birmingham and the Dixiecrat Convention of 1948." *Alabama Historical Quarterly* 32 (Spring and Summer 1970): 23–50.
Thornton, J. Mills, III. "Challenge and Response in the Montgomery Bus Boycott of 1955–1956." *The Alabama Review* 33 (July 1980): 163–235.
"Wallace's Man Taylor Tilts at Birmingham's Race Laws." *Alabama* (7 May 1948): 5.

Theses and Dissertations

Bains, Lee Edmundson, Jr. "Birmingham 1963: Confrontation over Civil Rights." Senior honors thesis, Harvard College, 1977.
Corley, Robert G. "The Quest for Racial Harmony: Race Relations in Birmingham, Alabama, 1947–63." Ph.D. dissertation, University of Virginia, 1979.
Eskew, Glenn T. "The Alabama Christian Movement and the Birmingham Struggle for Civil Rights, 1956–1963." M.A. thesis, University of Georgia, 1987.
Hobbs, Delores Ann. "States' Rights Movement of 1948." M.A. thesis, Samford University, 1968.
LaMonte, Edward S. "Politics and Welfare in Birmingham, Alabama 1900–1975." Ph.D. dissertation, University of Chicago, 1976.
Nichols, Michael Cooper. "Cities Are What Men Make Them: Birmingham, Alabama Faces the Civil Rights Movement 1963." Senior honors thesis, Brown University, 1974.
Snell, William Robert. "The Ku Klux Klan in Jefferson County, Alabama 1916–1930." M.A. thesis, Samford University, 1967.
Underwood, Anthony Paul. "A Progressive History of the Young Men's Business Club of Birmingham, Alabama 1946–70." M.A. thesis, Samford University, 1980.

Court Cases

Bergman v. United States, 565 S. Supp. 1353 (W. D. Mich. 1983).
Connor v. State ex rel. Boutwell, 275 Ala. 230, 153 So. 2d 787 (1963).
F. L. Shuttlesworth v. Gaylord, 202 F. Supp. 59 (N. D. Ala. 1961).
Gayle v. Browder, 352 U.S. 903 (1956).
NAACP v. Alabama ex rel Patterson, 357 U.S. 449 (1956).
New York Times Company v. Connor, 365 F. 2d 567 (5th Cir. 1966).
Orleans Parish School Board v. Bush, 268 F. 2d 78 (5th Cir. 1959).
Shuttlesworth v. Birmingham, 394 U.S. 147 (1969).
Smith v. Allwright, 321 U.S. 649 (1944).
United States v. Association of Citizens Councils of Louisiana, 196 F. Supp. 908 (W. D. La. 1961).
United States v. United States Klans, Knights of Ku Klux Klan et al., 194 F. Supp. 897 (M. D. Ala. 1961).

Books

Abraham, Henry J. *Freedom and the Court: Civil Rights and Liberties in the United States.* 2d ed. New York: Oxford Univ. Press, 1972.

Allen, Robert S., ed. *Our Fair City.* New York: Vanguard Press, 1947.

Atkins, Leah R. *The Valley and the Hills: An Illustrated History of Birmingham and Jefferson County.* Woodland Hills, Calif.: Windsor Publications, 1981.

Barnard, William D. *Dixiecrats and Democrats: Alabama Politics 1942–50.* University, Ala.: Univ. of Alabama Press, 1974.

Bartley, Numan V. *The Rise of Massive Resistance: Race and Politics in the South During the 1950's.* Baton Rouge, La.: Louisiana State Univ. Press, 1969.

Bass, Jack. *Unlikely Heroes: The Dramatic Story of the Southern Judges of the Fifth Circuit Who Translated the Supreme Court's Brown Decision into a Revolution for Equality.* New York: Simon and Schuster, 1981.

Black, Earl. *Southern Governors and Civil Rights: Racial Segregation as a Campaign Issue in the Second Reconstruction.* Cambridge, Mass.: Harvard Univ. Press, 1976.

Brownell, Blaine A., and David R. Goldfield, eds. *The City in Southern History: The Growth of Urban Civilization in the South.* Port Washington, N.Y.: Kennikat Press, 1977.

Caiden, Gerald E. *Police Revitalization.* Lexington, Mass.: D. C. Heath and Company, 1977.

Chalmers, David M. *Hooded Americanism: The First Century of the Ku Klux Klan 1865–1965.* Garden City, N.Y.: Doubleday, 1965.

Frady, Marshall. *Wallace.* New York: World Publishing, 1968.

Garrow, David J. *Bearing the Cross: Martin Luther King, Jr., and the Southern Christian Leadership Conference.* New York: William Morrow and Company, 1986.

Hamilton, Virginia V. *Alabama: A History.* New York: W. W. Norton, 1977.

Harris, Carl V. *Political Power in Birmingham 1871–1921.* Twentieth Century America Series. Knoxville, Tenn.: Univ. of Tennessee Press, 1977.

Jacoway, Elizabeth, and David R. Colburn, eds. *Southern Businessmen and Desegregation.* Baton Rouge, La.: Louisiana State Univ. Press, 1982.

Key, Vladimer O. *Southern Politics in State and Nation.* New York: A. A. Knopf, 1949.

King, Martin Luther, Jr. *Why We Can't Wait.* New York: Harper and Row, 1963.

Lewis, David L. *King: A Biography.* 2d ed. Urbana, Ill.: Univ. of Illinois Press, 1970.

Moore, Geraldine H. *The Black Side of Birmingham's Story 25 Years Later.* Birmingham: Help One Another Club, 1985.

Morgan, Charles, Jr. *A Time To Speak.* New York: Harper and Row, 1964.

Painter, Nell Irvin. *The Narrative of Hosea Hudson: His Life as a Negro Communist in the South.* Cambridge, Mass.: Harvard Univ. Press, 1979.

Raines, Howell. *My Soul Is Rested: Movement Days in the Deep South Remembered.* New York: G. P. Putnam's Sons, 1977.

Rather, Dan, with Mickey Herskowitz. *The Camera Never Blinks: Adventures of a TV Journalist.* New York: Ballantine Books, 1977.

Rowe, Gary Thomas, Jr. *My Undercover Years with the Ku Klux Klan.* New York: Bantam Books, 1976.

Schlesinger, Arthur M., Jr. *A Thousand Days: John F. Kennedy in the White House.* Boston: Houghton Mifflin, 1965.

———. *Robert Kennedy and His Times.* Boston: Houghton Mifflin, 1978.

Seay, Noble H. *Alabama Reports 199 So. 2d.* St. Paul, Minn.: West Publishing, 1967.

Sims, George E. *The Little Man's Big Friend: James E. Folsom in Alabama Politics 1946–58.* University, Ala.: Univ. of Alabama Press, 1985.

Sorensen, Theodore C. *Kennedy.* New York: Harper and Row, 1965.

Tindall, George B. *The Emergence of the New South 1913–1945.* A History of the South Series, no. 10. Baton Rouge, La.: Louisiana State Univ. Press, 1967.

Index